Leaving Home in Dark Blue

CHRONICLING OHIO'S CIVIL WAR EXPERIENCE THROUGH PRIMARY SOURCES & LITERATURE

BUCHTEL BOOKS

Miss Harriet Angel, editor, *Recipes by Ladies of St. Paul's Church: A New Edition with a Photo Insert and an Introduction by Jon Miller*

Glenna Snow, editor, *Glenna Snow's Cook Books: A New Edition with a Photo Insert and an Introduction by Kevin Kern*

Mark J. Price, *The Rest is History: True Tales from Akron's Vibrant Past*

Curt Brown, editor, *Leaving Home in Dark Blue: Chronicling Ohio's Civil War Experience Through Primary Sources and Literature*

Leaving Home in Dark Blue

CHRONICLING OHIO'S CIVIL WAR EXPERIENCE THROUGH PRIMARY SOURCES & LITERATURE

CURT BROWN, EDITOR

BUCHTEL BOOKS • AKRON, OHIO

16 15 14 13 12 5 4 3 2 1

ISBN 978-1-935603-01-6 (paperback)

LCCN 2011923722

The paper used in this publication meets the minimum requirements of American National Standard for Information Sciences—Permanence of Paper for Printed Library Materials, ANSI Z39.48–1984. ∞

Cover: Private William F. Bower of Company D, 21st Ohio Regiment Infantry Volunteers, with bayoneted musket, LC-DIG-ppmsca-36856, Library of Congress Prints and Photographs Division Washington, D.C. 20540 USA. Cover design by Amy Freels.

Leaving Home in Dark Blue was designed and typeset by Zac Bettendorf, with help from Amy Freels, in Adobe Caslon, printed on sixty-pound natural, and bound by BookMasters of Ashland, Ohio.

Contents

1864

1865

Publisher's Remarks

Many collections have been published about the Civil War. Over one hundred and fifty years after the war began, interest has not waned in the rebellion that pitted states and families against each other. What you are about to read is not a comprehensive look at the war, or even a comprehensive look at Ohio's role in that war; this collection brings together a variety of sources to provide a broad, personal picture of historic events. A range of resources—including personal letters, government resolutions, poetry, fiction excerpts, and more—touch on areas that are not always covered by battle reports and standard histories. The material is, by and large, created by Ohioans and remains contemporaneous to the events of the war.

Passages in this collection were transcribed as closely as possible to the original documents. Therefore, they may contain language and usage that is considered offensive today. The publisher and editors do not condone such language and have only reproduced such material in keeping with the book's broad, personal scope; this is a book of historical pieces and the language, usage, spelling, and grammar reflect that.

Foreword

The material collected in this book describes the immediate, human experience of Ohioans during the Civil War. The authors of the majority of these documents were individuals who lived through the war, both on the battlefield and on the home front. The documents often refer to specific historical events, but remain timeless because of the individual, human element. The result is an intensely readable, chronological overview of how Ohioans were affected by and involved in the war of the rebellion. Far from comprehensive, the focus in *Leaving Home* is on the common individual (although more prominent or recognizable characters also make appearances). These are the stories of men, women, and children from various walks of life and economic conditions who took part in military service or served on the home front.

Introductions and annotations are included to clarify the material and help modern audiences relate to these historical works. Prominent events are noted in the "A Nation at War" features, which provide a timeline to help contextualize the pieces. Much of the material is collected and published here for the first time; other material is republished for the first time since the initial publication over one hundred years ago. This collection serves as reminder of the roles that Ohioans played in the war and details the war on an intimate level through an overall emphasis on personal experience.

Many people helped see this project through from idea to completion and without their help this book would not exist. Special thanks to Nick Sturm, Abby Thompson, and Michael Goroff for meticulous research, compilation, writing, and editing. In addition, thanks to Zac Bettendorf for the design and Nathan Kemp, Kaana Lewis, Katelyn Mertz, David Poole, and Krystal Williams for research assistance. Thank you to the staff of The University of Akron Press—Thomas Bacher, Amy Freels, and Carol Slatter—for directing, refining, and guiding this book to completion. Most importantly, thank you to the authors of these materials for documenting their experience and allowing us an unparalleled view into the past through their words.

Curt Brown, Lead Editor

Introduction

From "Ohio in the Civil War" by General John Beatty
Source: Henry Howe, *Historical Collections of Ohio: In Two Volumes, An Encyclopedia of the State.* Columbus: Howe, 1889.

It would be impossible to make an exact estimate of the number of men who entered the National army from Ohio during the war for the preservation of the Union. Those embraced in regimental and company organizations of the State can, of course, be enumerated, and, with some degree of accuracy, followed to the time of their death, discharge, or final muster out; but these organizations did not by any means include all the patriotic citizens of Ohio who left peaceful homes to incur the risks of battle for the maintenance of national authority. Five regiments credited to West Virginia were made up in large part of Ohio men; the same may be said of two regiments credited to Kentucky; also of the Fifty-fourth and Fifty-fifth Massachusetts Colored Infantry, and of two regiments of United States colored troops [the 5th and 27th U.S.C.T]. In addition to those enrolled in regiments credited to other States, thousands entered the gun-boat service, of whom Ohio has no record, while other thousands enlisted in the regular army.

According to Ohio General J. Warren Keifer, "From the best prepared statistics of the Provost Marshal-General and Adjutant-General of the U. S. A. and the Adjutant-General of Ohio, excluding reenlistments, 'squirrel-hunters' and militia, and including a low estimate for regular enlistments in the army and navy not credited to Ohio, it is found that Ohio furnished of her citizens 840,000 men of all arms of the service for war; reduced to a department standard, they represent 240,000 three-years soldiers."

The State contributed in organized regiments:

26 regiments of infantry .... for three months.
43 regiments of infantry .... for 100 days.
2 regiments of infantry .... for six months.
27 regiments of infantry .... for one year.
117 regiments of infantry .... for three years.
13 regiments of cavalry .... for three years.
3 regiments of artillery .... for three years.

To these should be added twenty-six independent batteries of artillery, and five independent companies of cavalry.

6,536 Ohio soldiers were killed outright in battle.
4,674 were mortally wounded and subsequently died in hospital.
13,354 died of disease contracted in the service.
In brief, 84 Ohio soldiers out of every 1,000 enlisted men lost their lives in the war of the rebellion.

General Keifer also notes, "The total losses in battle of all kinds in both the American and British armies in the seven years' war of the Revolution, excluding only the captured at Saratoga and Yorktown, is 21,526. This number falls 4,000 below Ohio's deadlist [*sic*] alone during the late war. . . . The loss of Ohio officers is known to have reached 872, nearly ten per cent, of the grand total of officers. . . ."

No army ever had a more abundant and sympathetic support than that accorded by the loyal men and women of the North, who carried forward with intense energy the ordinary business of civil life, while sons, brothers and husbands were in the field. Indeed, when we consider that more than one-half of the adult male population of Ohio was in the army, and that probably one-half of those who remained at home were unfitted by age or physical infirmity for military service, and that very many others were held to their farms and offices by business obligations, which could not be honorably disregarded, or family ties it would have been cruelty to sunder, we shall be at some loss to determine whether those who by their industry and liberality made it possible for an army to live, are entitled to less or more credit from the country than those who fought its battles and won its victories. . . .

The population of Ohio probably represented more nearly than that of any other State, the people of all the older sections of the Union. Settlers from New England and New York predominated in the Western Reserve. Pennsylvania had peopled the eastern counties; Virginia and Kentucky the southern and southwestern; and so we find that [Ulysses S.] Grant's father and [William S.] Rosecrans's came from Pennsylvania; [William T.] Sherman's and [David] Tod's from Connecticut; [James B.] McPherson's and [James A.] Garfield's from New York; [Irvin] McDowell's, Kentucky; [William] Dennison's, New Jersey; [Quincy A.] Gillmore's, Massachusetts; [Edwin M.] Stanton's, North Carolina; while [Salmon P.] Chase was born in New Hampshire, and [Jacob] Ammen, [Benjamin] Brice, and [John C. Tidball] Tibball were natives of Virginia.

It was thus on Ohio soil that the people North and South first met and fraternized, and by their united and harmonious efforts transformed, within less than half a century, an unbroken wilderness into a rich and powerful State.

Editor's Note: General Beatty's introduction provides a brief but comprehensive overview of Ohioans' roles in the Civil War. Through these numbers and lists, it is possible to gain a view of exactly how encompassing and momentous the war was. With Ohio as microcosm, the ubiquitous transformation that the country underwent is clear, as are the devastating effects of war on a personal level. The individual's experience is the central theme of this book and is reflective of the experiences and accounts that are collected here.

1861

". . . no man, in the face of recent events, will have the hardihood to deny that the Government of these United States has proved a stupendous failure."

An Alabamian

1861.1

The Horrible Scourge of Civil War Shall Be Averted

From Clement L. Vallandigham, *Speeches, Addresses, and Letters of Clement L. Vallandigham,* New York: J. Walter & Co., 1864.

Prior to the war, rhetoric for and against secession was at an extremely high pitch. Clement Vallandigham, an Ohio Representative, made the case for compromise rather than engagement. Vallandigham envisioned a country that could have as many as four distinct governing entities with different laws concerning slavery. He would become a central character in Ohio during the war, even being tried for treason.

The passage of personal liberty laws prior to the war contributed to the heightened tension between the North and South. These laws were adopted to circumvent the Fugitive Slave Law, which required the return of runaway slaves to their owners. The personal liberty laws, which were passed by Northern states, indicated that slavery was abhorrent to the general population of the North and not only to Northern extremists.

Speech of Hon. C. L. Vallandigham, of Ohio Delivered in the United States House of Representatives,

February 20, 1861

Mr. Speaker: It was my purpose, some three months ago, to speak solely upon the question of peace and war between the two great sections of the Union, and to defend at length the position which, in the very beginning of this crisis, and almost alone, I assumed against the employment of military force by the Federal Government to execute its laws and restore its authority within the States which might secede. Subsequent events have rendered this unnecessary. Within the three months or more, since the Presidential election, so rapid has been the progress of events, and such the magnitude which the movement in the South has attained, that the country has been forced—as this House and the incoming Administration will at last be forced, in spite of their warlike purposes now—to regard it as no longer a mere casual and temporary rebellion of discontented individuals, but a great and terrible revolution, which threatens now to result in permanent dissolution of the Union, and division into two or more rival, if not hostile, confederacies. Before this dread reality, the atrocious and fruitless policy of a war of coercion to preserve or to restore the Union has, outside, at least, of these walls and of this capital, rapidly dissolved. The people have taken the subject up, and have reflected upon it, till to-day, in the South, almost as one man, and by a very large majority, as I believe, in the North, and especially in the West, they are resolved that, whatever else of calamity may befall us, that horrible scourge of civil war shall be averted. Sir, I rejoice that the hard Anglo-Saxon sense and pious and humane impulses of the American people have rejected the specious disguise of words without wisdom which appealed to them to enforce the laws, collect the revenue, maintain the Union, and restore the Federal authority by the perilous edge of battle, and that thus early in the revolution they are resolved to compel us, their Representatives, belligerent as you of the Republican party here may now be, to the choice of peaceable disunion upon the one hand, or Union through adjustment and conciliation upon the other. Born, sir, upon the soil of the United States—attached to my country from earliest boyhood, loving and revering her with some part, at least, of the spirit of Greek and Roman patriotism—between these two alternatives, with all my mind, with all my heart, with all my strength of body and of soul, living or dying, at home or in exile, I am for the Union which made it what it is; and therefore I am also for such terms of peace and adjustment as will maintain that Union now and forever. . . .

A Nation at War

After South Carolina secedes from the Union in December 1860, Alabama, Florida, Georgia, Louisiana, and Mississippi follow suit in January.

1861.2

The Mounting Tensions

From *Oberlin Students' Monthly: A Religious, Political, and Literary Magazine* 3, no. 5, 1861. Courtesy Oberlin College Archives, Oberlin, Ohio.

The following poem comes from an Oberlin College student publication and describes cadets at The Citadel firing on the steamship, *Star of the West*, as it attempted to bring reinforcements and supplies to Fort Sumter on January 9, 1861. The steamship was driven away by secessionist forces, who had occupied Forts Moultrie and Johnson and Castle Pinckney near Charleston, South Carolina, after Federal troops abandoned the sites. The poem's author is unknown.

The First Gun

The sun arose o'er Charleston bay,
Lighting the morn of the dark day—
The wavelets broke o'er sparkling sand,
And all was peace on sea and land.
Sumter reposed in misty air—
A sleeping lion in his lair—
And o'er its tower the breeze unfurled
The proudest ensign of the world;
Eastward, the Southern city lay,
Uncurtained by the light of day;
Before her, Pinckney's Castle, manned
By traitor flag and traitor band,
While rebel sentries watched the hours
On Moultrie's and on Johnson's towers.
Treason with guilty, jealous eyes,
Guarded her plunder from surprise;
Her sentries walked the beaten sand,
Before her guns on Cumming's strand.
A while sail o'er the sunny bay
Is gently wafted on her way—
A peaceful craft—no port-holes wide
Gape savagely from either side;

But quickly, as she clears the bar,
The guns are signaled from afar,
And 'cross her bow a ball is sent,
To warn her of a foe's intent.
To hoist our flag the word is given—
A standard owned and blessed of heaven—
By patriot fathers dearly won,
Revered by every patriot son.
Alas! Our flag has lost its charm—
For madness nerves the traitors arm!
From Cumming's point, the smoke, the roar—
Our *Union* banner is no more!
Methinks each hero in his tomb
Was startled by that cannon boom,
And living patriots breathed a sigh,
As echo passed the thunder by.
E'en treason, for a while, grew pale,
Her iron daring seemed to fail.
From her our fathers' God defend—
For He alone can mark the end!
But be the day to sorrow given,
When civil war was sent by heaven!
But be the traitor's name forgot,
Who fired the first, the fatal shot!

A Nation at War

On February 18, Jefferson Davis is inaugurated President of the Confederacy.

On March 4, Abraham Lincoln, at his inauguration as the 16th President of the United States, says, "I . . . consider that in the view of the Constitution and the laws, the Union is unbroken."

1861.3

Ohio Responds to Lincoln's Call for Troops

From Ohio Legislature, *Acts of a General Nature and Local Laws and Joint Resolutions passed by the Fifty-Fourth General Assembly of the State of Ohio,* Volume LVIII, Columbus: Richard Nevins, State Printer, 1861.

By early 1861, the states of South Carolina, Mississippi, Florida, Alabama, Georgia, Louisiana, and Texas seceded from the Union, forming The Confederate States of America (CSA), with Jefferson Davis appointed CSA president. The attack on Fort Sumter in Charleston Harbor, South Carolina, was a manifestation of the growing tensions between the North and South and marks the official start of the American Civil War or War of Rebellion.

Lincoln's call for troops was met with enthusiasm in the North, as shown by the following document. The object for Lincoln, at first, was simply to reclaim Union property seized by the South. After Lincoln's announcement, Virginia would secede, followed shortly by Tennessee and Arkansas.

An Act

To provide for the rapid organization of the militia of Ohio, enlisted under the requisition of the president of the United States.

Section 1. *Be it enacted by the General Assembly of the State of Ohio,* That the companies of militia volunteers raised in the state, under any requisition of the president of the United States, shall have the same company and regimental organization as the army of the United States, and when so organized, shall immediately proceed to elect their regimental officers—except the regimental adjutant and quartermaster, who shall be appointed by the colonel, and the regimental surgeons, who shall be appointed as hereinafter required.

Sec. 2. The regiments shall be organized into brigades and divisions, under the direction of the governor who is hereby authorized to appoint from the citizens of this State, the major-general or generals, and to appoint from the general officers in commission in the militia of this state, the brigadiers general to command such divisions and brigades respectively; also to appoint all surgeons and assistant surgeons to the regiments.

Sec 3. Immediately on the passage of this act, the governor shall appoint a medical board, to consist of not less than three skillful surgeons; and no person shall receive the appointment of surgeon or assistant surgeon unless he shall have been examined and approved by said board.

Sec. 4. The governor shall further be authorized to appoint such numbers of aids-de-camp as in his judgment may be necessary to enable him to discharge his duties as commander-in-chief. He shall also have authority to appoint such assistant adjutants general and assistant quartermasters general as may be necessary in his judgment; said officers to rank as lieutenant colonels.

Sec. 5. The militia accepted by the governor, and all officers thereof, and staff officers in actual service, shall be entitled to the pay and emoluments of the same grades of rank in the United States army, from the time of acceptance of troops by the state, and from the time of election and appointment of officers of the line, or the calling into actual service, and necessary for the defense of the state, and accepted by the governor.

Sec. 6. This act shall be in force from and after first passage; and sections two and three of an act entitled "an act relating to the militia of Ohio, mustered in the service of the United States, under any requisition of the President thereof," passed April 17, 1861 are hereby repealed.

P. Hitchcock, *Speaker pro tem. of the House of Representatives.*
James Monroe, *President pro tem. of the Senate.*
Passed April 23, 1861

1861.4

What a Motley Crew!

From Lawrence Wilson, ed., *Itinerary of the Seventh Ohio Volunteer Infantry: 1861–1864*, New York: Neale, 1907.

In April 1861, Camp Taylor, located near Cleveland, Ohio, was established as a training camp for Ohio volunteers. Camp life in the early part of the war reflected a naïve enthusiasm, because battles had yet to be fought and blood had not yet been spilled. Recruits envisioned a swift war that could bring a little adventure to their lives. A grand army was formed without much advance planning. The following letter can probably be attributed to William P. Tisdel, who was discharged from the service in April of 1864, after serving his three-year commitment.

One of the First Letters from the Camp
[to the *Painesville Telegraph*]
"Camp Taylor, Cleveland, O., April 27, 1861."

"We left Painesville at 12.40 Wednesday, and arrived in camp about 3 o'clock. Headed by the Cornet Band we were marched on to the parade grounds and rested until supper time, when we were called together and marched to supper, which consisted of bread, coffee and cold meat. After this we were marched near headquarters and received a good heavy blanket, thence to the barracks, where we stopped for the night.

"After a night's rest on Uncle Sam's *feathers* (straw) we were called by the reveille. Orderly Weed called the roll, and we broke ranks to prepare for breakfast, after which we were marched to the parade grounds, where we drilled until dinner. Our dinner consisted of meat and potatoes, bread and beans and water. From 2 until 6 o'clock visitors are allowed on the grounds. At 5 o'clock we all assemble around the center stand for prayer. The boys are all enjoying themselves first rate. There are between four and five thousand men in camp at present. Respects to all.

"W. P. Tisdel"

A Nation at War

On April 19, a fight between the 6th Regiment of Massachusetts Volunteers and citizens of Baltimore, Maryland occurs, leading to the first bloodshed of the war.

1861.5

Love Conquers All

From *The Cleveland Daily Herald*, "Romance of War," May 14, 1861.

The following story illustrates how a soldier's identity was not always apparent. During the war, accounts of women being discovered in the army were not prevalent, but became part of Civil War lore. Some put the number of battlefield woman at 400, but others thought that number was far too low. Since teenage boys were part of many units, serving as drummer boys, "delicate features" could not always be used to determine a soldier's gender. The stories of loved ones lost to conscription were continuously retold as the war dragged on.

A remarkable instance of female devotion has been recently divulged. It is said to have occurred in connection with the departure of the Seventh Regiment from this city a week ago last Sunday. We give the story as it was told to us, as showing that beside the many brave hearts in the gallant Seventh, it has a "reserved corps" of heroic women at home.

When orders were received for the marching of the Seventh to Columbus, one of the members of a —— County Company—known to the company during the short time they had been gathered together as a young and rather delicate, but spirited fellow went to the Orderly Sergeant and wished to make a confidant of him. The Sergeant promised profound secresy when the supposed young man made the astonishing revelation that her sex had been concealed. Her lover was an officer in the company, and unable to part with him she had assumed men's apparel, enlisted, and had been doing camp duty since the company arrived here. Her object in revealing her secret to the Sergeant was to appeal to him for assistance in enabling her to pass Columbus without exposure, as she had heard that a close medical examination was to be made of all the members. The Sergeant attempted to pursuade [sic] her to abandon the enterprise, but failing in that, promised his assistance in her endeavors. No sooner had the girl left him, however, than the Sergeant went to the officer who held her affections and informed him of the affair. Of course he was incredulous. The two went to the company's barracks, the Sergeant in hopes of finding something among the girl's baggage to determine the matter. A carpetbag belonging to her was found, and the officer nervously tore it open. The first article that met his eyes was a daguerreotype case, which, on being opened, was found to contain his (the lover's) picture. This, apparently, was conclusive; but the officer refused to believe until he had seen the girl. Even when she was brought to him, so effectually was she disguised that he would not have known her. The Sergeant was sent from the room, and the couple passed an hour in a manner that may be easily imagined.

The girl refused to give up her undertaking. She was confident her lover would rather have her go than expose her. Neither entreaties or threats were availing, and finally it became apparent that the only way to prevent her going with the regiment, and avoid an exposure, was to take her home by force. She was therefore compelled to quit the camp, and return to the town from which she came. Since then, however, she has come back to the city, with the full determination of rejoining the Seventh, in some capacity, and the aid of the authorities has been invoked to detain her.

The girl belongs to one of the first families in —— county, and is in every way a most estimable young lady. Her courage in endeavoring to follow her lover is certainly remarkable.

A Nation at War

On May 25, Union General Butler at Fortress Monroe, Virginia, refuses to return runaway slaves to their owners and designates the slaves as "contraband of war," since they were used to fortify Southern positions.

1861.6

Where O Where is My Joe?

Source: Rebecca Harding Davis, "Ellen," *Atlantic Monthly*, July 1865.

The following is an excerpt of a story, "Ellen," published in the *Atlantic Monthly* in 1865. The writer, Rebecca Harding Davis, gained fame in 1861 for her work, *Life in the Iron Mills*, a startling, realistic story about the laboring class. In "Ellen," based on actual events, Davis traces the journey of a young woman who grew up in Michigan and lost everyone in her family, except for her brother, Joe, a soldier in the 24th Ohio Volunteer Infantry. Against severe odds, especially for a woman travelling alone in 1861, Ellen sets out to find her brother.

In many ways, Ellen's story reminds one of a nineteenth-century catch-22. Each time Ellen is about to find her brother, circumstances prevent the meeting—he is always just a step away. Many of the prime characters in the piece are women. While not a suffragette, Davis's writing did examine social issues of the time.

[The excerpt begins with Ellen leaving Columbus, Ohio on her continuing search to find Joe. Joe's regiment has been sent to Bellaire, Ohio, a departure point for Virginia engagements. The story is retold by the author, who heard the story from Ellen herself.]

. . . It is but a few hours' ride from Columbus to Bellaire (the terminus of the Central Ohio Railroad); but at Lewis's Mills this day a collision or some other accident occurred, by which the train was delayed until late that night: no other harm was done, except to give time for poor Ellen's chance again to fail her. Joe's regiment crossed the Ohio that night and went into Virginia [what is now West Virginia].

Bellaire and Benwood, the opposite point on the other side of the river, are small railroad stations, which one or two iron-mills have rendered foul with ashes and smoke. The crossing of the river at that time was by a ferry, rendered purposely tedious by the managers of the Baltimore and Ohio Road, to force their passengers to the lower junction at Parkersburg. I mention this to account for the detention which ensued. When the train stopped at Bellaire, Ellen followed the crowd off the platform into a tavern consisting of a barn-like eating-room and a few starved little garret rooms over it. She stopped at the door uncertainly, while the passengers crowded about the eating-stands at the far end of the room. A fat, oily landlord came up with a hat driven down over his brows.

"Cross the river to-night, Ma'am? Slow work! Slow work! Not get this train over till morning. Better take a bite."

Ellen managed to interpose her brother's name and that of the regiment.

"Twenty-Fourth Ohio? Gone over to-day and this evening. Government has the roads and ferries now, and that keeps passengers back. Troops must be transported, you know,"—and then stopped suddenly, seeing Ellen's face.

"Where did you say he had gone?"

"Over," with a jerk of his thumb across the river,—"into Virginia. You are ill, young woman! I'll call Susan."

Virginia, the country of the man-hunters! A low moon lighted up the broad river and the hills beyond; they were mountains to Ellen, threatening and fierce. She looked at them steadily.

"All the stories I had heard of that country came up quick to me," she said, afterwards. "I thought it was death for me or Joe to venture there. Then he was gone! But I had a great courage, somehow, there at Bellaire. It came to me sudden. I said to the man it did not matter. I would have gone with Joe, and I could follow him. He spoke to me a minute or two, and then he went for 'Susan,' who was his wife. She was a sharp-faced woman, and she scolded her servants all the time; but she was very kind to me. When I told her about Joe, she brought me some tea, and made me lie down until it would be time to cross the ferry, which was not until near morning. She would take no money from me. She said, Sue Myers was no skin-flint to take money from the likes of me. Afterwards she said, if I found Joe and he did well, he could pay her some time again: these soldiers made money easy, lounging round camp. I was angry at that," Ellen said, reddening; "but she would not take the money from me. She told me not to be disappointed, if the regiment had left Benwood and gone out the Baltimore Road. She knew they were to camp at Piedmont, and to follow them up, for they had but a day's start of me. It was quite clear day before our turn came to cross the ferry, and then we had to wait for hours on the other side. When I came out of the ferry-house, I put my foot on the grass, and I thought, 'This is Virginia!' It was as if I had stepped on some place where a murder had been done. I was as silly as a half-witted person," blushing apologetically. "I have had great kindness done to me in Virginia since then."

Though Ellen said no more of this, as she was talking to Virginians, we readily understood the real terror which had seized her, added to the gnawing anxiety to see her brother. Caspar Hauser [a German youth of the early 1800s who claimed to have grown up in total isolation] was not more ignorant of the actual world than this girl, brought up as she had been in such utter seclusion. The last few days had shattered whatever fancies she had formed about life, and given her nothing tangible in their stead. Even Coldwater [her Michigan home] and Joe, and "them that lay up on the hill," [her dead family] were beginning to be like dreams, cold and far-off. It was just a wild whirling through space, night-storms, strange faces crowding about her from place to place; undefined sights, sounds that terrified her, and a long-drawn sickening hope to find Joe through all. No more warm rooms and comfortable evenings beside the fire with mother, no more suppers made ready for the boys, and jokes and laughing when they came home; there was no more a house to call home, no mother nor boys, only something cold and clammy under the muddy ground yonder.

"Ours had been a damp house on the lake-shore," Ellen said, "and we kept a fire always. Winter or summer, I always had seen a warm fire in the grate; but the morning I left Coldwater they put it out; and in all my travel, when I'd think of home, I'd go back to the thought of that grate, with a few wet ashes scattered over the hearth, and nobody to sweep them up, and the cold sun shining down the chimney on them. When I'd think of that, I'd say, 'It's all over!' It began to seem to me as if there was no more Ellen and no more Joe."

She had come, too, into the border region, where the war was breaking ground, with all its dull, gross reality of horrors, to which the farther South and North were strangers; the broken talk in the cars was even more terrifying to her, because half understood,—of quiet farmers murdered in cold blood, of pillaging and outrage, of anticipated insurrections among the slaves, and vengeance for their wrongs.

"I thought of the Lord Jesus and Joe, but they did not seem to be alive here," she said. "I would peep into my basket and look at the Testament and the spoons and Joe's collars, and that made things seem real to me." (Ellen's basket, by the way, was but another example of the singular habit which we find in persons of unsound intellect, the clinging to some one inanimate object as if it formed a tangible link to hold time and place together.)

When the train stopped at Littleton, the conductor, an old, gray-headed man, came up to Ellen as she sat alone. "Simeon Myers told me your story," he said, gravely. "He crossed the river to tell me. I'll take the matter in hand myself; I telegraphed before leaving Benwood, in advance. The Twenty-Fourth Ohio, they say there, have gone on to camp at Piedmont; but the movements of the troops are so uncertain, we will wait until the answer comes to my despatch at the next station. You go to sleep, Ellen."

"Yes, Sir," numbly. She sat with her hand over her eyes, until the name of the next station was called, then rose, and remained standing. The old conductor came in.

"Sit down," he said, gently. "Why, you shiver, and are as cold as if your blood was frozen!"

"My brother, Sir?"

"Tut! tut! Yes! Good news this time, Ellen. The Twenty-Fourth is at Fetterman,—has stopped there, I don't know why,—and"—pulling out his watch, but speaking slowly, and controlling her with his eye—"in two hours we will be there."

At this time (June 1861) Government, striking at the Rebellion wildly, as a blind man learning to fence, was throwing bodies of raw, undisciplined troops into the Border States, wherever there was foothold, to their certain destruction, though with an ulterior good effect, as it proved. Camps of these men were stationed along the road as Ellen passed,—broad-backed and brawny-limbed Iowans and Indianians, clothed in every variety of militia military gear, riding saddleless horses, with a rope often for a bridle, sleeping on the ground with neither tents nor blankets. Near one of these straggling encampments the long train stopped, with a trumpet-like shriek from the engine. "Here's Fetterman, and here's Joe, Ellen," said the conductor, his old face in almost as bright a glow as hers, as he hustled her off on the platform.

"It was just a few low houses, not so large as Coldwater, and soldiers everywhere, on the hills and in the fields and strolling along the road; and it was a clear, blue summer's day, and—oh, it did seem as the soldiers and the town and the sky were glad because I had got there at last, and were saying, 'Joe! Joe!'"

She went into the nearest house, a wide, wooden building, where two women sat shelling peas. Ellen propounded her usual question. The oldest woman took off her spectacles, and looked at her keenly.

"The Twenty-Fourth Ohio? How far did you say you had come? Michigan? Forgive me, (Jinny, bring a chair,) if I looked at you curiously; but I really fancied the people out yonder were savages."

Ellen laughed nervously.

"And you are Virginian? Yes! But my brother"—

The old lady's scrutiny grew graver.

"We are Virginians, in every sense of the word. So I know but little of the movements of the troops. But Captain Williams, the commandant of the post, occupies two of our rooms, and his wife is a gentle little body. Jinny, call Mrs. Williams."

So Jinny, a shy, kindly-faced little girl, disappeared, and speedily returned with the officer's wife (who had a dainty baby in her arms) and a glass of currant wine, which she pressed on Ellen. Mrs. Williams heard Ellen's story in silence, looking significantly at her hostess when it was finished.

"Yes, yes; of course you'll see Joe. Hold the baby, please, Jinny. Now let me take off your bonnet. But you won't mind, if there's a little delay,—a very little. I am not sure, but I am afraid. We'll send for Captain Williams; and know at once. But some detached companies went on to Grafton for special orders this morning, and I thought part of the Twenty-Fourth was with them. There! There! lie down a bit on my bed, or stay here with Mrs. Ford. Very well; it will all be right; only keep up heart."

So chattering, the little woman and the old one fussed about Ellen, soothing, patting her, administering tea, comfort, and hope, all in a breath, as women do to the healing of soul and body,—while Jinny, baby in arms, made off and brought in a moustached young man, with a pleasant, cheerful face, not unlike his wife's.

"It is an unfortunate piece of work," he said. "Yes, the detachment included that company to which Carrol belonged. They are at Grafton now; and I cannot send a message, for official despatches will be going over the lines until night. In the morning, though, it shall be the first word to go. I know the colonel of that regiment, and I do not doubt we will have Joe here on furlough to-morrow."

"They were very careful of me," said Ellen. "Mrs. Ford made me sleep in her spare room; and Mrs. Williams brought me in my supper herself, and sat by me with baby all the evening. I couldn't believe they were all Virginians, and fighting against each other too. The next morning was clear and sunny. Jinny came in, and opened the window, and said, 'Isn't such a clear day a good omen?' But I hadn't courage to laugh with her, I was so tired; I had to lie still on a settee there was there. Captain Williams came in, and said,—

"'By nine o'clock we will have an answer to my message, Ellen.'

"I said then, 'When it comes, if it is "No," will you just say, "No, Ellen," and no more,—not one word more, please?'

"He said, 'I understand,' and went out.

"I heard him tell them not to disturb me; so I lay quite still, with my hands over my eyes. He kept pacing up and down as if he was anxious; then I heard a man's step coming towards him. I knew he brought the message. Captain Williams came towards the door; his wife was there waiting. I heard him speak to her, and then he said, 'You do it, Mary.' So she came in, and kissed me, and she said, 'He is gone, Ellen,'—no more but that. I knew then I never should see my brother again. Mrs. Williams cried, but I did not. She told me, after a while, that he had gone by another road to the Kanawha Salines, where they were fighting that day. 'You cannot go,' she said. 'It is a wilderness of hills and swamps. You must stay with us; help me with baby, and presently Joe will be back.'

"I did not say anything. I lay there, and covered my face. She thought I was asleep presently, so rose softly and went away. I lay quiet all day. I could not speak nor move. They brought me some wine, and talked to me, but I did not understand. I knew I must go on, go on!"—with the wild look again in her eyes. "They would not disturb me, but let me lie still all night there. Early in the morning, before day, I got up softly, softly, I was so afraid they would hear me, and made a light. I wanted to bid Joe farewell before I started."

"Where were you going, Ellen?"

"On, you know,"—with that grave, secretive look of the insane. "I had to go. So I made a light. I wanted to write a letter to my brother, but my head was so tired I could not; then I took my little Testament, and I marked the fourteenth chapter of St. John. He knew that I liked that best, and I thought that would be my letter. I wrote alongside of the printing, 'Good bye, Joe.' Then I fastened it up, and directed it to Joseph Carrol, Kanawha Salines."

"That was a wide direction, Ellen."

"Was it, Sir?" indifferently. "So Joe has it now. I think all his life he'll look at that, and say, 'That was Sis's last word.' I went gently out of the door, and I put my book in the post-office, and then I went away."

She began, it appears, to retrace her way on the railroad-track on foot, leaving her money and clothes at Mrs. Ford's, but carrying the little basket carefully. The Williamses, thinking she had followed Joe, searched for her in the direction of Grafton, and so failed to find her. There are no villages between Fetterman and Fairmount,—only scattered farm-houses, and but few of those,—the line of the railroad running between solitary stretches of moorland, and in gloomy defiles of the mountains. Ellen followed the road, a white, glaring, dusty line, all day. Nothing broke the dreary silence but the whirr of some unseen bird through the forests, or the hollow thud, thud of a woodpecker on a far-off tree. Once or twice, too, a locomotive with a train of cars rushed past her with a fierce yell. She slept that night by the roadside with a fallen tree for a pillow, and the next morning began again her plodding journey.

I come now to the saddest part of the poor girl's story, gathered from her own indistinct remembrances. I mean to pass briefly over it. On the latter part of this day's travel, Ellen had passed several of the encampments which lined the road, but had escaped notice by making a detour through the woods. A mile or two east of Fairmount, however, coming near one, she went up to the first low shed; for the men had thrown up temporary huts, part wood, part mud.

"It was a woman who was there," she said, in apology; "and I was not very strong. I had eaten nothing but berries since the morning before."

The woman was a sutler. [See 1862.5.] She listened to Ellen's explanations, incoherent enough probably, and then, bursting into a loud laugh, called to some of the soldiers lounging near by.

"Here's a likely tale," she said. "I half suspect this is the Rebel spy that's been hanging round these two weeks, and kept Allan dodging you. See to her, boys, while I weigh out this sugar."

The regiment was made up of the offals [scraps] of a large city; the men, both brutal and idle, eager for excitement; this sutler, the only woman in camp. The evening was coming on. Ellen was alone in the half-drunken, shouting crowd.—Not alone. He was near who was real and actual to her always. When I think of Christ as the All-Wise and All-Merciful in this our present day, I like to remember Him as going step by step with this half-crazed child in her long and solitary journey. When I hear how her danger was warded back, how every rough face turned at last towards her with a strange kindness, and tenderness, I see again the Hand that wrote upon the dust of the Temple, and clearer than in the storm or battle which I know He guides I see again the face of Him who took little children in His arms and blessed them.

When the sutler went down to the end of the field she found Big Jake, the bully of the regiment, holding the girl by the shoulder, her clothes covered with mud with which the men had pelted her. She had given one or two low cries of terror, and stood shivering weakly, her eye alone steady, holding the man at bay, as she might a brute. She held out her hands when she saw the woman. "I am no spy," she cried, shrilly.

"We'll soon test that," growled the camp-follower.

"Here, you Jake, unhand the girl! Yonder's Captain C—— looking this way. If she turns out as I say, it'll be a lucky stroke of work for you an' me."

Jake flung her back with a curse, and the woman led her to her shed. She searched Ellen. I saw the girl, when she told it, turn ashy white with terrible shame and anger. She was one of the womanliest women I ever knew.

"I would have killed her then," she said gravely.

"When she could not find that I was a spy, she fastened me in an open pen outside her shed. I tore off the clothes she had touched, they seemed so vile to me. I was so shamed that I held my hands to my throat so that I could die, but she came and fastened them with a cord. She kept me there all the evening, and the men looked over the pen and laughed at 'Mother Murray's prisoner.' After awhile I did not heed them. The moon came up, and I cried then thinking if mother or Joe could know what had come to me. Then I made up my mind what to do. I prayed to the Lord Jesus; but I thought, through all, what I would do. She brought me some food, but I would not touch it, though I was sick with hunger. When the drum had beat and the camp was all quiet, there was a sentry came walking up and down before the pen. He had a kind, good face: he whistled to keep himself awake. Afterwards he stopped it, and, leaning over the log-fence, said, 'Forgive me. I didn't think of your being a prisoner, or I would not have whistled.' It was so sudden, his kind way of speaking, that I began to cry, sitting back in the corner. He bade me never heed, for that I would be free in the morning. 'You're no spy,' he said,—'only Captain Roberts heard Mother Murray's story, and put me here till he could see for himself in the morning.' Then he asked me questions, and somehow it did me good to tell all about Joe, and how I had not found him. He stood there when I had done, thinking, and whistling again, soft to himself. 'Just you wait, Ellen,' he says,—'I know what you want.' And with that he takes out a little Testament, and, sitting down, he reads to me. Then he asked me what verses I liked, and talked of the chapters, till I began to forget all that had happened. Then he put the book in his pocket, and talked of other things, and made me laugh once or twice; and at last he took a card out of his pocket, and thought for a good while. Then he wrote a name on it, Mrs. Jane Burroughs, Xenia, Ohio, and gave it to me. 'That is my mother,' he said, very gravely,—'as good a woman as God lets live. Do you go to her, Ellen, when you're out of this den, and tell her I sent you, and, if I should die in this bloody business, to remember I said to be good to you.' Soon after that another man came and took his place, and I saw him no more. He was very kind. But I knew what I would do,"—with the same dropping of the voice.

In the morning Ellen was released, and the soldiers forbidden to molest her. She hurried along the road to Fairmont. There is a long bridge there, spanning the Monongahela. "I saw it when I was in the cars, and the sight of the water below it came back to me through all my trouble. It was noon when I came to it again. I don't think I stopped at all, to think about Joe, or to think good-bye to him. But," her eye wandering vaguely, "I said good-bye to my little basket I had packed it at home for my journey, you know. I thought Joe would laugh when he saw some things I had there. But it was all over now. So I went down to the water's edge, and set it down; and then I went up, and climbed up on the parapet of the bridge, and then I heard a cry, and I was jerked down to the ground. When I came to myself, I was in a bed. They had ice on my head. They told me they had found my basket, and so knew my name. I laid there for several days. It was soldiers that found me. They paid for me at the tavern. But the regiment was going on. One day, when I was able to sit up, two of them said to me, they would take me to see Joe. They took me on the cars; all the way I had to lie down, with ice to my head. We came a long way; every time we stopped, they said we were going to Joe. I didn't know, my brain was like fire in my head."

Ellen was sent on by the officers of this regiment, and lodged by them for safe-keeping in the jail at Wheeling. The long-suspended brain-fever had set in. She was taken through the streets, her clothes ragged and muddy, her head bare, followed by a curious crowd of idlers, with just enough reason left to know what the house was in which they lodged her. Cruel as they were in act, it proved a kindness to the girl. The jailer and his family nursed her carefully, and gave her a large, airy room in the old debtors' prison.

After she had been there three weeks, a person who had accidentally seen Ellen that first day on the street went to the jail and asked to see her. A whim, perhaps, the fruit of idleness or curiosity. But Ellen thought otherwise. She was clothed and in her right mind now, and sat inside of the iron door, looking with her large, grave, blue eyes searchingly at her visitor. "God sent you," she said, quietly.

That night she told the jailer's wife that her new friend had promised to come the next morning and take her out.

"She may disappoint you, Ellen."

"No. I know God meant her to come, and I shall see my brother again."

She was strangely cheerful; it seemed as if, in that long torpor, some vision of the future had in truth been given to her.

"I shall see Joe," she would repeat steadily, a great glow on her face, "I know."

She carried her little basket, going to her friend's house. It was here I saw Ellen. She was not pretty,—with an awkward, ungainly build, and homely face; but there hung about her a great innocence and purity; and she had a certain trustful manner that went home to the roughest and gained their best feeling from them. Her voice, I remember, was low and remarkably sweet. It was curious to see how all, from the servants in the house to blasé young men of society, were touched by some potent charm, and tried in simple, natural ways to aid her. I used to think Ellen was sent into the world to show how near one of the very least of these, His brethren, came to Him. She grew restless,—her disease working with her. "She must go on to Columbus,—to the gate-keeper and his wife [earlier in the story they had aided Ellen]. She would live with them as their child."

Meanwhile every effort had been made to communicate with her brother, or to gain a furlough for him. But all failed; the regiment was in the wilds of the Virginia border in active service. No message could reach him. There was no system then in the army.

What could be done for Ellen's comfort in the future her friends did anxiously, and then sent her on to Columbus. She remained with the old people but a week, however. "She was very happy with us," the gate-keeper's wife said. Governor Dennison promised to procure Joe a furlough, and, if possible, a dismissal, as soon as the regiment could be reached by letter. In the mean while she busied herself in making a dress and little useful things for housekeeping, to please her brother when he should come; used to talk all day of her plans,—how they would live near us in some quiet little house. Her trouble seemed all forgotten.

But one day she went out and saw the camp. The sight of the armed men and the uniforms seemed to bring back all she had suffered in Virginia. She was uneasy and silent that night,—said once or twice that she must go on, go on,—got her basket and packed it again. The next morning she went across the field without it, as if to take a walk. When an hour passed we searched for her, and found she had gone into town and taken passage on the Western Railroad.

My story ends here. We never could trace her, though no effort was left untried. I confess that this is one, though almost hopeless. Yet I thought that some chance reader might be able to finish the story for me.

Whether Joe fell in his country's service or yet lives in some "little house" for Ellen, or whether she has found a longer, surer rest, in a house made ready for her long ago by other hands than his, I may never know; but I am sure, that, living or dead, He who is loving and over all has the poor "natural" in His tenderest keeping, and that some day she will go home to Him and to Joe.

1861.7

The Franklin Rifles

From *The Daily Cleveland Herald,* "From Camp Dennison," May 24, 1861.

The Franklin Rifles were organized by John Morris, a well-known businessman and attorney who lived in Franklin Mills, Ohio (renamed Kent, Ohio, in 1863).The enlistment of this unit is indicative of how towns and localities organized troops for the war—local men of prominence called on the citizenry to fight alongside each other for the good of the Union. Unfortunately, depending on the results of battle, a town might lose a large portion of its male population to the ravages of the fighting. The following letter, probably written by Alfred H. Day, depicts the patriotic spirit at Camp Dennison, a Union recruitment and training post located near Cincinnati, Ohio.

Letter From Company F. (Franklin Rifles)
Seventh Regiment.
Camp Dennison, May 22.

Believing that an account of the varied and changing scenes of camp life would not be uninteresting to your numerous renders, and especially that part closely connected with the interests of Northern Ohio volunteers, I presume to again address you a few hasty lines. After a number of weeks of unchanging fidelity for our dear and beloved country on the part of our little band of riflemen, we find ourselves at precisely 9 o'clock P.M. sitting by our Camp fires in usual good health, pleasantly engaged in writing to our friends at home, and as I cast my eyes around upon our little group, I cannot fail to discover in their open and honest countenances, (which are all aglow, with enthusiasm) indelible traces of pure and undying patriotism for the great and glorious flag of our Union, which was proudly unfurled to the breeze nearly a hundred years ago, to

"Wave o'er the land of the free and the home of brave, and which was never—never struck down until that hateful day of Sumter!

Since we arrived here we have, as a company, had excellent health. It is true that a few from different companies belonging to the 7th Reg't have been incarcerated in our unwholesome hospital and a very few, from some unknown cause, fell prostrate upon parade grounds, but as yet I do not know of but three deaths in our camp of fifteen thousand men. Truly our good Master on high favors the bravo and true hearts of our nation. I make these remarks in order to correct a mistaken idea which has gone abroad in regard to the state of our health.

Since I last wrote you, our Franklin Rifles have elected a new captain in the person of Representative Steadman, from Portage, a gentleman in every sense of the word, possessed of a noble and generous nature, a pure and undefiled heart, and well calculated to lead us on from victory to victory and to great and noble deeds, and as for our other officers Col. Tyler, Lieut. Col. Creghton and Major Casement—they are, without an exception, just the men calculated to fill the position in which they are destined to move, acceptably to all concerned.

Yesterday your humble servant received a large box of provisions from his lady friends of Franklin, and knowing that its contents would be received by all in the name spirit in which it was sent, I invited officers Tyler, Creighton and Casement to join our mess at tea. Everything passed off pleasantly, and at the conclusion Col. Tyler being called upon responded by giving—"Ten thousand thanks to the fair hands and warm hearts of the Ladies of Franklin for their kind remembrance of us, manifested by their munificent donation. God bless their souls." Others being called upon, responded with equal warmth, all of which indicated our great appreciation of our friends' kindness.

But the tattoo [drum] is beating and I must bid you farewell for a season I will write you again soon.

A. H. D.

Members of 7th Ohio Volunteer Infantry leaving for Dixie. (Wilson, Lawrence, ed., *Itinerary of the Seventh Ohio Volunteer Infantry*. New York: Neal Publishing, 1907.)

1861.8

What are Contraband Goods?

From *The Summit County Beacon,* "What are Contraband Goods?" May 23, 1861.

The following announcement was published in the *Summit County Beacon* in the early stages of the war. The Federal government was obviously concerned with the supply of materials to the South that could aid its cause. Some Northerners were not fully supportive of the war, forcing Ohio and other states to monitor possible traitorous activity closely.

Ball would be involved in the treason proceedings brought against Clement Vallandingham. A prominent member of the bar in Cincinnati, Ball was also an inventor, receiving a patent for improvements to electric headlights for locomotives after the war. He was appointed to many positions, including the presidency of the Board of Trustees of the Medical College of Ohio.

Flamen Ball, United States Attorney for the Southern District of Ohio, has written an opinion regarding contraband goods. He includes in this class the following articles, which he says should not be allowed to reach the seceded States directly or indirectly through disaffected persons in Kentucky or Tennessee:

All gold and silver coin; all checks or bills of exchange for money; all articles of food, clothing and the materials for the manufacture of clothing; all rifle, pistol, and cannon balls and shells; gunpowder and all materials used in its manufacture; all amunitions [sic] and munitions and implements its of war of every discription [sic]; all books of military education; all saddles, harness, and trappings for flying artillery, field, and staff officers, and cavalry troops; all horses; all gun carriages; all timber for ship building; all kinds of naval stores; all engines, boilers, and machinery for boats, all locomotive engines and cars for railroads, and other goods and commodities which might be useful to the enemy in war.

He adds:

It may be well for me to say, that all persons anywhere in The United States, as in those States which pretend to have seceded from the Union; whether they be venders, brokers, manufacturers, merchants, shippers, express agents, or freighters, who make or send forward any of those articles to the rebel forces, incur alike the penalty of treason, and must be dealt with accordingly.

1861.9

Secession and Schools

From Ohio's Teacher's Association, *Ohio Educational Monthly: A Journal of School and Home Orientation* 2, no. 6, June 1861.

The War of the Rebellion had a great impact on educational systems across the divided country. Institutions of higher learning saw a great decrease in students as they enlisted and fought during the war. Many teachers also joined the ranks of both armies. The Ohio Commission of Common Schools noted in its 1863 report that "one-half [5,000] of young men who were teaching in the State two years ago, have obeyed their country's call and volunteered to fight its battles." As resources were used to finance the war, public schools lost monetary support from their states.

The rebel Legislature of Missouri has appropriated her School fund to arm the State and hoist the flag of secession. From late dispatches, we learn that the Public Schools of St. Louis have been closed in consequence. This sacrilegious plunder of the heads and hearts of the children of that loyal and patriotic city, by traitorous law-makers, will add a deeper shade to the infamy of this infamous rebellion. An Exchange truly remarks that if the State had given more liberally to her Schools in the past, the intelligence of her people would now direct to a safer and wiser policy. Thanks to Gen. Lyons and the brave United States volunteers, secession is not much profited by this desecration of a sacred fund.

We have instanced this action of the Missouri Legislature to call attention to the intimate connection in our country between loyalty and the school-room.

We once heard a celebrated Kentucky orator and journalist lament the decay of the spirit of nationality and loyalty among our scholars and in our institutions of learning. In his imagination, disunion even nestled in our school-rooms. How often have we been told, in the same spirit of wisdom, that the South was more loyal and law abiding than the North "with all her Yankee Schoolmasters." How stands the record now? Take a map of the United States and draw a white line around every State which has had, for any length of time, an efficient system of Free Schools; then, with black pigment, color every State now in open rebellion against the government; and how many black States do you find surrounded with a white border? *Not one.*

The truth is there is no influence, save the Bible and the Church, more potent in securing the growth and perpetuity of our civil institutions than our

Schools. They are the very nurseries of law and order. Intelligence and virtue diffused among the people, by the pulpit, the press and the teacher, form the very atmosphere in which alone loyalty to law and free institutions can long exist. The noisy patriotism of the beer barrel and the whiskey cask, of ignorance and corruption, is the very wail of civil distress. Whatever, therefore, tends to the cultivation of intelligence [sic], virtue, and manhood in the citizen is a preserver of civil liberty and the State.

Some one has well said that the decay of civil institutions always begins at the *core*. Disloyalty and rebellion are only the outgrowth of social and private wrongs and vices. Loyalty and patriotism—those twin public virtues, begotten of heaven—feed on personal morality and intelligence.

The saddest page of political history is that which records the downfall of the Roman Republic; but he who sees in the decisive battle of Philipi, the Waterloo of vigorous government, has not yet read that history aright. Private vice and corruption, ere this, had eaten out Roman manhood and virtue. Then consolidated and organized by ambitions demagogues and conspirators, they reared their hydra-head and fastened their fangs in the very vitals of the Republic.

Philipi was the grave of the Roman Republic, because there fell the last of Roman virtue—her Cassius and her Brutus whom history styles, "the last of the Romans."

The lesson we would draw from this is the importance of keeping our Schools in vigorous operation during this "Rebel War." Our youth now, more than at any other time, need the discipline and instruction of the school-room. One of the most serious consequences of a civil war is its demoralizing influence upon the young.

At the close of the late session of our General Assembly, a vigorous effort was made to reduce the State levy for Schools to *one mill* (a reduction of *four-tenths* of a mill). A bill to that effect, under the intense war pressure, passed the Senate; but the House, by a decisive vote, amended the Senate bill, by restoring *four-tenths* of the a mill, and the Senate was obliged to recede from its position. This action of our Legislature affords a marked contrast to that of Missouri. Ohio refuses to despoil the souls of her children even to evince her patriotism. It is suicide for a State now to dismiss her Teachers and close her Schools.

1861.10

A Fighting They Will Go

From *The Daily Cleveland Herald,* "Departure of the Second Enlistment of Volunteers," June 18, 1861.

Coming exactly two months after Lincoln's initial call for troops, the following account from Chagrin Falls, Ohio, just outside Cleveland, describes the pomp preceding the departure of troops for training. The citizens and town dignitaries paraded with the troops. Speeches were given and bands played. The town's ladies provided clothing and food. The 7th Ohio Volunteer Infantry was initially composed of 1,800 men in 10 companies. The regiment fought at Cedar Mountain, Antietam, Chancellorsville, and Gettysburg. The unit lost 12 officers and 261 men during the war.

CHAGRIN FALLS, CUYAHOGA CO.
JUNE 14, 1861.

In answer to the proclamation of the President for 75,000 volunteers, Capt. Sessions organized a company of 84 men in our village, and offered them for service. But like many other companies in the State, they were, after waiting three or four weeks, disbanded, because the number of troops that offered themselves was so much larger than the demand. But our young men were not satisfied, and eighty of them enlisted at Camp Taylor for three years service, and are now in the army. To-day thirteen more have gone to Camp Dennison, having enlisted to serve in the Seventh Regiment. These thirteen recruits are sons of our old citizens, and are as fine a set of fellows as can be found in any camp....

The ladies provided for them a sumptuous ovation last evening, after which the citizens provided them each with a red shirt and Havelock cap [cloth headgear with a tail piece shielding the entire neck], $5 each in money, and 13 large cheeses, and the little Misses presented cushions and needles, buttons pins, thread and other fixins [sic]....

This morning our village Brass Band and Capt. Wyckoff's village Zouaves [American militia groups who emulated the traditions of native North African troops serving in the French Army. The Zouves were known for their bright uniforms with fancy trimmings] and the Chagrin Guards, under Capt. Hall, together with a large concourse of our citizens, male and female, accompanied the volunteers to Solon station. There they were addressed by J.W. Williams,

Esq., and Rev. Mr. Prosser. Then after a general shaking of hands, and the heartfelt "Good bye," and the hearty "God be with you," they entered the cars, accompanied by the Band and the Chagrin Guards, and started for Cleveland. They met at the Burnet House, Lieut. Williams, from Painesville, with more than his full complement of noble volunteers, to fill up Company D. to the maximum number. The remarks of J.W. Williams, Esq., at Solon Depot, were appropriate and appreciated by those young men, one of whom was his oldest son, and will be remembered in camp by them all. He expressed full confidence that victory would crown the efforts of the soldiers who volunteerily [sic] come forward to fight the battles of freedom, and that they would oblige the traitors to again honor that flag of our nation which they have insulted; and that the volunteer young men in, and going into our army, were the pride of our country, who the people never expected to return till treason should have been crushed out and the country safe. He referred them to the pledges of affection and esteem they had received from their friends they were leaving behind, as a guarantee that their safety and good behavior morally and as soldiers, would be prayed for, and their return victorious from the war would be expected in due time, and that too, uncorrupted by the vices of ordinary camp life, as their early moral and religious training it was hoped would save them in the hour of temptation.

W.I.S.

A Nation at War

On June 25, a section of Virginia, whose residents do not wish to secede, agrees to furnish troops to the Union.

1861.11

The Sounds of War

From John James Piatt and Sarah M. Bryan Piatt, *The Nests of Washington and Other Poems,* New York: Walter Low, 1864.

Many Ohio poets reflected on the war as it progressed. This particular verse comes from Sarah Piatt, who lived near Cincinnati, and describes the sorrow that arises when young men are sent into battle. Largely forgotten today, Piatt was compared in her time to Elizabeth Barrett Browning. This poem was written during her stay in Washington, DC, where her husband, John, held a post in the Treasury Department.

Hearing the Battle – July 21, 1861

One day in the dreamy summer,
On the Sabbath hills, from afar
We heard the solemn echoes
Of the first fierce words of war.

Ah, tell me, thou veiléd Watcher
O the storm and the calm to come,
How long by the sun or shadow
Till these noises again are dumb.

And soon in a hush and glimmer
We thought of the dark, strange fight,
Whose close in a ghastly quiet
Lay dim in the beautiful night.

Then we talk'd of coldness and pallor,
And of things with blinded eyes
That stared at the golden stillness
Of the moon in those lighted skies;

And of souls, at morning wrestling
In the dust with passion and moan,
So far away at evening
In the silence of worlds unknown.

But a delicate wind beside us
    Was rustling the dusky hours,
As it gather'd the dewy odors
    Of the snowy Jessamine-flowers.

And I gave you a spray of the blossoms,
    And said: "I shall never know
How the hearts in the land are breaking,
    My dearest, unless you go."

A Nation at War

On July 21, Confederate troops win the first Battle of Bull Run in Virginia.

1861.12

The Escape Route

From Frank Moore, ed., *The Civil War in Song and Story 1860–1865*, New York: P.F. Collier, 1889.

The account of De Villiers escape provided, in today's terms, great public relations for the North. The story saw wide distribution, even being reported in the December 8, 1861, issue of *The New York Times*. After all, De Villiers pulled the wool over the Confederates' eyes and escaped heroically.

Part of De Villiers' success can be attributed to the fact that he had been an officer in the French Army, which added to his authentic portrayal of a displaced Frenchman. After his discharge in 1862, De Villiers returned to France. (See 1863.13 for an account of De Villiers and the problems that led to his discharge.)

The experiences of Col. De Villiers, of the Eleventh Ohio regiment, who was captured with others, in Western Virginia, in 1861, and conveyed to Richmond, and who afterwards made his escape, is thus detailed:

"Arrived at Richmond, they were taken to a tobacco warehouse, where they found forty other prisoners. In the room there was neither table nor bed. They were kept without food; no breakfast given them the next morning after their arrival—and when, finally, a little bread was brought them, it was thrown upon the floor as to a dog; and the quantity so small, that every man must make double-quick in grabbing it, or he got none, and was compelled to beg from the others. But there were rich officers, who could *buy* something to eat for if the rebels did not love the Northerners, they loved their gold. But to shorten, he got the brain fever in prison, and was removed to the hospital; and here the Colonel took occasion to affirm, that the kindness which had been spoken of, as practiced by the physicians, was not from rebels, but from our own surgeons.

"Being by profession a physician, Col. De V., when he had sufficiently recovered, was asked by the hospital doctor to assist, which he consented to do; and he was thus permitted to enjoy more liberty. By good fortune, one day the commanding General gave the physicians liberty to go into the city several times. They wore, as a distinguished body, a red ribbon, or badge, fixed in their button-hole. When he encountered the sentinel, he was challenged, and forbidden to pass on the ground of being a prisoner; the order of the General did not include him. Now, as they called him a French Yankee, he thought he would play them a Yankee trick; so he wrote a note stating that he was included. When he returned to the hospital, the rebel physician said he had been practicing deceit, and must consequently go back among the prisoners. He was again incarcerated and put in irons. He soon made up his mind, however, to escape from there, or die. He was asked to take an oath by the rebels; but, said he, 'I have taken an oath as a naturalized citizen of the United States, and I will never take another to conflict with it.' He had been tempted by the offer of position, but he abhorred the enemies of this Union, and could never forget that he came here for Liberty's sake. He told Col. Woodruff of his determination to escape, for his time had come. Col. W. wished him well, and hoped that he would escape. He set about it, and devised a lie, and stole; for which he felt assured he would be forgiven. He stole the coat and hat of a secession officer, and in that garb passed the guard.

"Col. De Villiers, while Brigade Inspector at Camp Dennison, Ohio, learned a lesson from the soldiers who wanted to go to Cincinnati. They were in the habit of lying in the bushes to hear the countersign, and having obtained it, passed the guard. Without the countersign he could not get out of the gate, even with his full uniform.

"So he lay for about two hours behind the guard-house, (in the night, as should have been stated,) until he was happy by hearing it. The guard called at his approach, 'Who comes there?' 'A friend, with the countersign.' He passed the guard, the gate was opened, and he was once more free. He made his way to Manassas Junction [near the site of the recent rebel victory at the First Battle of Bull Run], which is nothing but a swamp. About six miles from Richmond, he was encountered by a guard, and to his challenge replied, 'A friend, without the countersign.' (He had the precaution to lay the double-barrel shot gun, which he contrived to get before he escaped from Richmond, down, before he approached this guard. He had, besides, a revolver and a bowie knife.)

"Approaching, they asked him where he was from and whither he was going. He replied from Richmond to Petersburg. They then asked why he did not take the railroad, and he said he missed the cars. They then took him in custody, and marched one on each side of him upon a narrow bridge crossing a stream near at hand. The situation was desperate, but he was determined never to go back to Richmond alive; so when he got to about the middle of the bridge, he struck to the right and left, knocking one of the guards on one side and the other on the other side, and giving them both a good swim. Hence he made his way towards Petersburg, subsisting for three days upon nothing but a few raw beans, 'which was not very good for his digestion.'

"Upon this tramp, for a distance of sixty-five miles, he carried his skiff for crossing rivers (a pine board) upon his shoulder. During his travels he was several times shot at. When he got in the neighborhood of [John B.] Magruder's forces, his hardest time began. He tried to pass sentinels several times, and at one time was twice shot at in quick succession. He shot too. He did not know whether he hit the two sentinels or not, but they never answered. But the whole brigade was aroused, and he took to the James River in what he called his skiff, viz., his pine-board companion. He landed on the other side in a swamp, recrossing again near Jamestown, where he lost his gun. He had cast away his officer's coat, and what remained of his suit was rusty enough. So he took an open course, and resolved to ask for work; but like the poor men in the South, when they ask for work, they are told to go into the service. Even the ladies do not look upon a young man unless he is in the service; viewed from this test, there were more patriots in the South than in the North; they were all soldiers, old and young.

"He hired with a German blacksmith, at $1.50 per week, having concluded to remain a while, and learn something of the condition of the rebel forces. He staid a fortnight, observing all the rebel movements. At the expiration of this time, he got tired of blacksmithing, and wanted to go home. He found a good German Union man, to whom he told his story, without reservation, just as if he was telling it here to-night. This was of great service to him; he led him for nine days, the Colonel having adopted another Yankee trick, and made a blind man of himself; he couldn't see, and the German was his guide. Dropping the Yankee French, he became a French subject, and wanted to go back to France, because he could not get any work to do here; and so he told Gen. [Benjamin] Huger, when he got into his command. This General promised to send him to Fortress Monroe with a flag of truce. The next flag of truce that was sent he accompanied, blind still, and led by his faithful German Union man.

"He contrived, unobserved, to tell the Captain of the flag party that he was a prisoner, a Union officer, and had assumed blindness as a disguise, and that he should take him: but the young officer said he could not understand it, and said he would inform Gen. [John E.] Wool. He did so, and Wool, being an old soldier, comprehended the matter at once, immediately sending another boat out to bring him; but it was too late, for the rebel officer said it was not worth while waiting on the Yankees, and hastened off. Having lost his German guide, Gen. Huger himself led him (the poor old blind man) with unaffected sympathy, to the hotel, and he assured him that he should go with the next flag of truce which was sent; and he further took the trouble of writing a special letter to Gen. Wool about the old French blind man who wanted to go home. Col. De Villiers remarked that Gen. Huger evinced true kindness towards him.

"With the flag, there were, besides, a number of ladies, who 'left the South for the purpose of going North to do business.' Though he was blind, he could see the glances they exchanged; and though old and somewhat deaf, he could hear the officers tell the ladies to learn all they could, and come back with the information—wishing them much success. 'It is surprising what fine spies they make!'

"When he got into safe quarters, he threw off his disguise, his decrepitude—saw and was strong—observing, without surprise himself, the astonishment of the ladies at the change."

1861.13

You're a Captain Now

From Civil War Service Records of Giles Waldo Shurtleff; Military Papers, 1861–1865; Oberlin College Archives. Courtesy Oberlin College Archives, Oberlin, Ohio.

William Dennison was the Governor of Ohio during the early stages of the Civil War and had the authority to commission officers to the Ohio militia. Giles W. Shurtleff was a theology student and tutor at Oberlin College in April 1861. He took the official oath in June of the same year at Camp Dennison and became a Captain in the 7th Regiment of the Ohio Volunteer Infantry.

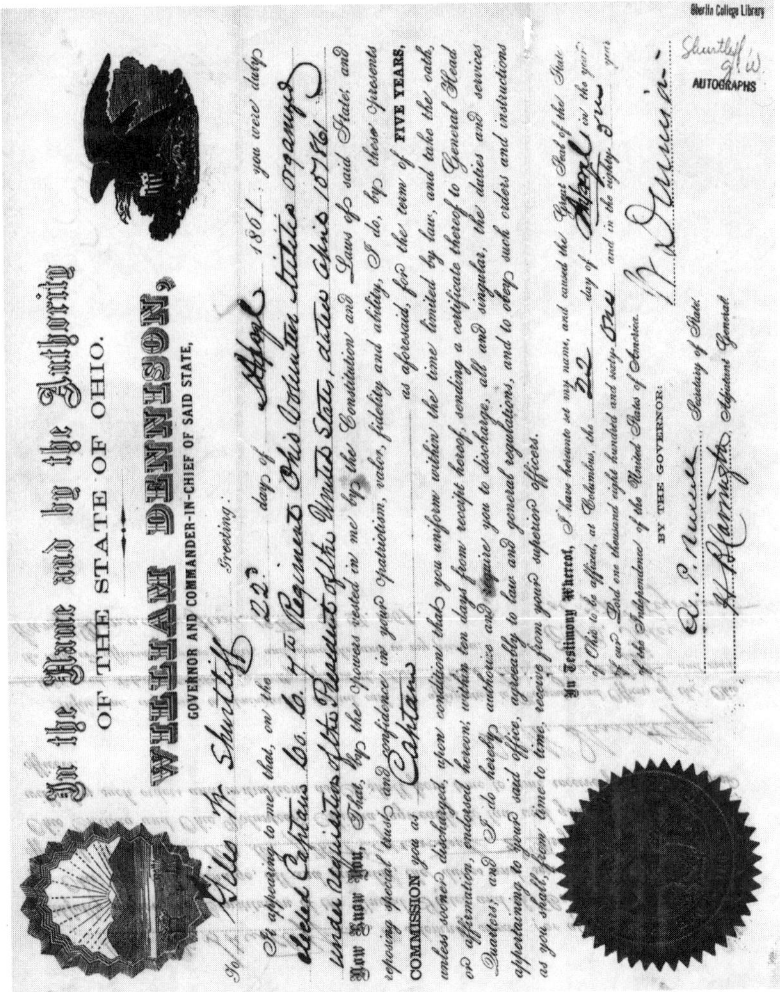

In the Name and by the Authority
OF THE STATE OF OHIO.
WILLIAM DENNISON,
GOVERNOR AND COMMANDER-IN-CHIEF OF SAID STATE,

To Giles W. Shurtleff Greeting:

It appearing to me that, on the 22d day of April 1861 you were duly elected Captain Co. C 7th Regiment Ohio Volunteers titles organized under requisition of the President of the United States, dated April 15 1861

Now Know You, That, by the powers vested in me by the Constitution and Laws of said State, and reposing special trust and confidence in your patriotism, valor, fidelity and ability, I do, by these presents COMMISSION you as Captain as aforesaid, for the term of FIVE YEARS, unless sooner discharged, upon condition that you uniform within the time limited by law, and take the oath, or affirmation, endorsed hereon; within ten days from receipt hereof, sending a certificate thereof to General Head Quarters; and I do hereby authorize and require you to discharge, all and singular, the duties and services appertaining to your said office, agreeably to law and general regulations, and to obey such orders and instructions as you shall, from time to time, receive from your superior officers.

In Testimony Whereof, I have hereunto set my name, and caused the Great Seal of the State of Ohio to be affixed, at Columbus, the 22 day of April in the year of our Lord one thousand eight hundred and sixty-one and in the eighty-fifth year of the Independence of the United States of America.

W Dennison

BY THE GOVERNOR:

A. P. Russell Secretary of State

H. B. Carrington Adjutant General

Shurtleff G. W.

AUTOGRAPHS

(Front)

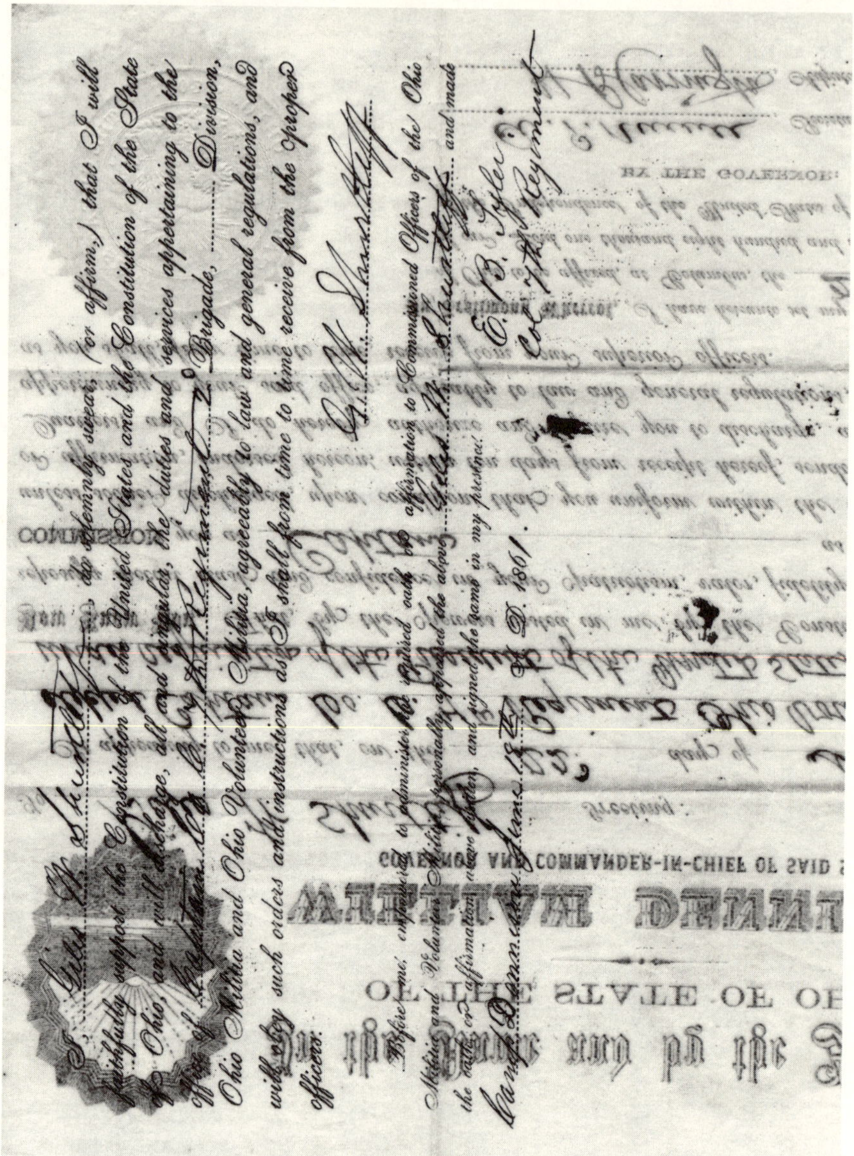

I, Giles W. Shurtleff, do solemnly swear, (or affirm,) that I will faithfully support the Constitution of the United States and the Constitution of the State of Ohio, and will discharge, all and singular, the duties and services appertaining to the office of Captain Co. A 7th Regiment 2nd Brigade, ... Division, Ohio Militia and Ohio Volunteer Militia, agreeably to law and general regulations, and will obey such orders and instructions as I shall from time to time receive from the proper officers.

G. W. Shurtleff

Before me, empowered to administer the oath or affirmation required of Commissioned Officers of the Ohio Militia and Volunteer Militia, personally appeared the above named Giles W. Shurtleff and made the oath or affirmation above written, and signed the same in my presence.

Camp Dennison June 18th A.D. 1861.

E. B. Tyler
Col 7th Regiment

(Back)

1861.14

1861.14

A Degree in Prison Life

From Lawrence Wilson, ed., *Itinerary of the Seventh Ohio Volunteer Infantry: 1861–1864,* New York: Neale, 1907.

This account, written by Giles W. Shurtleff, details his capture and imprisonment during the early part of the war. Shurtleff remained prominent throughout the war—beginning with his capture and erroneous notices of his death in papers like the *Cleveland Daily Herald.* Upon his release, he remained in service and was instrumental as lieutenant colonel in the organization of the 5th Regiment of United States Colored Troops. After the war, Shurtleff reurned to Oberlin College and taught Latin. His statue at the college is inscribed with following, "Freedom can not be given, it must be earned." He died on May 6, 1904.

At the outbreak of the Rebellion I was a tutor in Oberlin College and a student in its Theological Seminary. When Sumter was fired on and troops were called for, the young men were ready for the fight. Professor Monroe, who was in the State Senate, came to Oberlin and addressed a mass-meeting and called for volunteers. A company was at once filled and many offered themselves who could not be received. The Seventh Ohio Regiment, to which our company was assigned, had two candidates for the colonelcy, E. B. Tyler and James A. Garfield. Garfield was a prominent member of the State Legislature, and already gave promise of the greatness which he afterward achieved. Tyler was a man of little prominence, but an active politician. He was also a brigadier general of the Ohio State Militia, and appeared in camp in military uniform, and this won him the election. Three months after the organization of the regiment, it was surrounded in the mountains of West Virginia and a large portion of it captured. The Oberlin company held an outpost long enough to allow the main body of the regiment to retreat, but too long for its own safety. Thirty-five of the company were captured and six wounded, two of them mortally. One, a talented member of the freshman class, died the next day in the hands of the enemy. It was my privilege to be at his side during his last hours and receive his dying message.

After two days we started over the mountains for Richmond. The enlisted men were tied together with a rope like a gang of slaves. After marching from daylight until dark, dry flour was issued and two skillets in which to cook supper for more than a hundred men. A few of them built a fire, wet up the flour with water, and without salt, and cooked it. The process was slow and the result so unsatisfactory that most of the men went to sleep supperless. Lieutenant Wilcox and myself, the only commissioned officers among the prisoners, having given our parole of honor not to escape, were permitted to go ahead of the marching column. On the second day we learned where the night was to be passed and hastened on hoping to make some provision to prevent starvation. All we could do was to beat water in a large kettle ready to boil the flour when it came. After four days we reached Jackson River, where we took the cars for Richmond.

We had marched more than one hundred miles, and were so weary and. starved that many were scarcely able to stand. Upon arriving at the depot in Richmond, Lieutenant Wilcox and I started to walk into the city, and were arrested by a rebel sergeant and taken to the tobacco warehouse which was used as a military prison at that time. This sergeant proved to be [Henry] Wirz, afterward so infamous for the cruelty he practiced upon prisoners at Andersonville [Wirz was later tried and executed for war crimes at Andersonville. A monument honoring Wirz stands in Andersonville, Georgia. Many Southerners felt Wirz was judicially murdered under false charges of cruelty to prisoners amid the reaction to Lincoln's assassination.]. The commissioned officers were placed on the first floor and the enlisted men on the second and third.

Our room was about forty by sixty feet, and one-half of this space was occupied by the machinery connected with the factory. There were more than eighty officers. Our food was wheat bread and boiled fresh beef for breakfast and dinner, and bread alone for supper. Those who had money bought other articles—tea at four dollars a pound, coffee at one dollar, butter, sixty cents. Confederate money and greenbacks were at this time on a par in the South. No beds or bedding of any sort were furnished. A few officers had purchased blankets and mattresses but most of us slept on the bare floor with a block of wood for a pillow. I sold my watch to a rebel officer and used the proceeds to purchase Thiers's "Consulate and Empire," two of Thackeray's novels, and copies of Livy and Virgil.

Orders prohibiting a near approach to the windows were rigidly enforced. On the floor above us a New York sergeant thoughtlessly stood nearer the window than was pleasing to the guard below and was shot through the head without warning. Roll was called at 9 in the morning by a young rebel, Lieutenant Withers. He was very small, wore a long sword that dragged on the floor, and was a dude generally. He came in one morning and gave the usual order to "fall in for roll call." We arranged ourselves, according to custom, by standing with our backs to the wall in an irregular line reaching the whole length of the room. I happened to be sitting on the block which I used for a pillow, reading "Pendennis," and when the order to fall in came, I stood up, leaned my back against the wall and kept on reading. The Lieutenant was directly in front of me, and when I responded to my name without lifting my eyes from my book, he asked with an oath of execration why I did not get into line. The question seemed ludicrous and I glanced up and down the room and asked what line he referred to. My fellow prisoners laughed and the Lieutenant was enraged, and left the room in great haste and returned with a corporal and two private soldiers with fixed bayonets, halted them before me, and with his own hands put handcuffs upon my wrists. His triumph, however, was of short duration. The officers of the prison association wrote a note to the commanding officer asking him to come in and investigate. He did so, apologized to me and required Withers to remove the irons.

All the officers were searched immediately after this, and we learned that Withers believed that there was a conspiracy among the prisoners to mutiny, kill the guards, and get away, and that we had in some way obtained pistols.

Early in September an order came to transfer thirty officers to Charleston, South Carolina, to be placed in Castle Pinckney, a dismantled fort in the harbor. Major Potter, one of our number, was well acquainted in Charleston, and represented the fort as a delightful place. We started on the journey with hopes of better quarters. Reaching Petersburg, we had to march through the city from one depot to another. A crowd of citizens followed us, using abusive epithets and appealing to the guards to shoot us. Women shook their fists at us from windows. The trip lasted twenty-four hours and no food was furnished us. Reaching Charleston early in the morning, we were kept waiting for hours, that our march through the city might be witnessed by the people. When we finally moved we were escorted by a brass band, a troop of cavalry in gala attire, and thousands of citizens, men, women, and children. We were paraded through the streets of the city, and when we finally came to a halt, it was not at Castle Pinckney, but in front of the city jail. We filed into the jail, climbed the dark and dirty stairs, and passed along a dingy hail with grated cells on either side. Five of us were thrown into one of these cells. The first sight that caught our eye through the only window was a huge gallows, and I said to Major Potter, "There's our castle, and it is a veritable 'castle in the air.'

The rebel officers in charge of us knew that we had been twenty-four hours without food and yet several hours more passed before anything was brought us, and when it came consisted of raw coffee in the kernel, sea biscuit, and salt pork full of maggots. Our cell had a small open grate and our cooking utensils consisted of a single skillet. We succeeded in borrowing from the guard a kettle to cook our raw coffee in, and boiled it unground and unburned, fried our bacon over the coals, and had our dinner at 2 o'clock. And so we settled down to life in cells for four months. Some features of our life here are too shocking to relate.

The ration issued to us was this same maggoty pork and sea biscuit. No coffee, ground or unground, after the first day. We resorted to various methods of serving up sea biscuit. One day we boiled it until soft and served it with fat as a dressing. This we called lobscouse. The next day we softened it in hot water and fried it in fat. This we called dunderfunk. Occasionally we took up a collection and sent out for sweet potatoes and white bread. The rebel officers told us we were only temporarily in jail, until Castle Pinckney could be put in order. After about a month we were sent to Castle Pinckney. At first this seemed a great improvement.

We had a large court-yard for outdoor exercise. We soon found, however, that our rooms were so damp as to make them exceedingly unwholesome. The fort was built on the shore of an island in the midst of the bay which constitutes Charleston Harbor. When the tide was out the island was bare, but when the tide was in it was covered with five or six feet of water. The outside walls of the fort were solid masonry and we occupied the casemates, which are nothing more than great recesses in the walls, arched at the top and opening into the central court. Bunks had been built up on the walls and blankets were furnished us. But this solid masonry was full of water that had been gathering for generations, and we soon began to have coughs and rheumatism and fevers and after a few days were glad to be moved back to the stifling cells of the jail. In the early part of the winter there came an exciting episode to break the monotony of our prison life. This was the great Charleston fire, which swept away one half of the entire city. It commenced in the night at a point quite distant from us, burned all the next day, and kept coming steadily toward us. It seemed as if the whole city was doomed. We learned from one of the guards who was friendly to us that it was the purpose of the officers in charge to leave us locked in our cells if the jail burned.

We managed to smuggle an ax into our cell, through the aid of a guard, determined to make at least a vigorous effort before surrendering ourselves to the flames. During that terrible night all the buildings in the neighborhood of the jail burned. Our cell was brilliantly lighted, so that one could read without difficulty, and for some hours the gratings of the windows were so hot as to burn the hands that touched them. Great fire-brands were driven against the windows, but the jail escaped.

Soon after this fire we were removed from Charleston to Columbia, and placed in the city jail, the officers in a large room and the enlisted men in barracks adjacent. Our quarters were better than we had had before. Each officer had a bed, consisting of a plain pine bedstead with straw mattress, and our Government sent us warm clothing and army blankets.

Among the enlisted men were several members of a New York company which was made up of skilled engravers. Every night they manufactured Confederate money sufficient to furnish all our tables comfortably the next day. I have sometimes feared when I have related this circumstance that I should be regarded as drawing on my imagination, but it is, nevertheless, true.

One of the methods for passing time was to make trinkets from bones. The rebels were surprised at our skill, and eagerly purchased every article made. These engravers managed to buy necessary tools on the pretext of needing them for working in bone. Some that they could not get they made themselves. The officer in command of this prison, Captain Shriver, was a Christian gentleman, and treated us as honorable prisoners of war (which cannot be said of the officers of any other prison in which I was confined).

The rector of the Episcopal Church came in one Sabbath, and invited all who would like to attend divine service to go into an adjoining room. Some forty or fifty officers and soldiers went. Everything moved pleasantly until he reached the prayer for the President, which he had changed to a prayer for the "President of the Confederate States." The moment those words were uttered, we all jumped to our feet and shouted in confusion: "We are not Confederates!" "We are not traitors!" "We are not praying for Jeff Davis!" The poor rector seemed frightened, and slipped out at the side door and gave us up as a hopeless lot.

Before winter was fairly over an order came to parole all the prisoners at Columbia and send them to Richmond to be exchanged. We were wild with excitement and delight, too happy to sleep. Most of the night before starting was spent in an extemporized banquet, with toasts and speeches. Reaching Richmond, we were told there was an interruption in the negotiations for exchange. We took quarters in Libby Prison and had full opportunity to experience that deferring of hope that maketh the heart sick. We stayed about three months in this famous prison, in many respects the most trying period of my prison life. Libby Prison had been occupied by a wholesale ship chandler and grocer. It was three stories high with three rooms on each floor, extending from one street to another. The officers occupied the middle room on the first floor. The whole room was about forty by one hundred feet, of which nearly one third was partitioned off from the front as quarters for the guard. The only light and air came from the windows at one end. In this space, perhaps forty by seventy feet, there were at this time about one hundred and fifty officers. The air was extremely foul, and the room filthy and infested with vermin.

Our windows looked out upon James River and sloping fields beyond, and as spring advanced the water and the green fields were made beautiful by the bright southern sun, and presented a marked contrast with the filth, the squalor, and the stifling air of our prison.

Occasionally we could hear the distant boom of our cannon. We learned from the Richmond papers and from the arrival of new prisoners that McClellan's army was approaching Richmond.

Rebel troops were daily passing our window on their way to the front. To get out of prison and get to work became an absorbing passion. Lieutenant Wilcox of my own regiment, Lieutenant Kent of the Regular Army, and myself made an elaborate plan for escape. We managed to exchange our army clothing for citizen's dress, procured a pocket compass, and made from the mainspring of an old-fashioned watch a steel saw with which to cut the bars of a window. The plan involved cutting a hole through the floor, then through the brick partition beneath so as to pass from our room to the basement of the adjoining room. That room was occupied by loyal Southern men, and had a window that opened to a side street which was not guarded. The floor had to be cut with an ordinary pocket knife. It was hard oak plank two inches thick and thoroughly seasoned. We worked on that hole in the floor two hundred and twenty hours. It was cut under the head of my iron bedstead, and the work had to be done lying flat on the floor face down. After we had taken out some pieces of the plank, I was lying there one day at work when a rebel officer came into this unused basement directly under me. I could have reached down and taken his hat from his head. I held my breath during the few minutes he stood there, but fortunately he did not look up, and went out without seeing me.

The opening through the brick wall was made much more speedily. I think we did the whole work on the wall in three days. Now we were ready to move. But the night before we were to start some loyal Southern men on the upper floor cut a hole through the roof and let themselves down by a rope to the street into which we were to escape. A guard was immediately placed in this street; and thus all our plans came to naught.

Whenever any one was sent North we sent a large secret mail with him. On the 21st of May a large number of private soldiers were sent from Salisbury. One of them brought North a half dozen letters for me. Most of them were put between the lining and the outside of the boot-leg.

One letter I sent by writing on tissue paper, taking the cap from a brass button of the New York State Militia, wadding my letter into it, adjusting the cap again upon its base, and sewing the button on the coat. When the militia-man reached New York he cut the button off and sent it to its destination. There was nothing important in these letters, but there was diversion in the effort to get them through. We were permitted to send short letters of six lines, through the mail, but they were all read by a rebel officer.

One of the hardest things we had to endure in Richmond prison was the great number of visitors who came to see the "Yankees," and their unvarying assumption of superiority. After the disaster at Ball's Bluff [where Union forces mistakenly advanced on a non-existent camp and became trapped, leading to defeat] Howell Cobb came in, and with the greatest gusto told how many "Yankees" had been killed and captured, and with cool nonchalance assured us that one Southerner could whip ten "Yankees." The absurdity was only equaled by the meanness of the spirit which could prompt such insults to prisoners of war.

A Presbyterian minister of Richmond, with the most insolent and overbearing tone, descanted upon the chivalry of the South and the fanaticism of the North. There were some Southerners who treated us with kindness and courtesy. I have already spoken of Captain Shriver of Columbia. Archbishop Hughes, of the Catholic Church, called several times at our quarters while we were in Charleston, and though he indorsed the doctrine of secession, he always manifested a genuine Christian spirit and kindly disposition.

Early in May we were sent to Salisbury, North Carolina, where there were already several thousand prisoners, and among them were the members of my company who had been sent from New Orleans before that city was captured by General Butler. The prison at Salisbury consisted of a brick factory, perhaps forty by one hundred feet, four stories high, together with several small frame houses that had been used as residences by those who ran the factory. A stockade ten feet high had been built, enclosing these buildings and four acres of ground. The dead line was ten feet inside this stockade, and a line of sentinels with loaded muskets and fixed bayonets traversed this line day and night. The officers occupied the frame houses and had free use of the yard. This was a great improvement upon previous quarters. After the close confinement in filthy and stifling pens for nine months, the privilege of moving about in the free air and sunshine was an unspeakable blessing, and it apparently came just in time to save the lives of some of our members. We organized various kinds of outdoor sports. Baseball had come into vogue in Oberlin two years prior to the war, and I had played it. Many of the soldiers from New York were expert players. We formed an association and played every day.

About the first of June a staff officer of Jeff Davis came to our quarters with an order to select two captains, place them in confinement, feeding them on bread and water only, and treating them in every way like criminals condemned to death, thus to be held as hostages and to be immediately hanged in case our Government should hang a rebel captain who had been condemned as a spy. There were ten of us with the rank of captain. The method of selection was left to us. We numbered ten slips of paper with the numbers from one to ten, dropped them into a hat, shook them thoroughly, placed the hat in the hands of Chaplain Eddy (one of the prisoners), and agreed that we would one by one draw out the numbers, and that the two who should draw numbers nine and ten should be elected. The whole process did not occupy more than twenty minutes, and two of our number were placed in a dungeon, with every prospect of speedy execution. Our Government decided not to hang the rebel captain, and after two weeks our friends were returned to us, a little paler from the confinement and the starvation, but no less loyal or determined.

There were about one hundred Southern loyalists in close confinement in a small stockade within our prison-yard. They were held simply because they were loyal. They planned an escape, digging a tunnel under the interior stockade and beyond the guard line which surrounded it. They had provided themselves with rope ladders with which to climb the outside stockade. To reach this they had to cross an open field of about two hundred yards. We all knew they were to make the effort at midnight and we were on the watch to see how it would come out. We had not much confidence in the success of the effort, as we were more than two hundred miles from the Union lines. At the hour agreed upon there was a terrific thunder storm in progress. The night was utterly dark, except as it was lighted up by flashes of lightning.

There was a rebel regiment encamped within the yard, but without experience or discipline. Promptly at 12 o'clock these loyal men rose up out of the ground, at the end of their tunnel, in the darkness, and started across the field. The sentinels nearest yelled "Halt!" the long roll was beaten at regimental quarters, and the soldiers of the regiment became an uncontrollable rabble. They evidently supposed there was a general insurrection of prisoners. Our Union friends ran across the yard, the guards continuing to shout "Halt, halt!" and pursuing them, but apparently forgetting to fire at them. It was a novel scene as the flashes of lightning revealed it to us at frequent intervals. Every man succeeded in getting out of the enclosure and escaping into the woods. The rebel regiment succeeded in getting a line formed about three-quarters of an hour after the prisoners had escaped. Within a few days the escaped prisoners were all brought back, some of them mangled by hounds.

As the Fourth of July approached we determined to have an old fashioned celebration. The commanding officer consented on condition that we would not abuse the Confederate Government or say anything about the war. In the afternoon we read the Declaration of Independence, sang "My Country, 'Tis of Thee," and had some spirited, patriotic addresses. The afternoon was given up to games, among which were the greased pig, the sack race, wheel-barrow race, and some burlesque games, ending with a grand match of baseball. We had a crowd of spectators from the town. The players on both sides had been practicing for a month. After playing two hours the score stood five to six in favor of my club. We had had our last chance at the bat and two were out on the other side, while two men were on bases. My position was right field; the ball was batted directly over my head and across the dead-line. The game depended upon catching the ball on the fly or getting it in time to prevent a tally. Of course I ran across the dead-line, caught the ball, and saved the game. The guard cried "Halt!" but did not shoot, and after what I had seen a few nights before, upon the occasion of the escape of our Union friends, I did not believe he would shoot.

The better treatment in Salisbury, of which I have spoken, did not include the private soldiers. They were kept in close confinement in the great factory, when they might just as well have had the use of the yard. Sickness was very prevalent among them and there was no proper provision for their care. The percentage of mortality among these private soldiers was enormous. The dead-house was near my quarters. Several dead bodies were brought there every morning. Sometimes as many as a dozen. About 10 o'clock a cart drawn by a mule was backed up to the door and the dead were tumbled into it with no show of feeling, hauled off to the woods, and thrown indiscriminately into a ditch and covered up. During the war the bodies of 12,000 soldiers were thus carted from this dead house, and less than one hundred of them have any sign to mark the spot where they lie.

Early in August the order came to send all Union prisoners in Salisbury to Richmond for exchange. Most of the private soldiers had already been sent North. There were several in the hospital who had been unable to move, but they were all sufficiently recovered now to go with the rest, except one.

I had been visiting the hospital daily for more than a month, leading in religious exercises, and giving such attention to the sick as I could. Our chaplain, Hiram Eddy, and all the physicians among the prisoners had been exchanged. As soon as this order came I went to the hospital to aid the sick ones in getting ready to leave. One boy, barely seventeen years of age, had typhoid fever and was not fit to make the trip, but he insisted that he must go. His entreaties were so earnest and so touching that Capt. Thomas Cox, of Cincinnati, and myself, made the effort to take him along. We carried him on a rude stretcher to the depot. There the officer in charge refused to take him aboard unless he could stand, as every foot of room was occupied. A crowd gathered about us and our poor sick boy fainted. The disappointment of finding that he could not go had completely overcome him.

A lady came forward, and with the quiet dignity of one who has authority made her way through the throng and asked the crowd to stand back and give him air; sent a boy for cold water, and tenderly lifted his head and bathed his brow and nursed him back to consciousness. The train was about to start. I said to Captain Cox: "What shall we do? He must not be left here alone," and the Captain answered: "We must stay"—and so the train pulled out; the train that was headed toward the North! toward the Stars and Stripes; toward home and friends and the stirring activity that was so attractive to us; and we were left alone with this poor dying comrade in the very center of rebellion and treason.

On this good woman's invitation we took the lad to her home, bathed his fevered body, exchanged his hard and ragged clothing for clean, soft linen, furnished by Mrs. Johnson, and laid him in a comfortable bed. (Mrs. Johnson was warned by the rebel Major in command that manifestation of such interest in a "Yankee" would bring her into suspicion of being a Union woman, but this did not turn her from the path of duty.) Tenderly she cared for that stranger boy, and when he died the next day she wept over him as if he had been her own child. Captain Cox and I were not allowed to remain in her home during the night, but had to go back to our prison. The next day we obtained permission to go to the house and found that he was dead. Mrs. Johnson went to the city authorities and asked permission to bury him in her own lot in the public cemetery, but this was indignantly refused, with another coarse warning against the interest she was manifesting in a "Yankee." She said to us: "He shall not be buried in the brutal way of other prisoners." We placed him in a plain pine box, Captain Cox and I dug the grave, and reverently laid him beneath the sod in the garden of this Christian woman.

When our cavalry captured Salisbury near the end of the war, Mrs. Johnson was still there, an object of hatred and persecution. Our soldiers learned the story of her loyalty and love, furnished her money with which to go North and erected a monument over that grave and inscribed upon it not only the name of the soldier, but the heroic deed of this good Samaritan woman who soothed and comforted his last hours and gave him Christian burial. Captain Cox and I were allowed to start at once for Richmond, having given our parole that we would not attempt to escape. We found that our friends had not yet gone North, having again been delayed by negotiations in the business of exchanging. And so our staying with the dying soldier did not in the end delay us in the matter of our exchange.

While we were in Libby Prison a Federal officer was brought in who had secreted on his person a small battle-flag. We hid it and made daily pilgrimages to it and secretly feasted our eyes and comforted our hearts by looking on its Stars and Stripes undimmed and untarnished. For eight months we had not seen the national colors, had heard only of defeat of our arms, and had been in the power of those who expressed contempt for our Government and our flag. Despondency and gloom had been slowly taking possession of us. These officers, fresh from the battlefield, brought us tidings of the rallying thousands of the North and the deep determination to defend the flag; and there in the midst of the gloom and filth of Libby Prison we laid our right hands upon the emblem of national authority, and each for himself swore a solemn oath that he would use all his powers and shed his last drop of blood in defense of the national surpremacy.

It was just at sunset of a bright Sabbath day in August that we stepped from rebel soil upon the flag of truce boat on the James River and saw the Stars and Stripes waving over our heads. We gathered beneath that flag, reverently uncovered our heads, and sang "Praise God from whom all blessings flow.

A Nation at War

On August 29, Fort Hatteras at Cape Hatteras, North Carolina, falls to Union naval forces.

1861.15

The Enemy in Our Streets

From *The Summit County Beacon,* "Traitors about How to Recognize Them," September 19, 1861.

Copperheads were Northern sympathizers of the Confederate cause. Their name derived from the fact that they were regarded as attacking the Union treacherously from the rear, as the snake of the same name was said to strike. Ohioan Clement Vallandigham was considered a prominent Copperhead. The advice given in this article was probably already known by the *Beacon*'s readers. Obviously, Confederate spying was a concern in Northern states. Though not widespread, Confederate infiltration did occur in Ohio—a relative of Jefferson Davis was tried as a spy. As a result of the trial, several Columbus residents were placed under surveillance.

When you hear a man say that "this is nothing but an Abolition war," mark him well, for he is a foul traitor at heart.

Whenever you hear a man assert that "this war is only intended to free the niggers," keep your eye on him, for he is a full blooded secessionist in disguise.

Whenever you hear a man declare that "this is a Lincoln war," watch him well, for he is an incipient, if not a full fledged traitor.

Whenever you hear a man constantly harping about the "enormous expense of war," don't lose sight of him, for he would join the Secesh army if he dared to.

Whenever you hear a man declaring that this is "an unjust war, and might have been avoided," you may "bet your pile," that his treasure and his heart are both in the kingdom of Jeff Davis.

When you hear a man who is constantly endeavoring to build up an opposition to the vigorous prosecution of the war for the preservation of the Union, nail him to the counter as a disunionist.

Reader, don't you know some persons to who these rules apply exactly? If you don't, you must have carried your eyes in your pockets during the last two months.

A Nation at War

On September 20, Lexington, Missouri, falls to Confederate forces.

On October 21, Union troops are routed at the Battle of Ball's Bluff, Virginia.

1861.16

Caring for the Spirit

From Alfred E. Mathews, "Rev. L.F. Drake, chaplain 31st Ohio volunteers, preaching at camp Dick Robinson, KY, November 10th 1861," Cincinnati, OH: Middleton, Strobridge & Co.

Alfred Edward Mathews (1831–1874) was an English immigrant whose early career was that of a traveling bookseller and artist. During his service in the 31st Ohio Volunteer Infantry, he drew scenes of the conflict which were published as lithographs. This particular image is of a service given by Reverend L.F. Drake, who remained in the army for the duration of the fighting.

Some 3,694 commissioned chaplains, Union and Confederate, are known to have served during the Civil War. Most were regimental chaplains in the infantry, cavalry or artillery, but more than 200 also served as hospital or post chaplains. Methodist preachers made up the largest contingent of chaplains (at least 40 percent), followed by Presbyterian and Baptist preachers.

The service depicted below was conducted at Camp Dick Robinson, which has a special place in the history of the Civil War. When the camp was established in August 1861, Kentucky was attempting to stay neutral in the conflict. Although Gov. Beriah Magoffin complained to Abraham Lincoln about the site, Lincoln responded that since the camp "consists exclusively of Kentuckians" and that it was not the "popular wish of Kentucky" to close it, he refused to remove the soldiers. This action probably kept Kentucky on the Union side.

Union service at Camp Dick Robinson.

1861.17

Build a Prison and Confederates Will Come

From *Executive Documents Printed by Order of the House of Representatives during the Second Session of the Thirty-Seventh Congress, 1861–1862*, Washington, DC: Government Printing Office. From Lydia J. Ryall, *Sketches and Stories of the Lake Erie Islands*, Norwalk, OH: American Publishers, 1913.

In the fall of 1861, William Hoffman was appointed the commissary general of prisons. In that role he selected Johnson's Island, near Sandusky in Lake Erie, to build a prison for Confederate troops. The island's location made it almost immune from rescue and escape attempts. The island began to accept prisoners in April 1862. During the hostilities, the island held 3,000 prisoners; almost all were commissioned officers.

One grand conspiracy did involve the Johnson's Island prison. In September 1864, a plan was undertaken to capture a Union man-of-war, the *Michigan*. With the gun-boat under Confederate control, rebel forces, assisted by armed prisoners, were to break out of Camp Douglas, near Chicago; Camp Chase, near Columbus; Camp Morton, near Indianapolis; and Johnson's Island. The officers from Johnson's Island would organize the 20,000 freed prisoners and wage a campaign across the unprotected Northern states. The plot was foiled and among those captured was famed Confederate spy, Annie Davis (see 1865.2).

The document on page 51 lists the details of the government contracts for the Johnson's Island property and facilities. Hoffman found the $500 yearly lease a true bargain. The Johnson's Island prison is depicted below in a sketch from the period.

Prison grounds during the war (Ryall).

Government Contracts			
744	Sandusky Ohio, November 11, 1861	Lieut. E.W.H. Read, a.a.q.m. [Acting Assistant Quartermaster], with West & Gregg	Lease of part of Johnson's island, Sandusky bay, Lake Erie, for building a prisoners' depot, for one year or as long as the war continues, at a rate of $500 per annum.
745	Sandusky Ohio, November 11, 1861	Lieut. E.W.H. Read, a.a.q.m., with West & Gregg	For erecting the following buildings on Johnson's island, Lake Erie, as a prisoners' depot, 3 buildings marked A on the plan for officers' quarters, at $1,290 each; 1 building, B, for soldiers' quarters, at $1,020; 4 buildings, C, for imprisoned officers, at $2,100 each; 4 buildings, D, for imprisoned privates, at $1530 each; 1 hospital, E, at $850; 1 storehouse, F, at $550; $1500 for the additional expenses of getting materials on the island.

1861.18

How Many Ohioans Can Fight?

From Commissioner of Statistics, *Fifth Annual Report of the Commissioner of Statistics to the Governor of Ohio for the Year 1861*, Columbus, OH: Richard Nevins, State Printer, 1862.

Edward Deering Mansfield was Ohio's first commissioner of statistics, serving from 1857 to 1868. He was a professor of constitutional law and history at Cincinnati College and a frequent contributor to *The New York Times* under the pen name, "The Veteran Observer." Statistics, as a tool to gauge the characteristics of society, was in its infancy; many citizens dismissed the discipline as a mere mass of figures. In the introduction to his report, Mansfield concluded that statistics were consulted by historians and statesmen to "determine the basis of civilization and the wisdom of laws." The following portion of the report is a very straightforward, and perhaps cold, analysis of how many troops Ohio could send to war without damaging its economy.

Number Capable of Bearing Arms.—The old rule of the laws regulating the militia service was to require only those between the ages of 18 and 45 to bear arms. Undoubtedly this includes those who would be most serviceable, and there are few men over fifty years who are really capable of hard service in the field. In the exigencies of war, men of all ages may be called out; and the best mode of ascertaining those capable of bearing arms is to take the whole number of men over 18 years of age, and then deducting from them those of extreme age and a certain proportion of the infirm. The censuses of the United States have determined with exactness the number of these at each period of life, and this is an invariable ratio. Applying this proportion to the population of Ohio in 1860, and we have these results :

1. The proportion of males *over* 18 years is 49 per cent.
2. The whole number of *males* in Ohio is 1,169,799.
3. The number of males *over* 18 years of age—49 per cent of the whole—is 573,202.

The proportion of *males* over 70 years of age to the whole male population is 4 per cent., which, being deducted from the last number, leaves (able-bodied) 523,566. The proportion of those which may be kept in military service, without seriously *impairing the industry of the State*, is the important question in raising troops for the war. Until there is such a reduction of labor as will reduce the amount of agricultural and manufacturing products, the draft on the male population does not seriously injure the prosperity of the State. In Europe, about *one-fiftieth* part of the whole population are *in the regular army in time of peace;* and this is not a draft on the labor of one, two, or three years, but a *continuous draft on the industry* of a State. For a war of two or three years there is no doubt threefold that number may be maintained, and industry not materially reduced; but, when it becomes continuous, it is exhausting, and society must decline under it. This was the case with France in the wars of Napoleon, and it was the *exhaustion* of France, rather than the snows of Russia, which ultimately caused his downfall. When Napoleon returned from Moscow he found France exhausted of men, and he was unable to raise new armies on a large scale. Could he have done what he could ten years before—raise half a million of men in a short time—there is very little doubt the allies would have been driven back, and Napoleon have made a favorable peace. War is exhausting, but in nothing so much as of human strength. For every soldier who dies in battle, there are ten who sink beneath typhoid, dysentery, and pneumonia. Looking to the industry of Ohio, the increase of agricultural machinery, the number of those who can be spared in large towns, and the immigration, I think it safe to say that *one fifth* of the able-bodied men of Ohio can be spared for the army for two or three years. Beyond that period, so large a proportion would undoubtedly tell on the industry of the State. The surplus crops would be gradually exhausted, and thus *the wealth of the State be diminished.* This wealth—the accumulation of labor—is the basis of taxation, and no taxes would be felt half so severely as the exhaustion of labor. So long as we can maintain an annual surplus of crops, we really accumulate wealth, and thus we are able to bear the heaviest taxes. *One fifth* the able-bodied men of Ohio is 114,800 men. We have now less than 85,000 *actually in the field;* so that we have not yet arrived at the point when the draft of men becomes exhaustive. For a period of two or three years we could spare 30,000 more, and a similar proportion for the loyal population of the United States would produce an army of a million of men in arms—a number greater than will probably be ever needed in this generation.

A Nation at War

On November 1, General McClellan is appointed general-in-chief of the Union Armies.

1861.19

Buried and Betrothed

From L.C. Walton, *Reminiscences of 1861*, Tallmadge, OH: Tallmadge Historical Society, 1862. Lawrence Collection, Akron-Summit County Public Library. Used with permission.

Although town life was affected by war, in the early stages of the fighting the numbers of killed and wounded were relatively small. In reality, both armies were gearing up, training troops, and working out logistics; the real war had not yet arrived.

The following list from Tallmadge, Ohio, located near Akron, Ohio, details those from the area who were fighting for the Union cause. A few soldiers had perished. Unlike the way the dead are treated today, burials were not done locally. Relatives probably never had a chance to visit a fallen soldier's resting place. Life went on, however, and people still got married.

The following is believed to be a correct list of persons who have volunteered to sustain the authority of our government from this township and the regiments or companies in which they serve, viz:

Perez Clark	Konkle's battery	
Daniel Sullivan	" "	
John Patterson	" "	Died at Louisville, Ky.
Ambrose Hinds	" "	
William Patterson	" "	
Adam Taggart	" "	
George Blakelee	" "	
Alfred Sperry	" "	
Edward H. Butler	" "	Died in Hospital prison at Charleston S.C. Oct 8, 1864
Ashbel Root	" "	
Albert B. Clark	" "	
Edward Geerhart	" "	
Wesley Wells	" "	
Thomas Dixon	" "	
John Condon	" "	
Michael Honoddle	" "	
Zebulon McAlpine	" "	
Daniel Schaaf	" "	
George C. Ashmun	2d Cavalry Band	
Charles H. Sackett	" "	

Frederick Rexford	" "	
Frederick Spafford	" "	
Whitney	unknown	
W.H. Murray	Marines	
Geo. Patterson	" "	
Jas. Morris Walton	6th Battery	Died Feb 10, 1862 of fever at Jamestown, Ky. where he is buried in a cemetery.
T.W. Screen	" "	
William Warren	Sherman's Brigade	Died at home in Aug.
Otto Limber	" "	
Allen Limber	" "	
Alexander Carr	7th Infantry	
Frank Falkerson	" "	
S.W. Bettes	" "	
Amos Wills	" "	
Albert Reeves	Hazen's battery	
Henry McClelland	" "	
Oliver Wright	29th Infantry	
Alfred Palmer	" "	
John Randall	" "	
William Boyd	unknown	

Notwithstanding the war and the hard times there have been the usual number of marriages: the following are the names of the parties

Mr. Samuel C. Taylor	to	Miss S. Hagenbaugh
Mr. Bruce Baldwin	to	Miss Fannie Sackett
Mr. Henry N. Grant	to	Miss Sarah Sackett
Mr. Rufus Upson	to	Miss Mary M. Upson
Mr. Orange S. Treat	to	Miss Sarah Lyman
Mr. David B. Treat	to	Miss Katie Pierce
Mr. Treat Fenn	to	Miss A.F. Wright
Dr. Houghton	to	Miss M.E. Seymour
Mr. Permenas Sprague	to	Miss ?????
Mr. Philo E. Wright	to	Miss Fannie E. Pettibone
Mr. Clark A. Sackett	to	Miss Katie Ashmun

The deaths in town have been the following

Miss Sally Foster	January	aged 80
Mrs. Milo Stone	February	aged 69
Rev. William Hanford	May	aged 73
Almira Parsons	June	aged 21
Mrs. Richards	August	aged 57
Mr. George Patterson		
Mr. Edgerton child		aged 1
A child and hired girl of Mr. Lyman Brown	October	aged 1 and 57
and Rev. E. S. Scott		

A Nation at War

In mid-December, Julie Ward Howe writes a poem that provides the words for the "Battle Hymn of the Republic."

1862

"Even supposing the war should end to-morrow, and the army melt into the mass of populations within the year, what an incalculable preponderance there will be of military titles and pretensions for at least half a century to come."

A Peaceable Man

1862.1

A Calm before the Battle

From William H. Venable, ed., *Poems of William Haines Lytle*, Cincinnati, OH: The Robert Clarke Company, 1894.

William Lytle was born in Cincinnati in 1826. He was a graduate of Cincinnati College, where he studied law. During 1862, Lytle was in command of Camp Morton in Bardstown, Kentucky. In October, he would be wounded at the Battle of Perryville and taken prisoner. After returning to active duty, Lytle was killed at the battle of Chickamauga on September 20, 1863.

Lytle's most famous poem was "Antony and Cleopatra," which he wrote in 1858. Critics always held up that piece as the standard to which his other work did not always rise. The following selection echoes the calm, pristine wait for a coming battle.

In Camp

I gazed forth from my wintry tent
Upon the star gemmed firmament;
I heard the far off sentry's tramp
Around our mountain girdled camp
And saw the ghostly tents uprise
Like specters 'neath the jeweled skies.
And thus upon the snow clad scene,
So pure and spotless and serene,
Where locked in sleep ten thousand lay
Awaiting morn's returning ray,—
I gazed, till to the sun the drums
Rolled at the dawn, "He comes, he comes."

1862. Bardstown, Ky.

1862.2

Please Write. It's Cold and Lonely Out Here.

From Aron Allyn to Kate Allyn, January 8, 1862; The Allyn Civil War Papers (1859–1876); Aron Allyn, 1861–1863; Hiram College Archives. Courtesy Hiram College Archives, Hiram, Ohio.

This letter, written by Aron Allyn to his sister, Kate, is likely a description of the 42nd Ohio, which was led by Colonel James Garfield, during a skirmish in Kentucky. The letter is quite matter-of-fact and describes some of the drudgery of war—bad weather, little food, long marches, and lack of sleep. The writer also points out how easy it was to be mistaken for the enemy. Allyn died on May 1, 1863, after the battle of Thompson's Hill, Mississippi.

PAINTSVILLE [KENTUCKY]
JAN. 8TH 1862

Dear Sister,

Not having a chance to send my former letter I will endeavor to send a little more of what is going on in this part of the world. On Monday last we left camp Pardee and advanced 4 miles on our course. There was nothing of any account except it was muddy and was growing cold with a little [snow] of flying and at night it had froze up the mud a little. We pitched tents and cooked a rather poor meal. I laid down at half past nine tired and sleepy. I never slept any better in my life than I did till midnight when we was called out to go up to this place and see what we could about the rebels. We was gone till 3 o'clock when feeling as though we had done enough. On the next morning I got up and felt like a man of sixty more than a boy. At noon we was ordered to march to this place when we arrived here we heard the report that the rebels had run. Their camp being about 3 miles distant the Colonel decided to make them a visit at their own camp. The cavalry boys some 500 strong was sent one way and the 42nd went another so that if we had struck together we would have made a good thing of it. But we did not know their position the [unknown word] thing that we had for to do was for to make a bridge over a milldam a little larger than the Garrettsville [Ohio] mill dam which took us about an hour making the bridge of saw logs which was in the shape of a raft. We crossed the stream at about dark and commenced our first hard march for that is what this kind was called.

In the first place our boys had nothing for supper a few homony, one hard bread and some not a bite. We marched to the enemy's camp which we found deserted. I had a dispatch from Colonel More who was left in charge at our camp. The dispatch stated that there was a force of 500 cavalry about 4 miles from our present position and wanting to know whether he should move up and attack them at night or wait till morning. Our Colonel decided that he would have the fun himself. We started on the march with caution. When we came near the camp we saw their fires and taking them to be the picket the Colonel sent out 12 men to capture them while we was standing waiting for the result of our boys who was sent ahead. The boys of Co. B while moving around to keep from freezing discovered a dead horse nearby us which in examination proved to be U.S. cavalry horse.

On further examination they found a man's body which on examination was found to be a secesh cavalry man which excited us a little you may expect. Besides attracting some cheers from the boys we marched on through the rebel's camp their fire a burning yet and things looking as though they had left in a hurry. They was camp kettles clothing and everything scattered here and there but on we went making the best of our way in to camp which was a long way off yet. We arrived in camp at day break this morning. After making a march of 12 miles over as bad marching as it would be in marching through the worst part of Hiram not in the road but in the woods cross lots bridging two good size streams in order to cross. The ground was frozen hard only in deep mud which was plenty. The roads being tracks with cav where it was froze it was so slippery that a man would slip and sprawl about as though he was on ice. Many a boy got a fall but not hurt. Pem Cowles [mustered out on September 30, 1864] and a friend got foot sore and went to an old deserted house to stay. They have not come yet. We fear that they are taken or killed. The Joys boys have just come in. They endeavored to capture a flat boat but could not find it on the account of it being sunk and the goods hid. When we arrived near camp our pickets took us to be the enemy and fired on us. We took them for the same and fired on them. There was all of 150 shots fired on both sides and strange as it was they was no one hurt. All of the shots going over their head. There was one ball went near my head and I sent one back as well as I could for we had to fire at their flash. When we arrived in camp we found out the cause of the dead rebels. Our cavalry in scouting run into their cav and made a charge on them and run them in under the cover of their infantry who was entrenched in ambush. When our cavalry received the fire of the infantry and found their position they retreated but not till it was too late for the infantry fire killed one of our men and wounded another and killed the horse I spoke of. They was 6 of the rebel's cavalry killed. Don't know how many wounded . . .

The enemy got the worst of it and though they set their trap and our men spring it they was completely [unknown word] and had to make a hasty retreat. We marched through their entrenchments and burned their deserted camp. The devils are in full retreat and our cav are in pursuit of them but so far [if] the plan had worked the rebels would have got awfully whipped or else we would for the cavalry was not to attack them till it would have been impossible for them to have retreated unless they had cut their road through us which would have not been an easy job. . . . The 40th Ohio arrived here today. We met them with loud cheers. I am as well as ever but most awfully tired and I have not heard from home yet and I want to have you write soon for I shant write till I hear from home. I have no more now but may have before I can send it.

Yours,

Aron

A Nation at War

On January 19, Union forces are victorious at the Battle of Mill Springs, Kentucky, an outcome that provides a morale boost to the North.

1862.3

A Marching We Will Go!

From "73rd Ohio Leaving Chillicothe, 1862;" Albums of the War of the Rebellion; Photographs; Western Reserve Historical Society. Used with permission.

This image was likely taken in January 1862 (some sources date the image to 1864), after the 73rd Ohio Volunteer Infantry trained at Camp Logan near Chillicothe, Ohio. The 73rd was one of the Ohio regiments that saw almost continuous action in the war. Two companies of the 73rd were the first to enter Atlanta during Sherman's March to the Sea.

Of the approximate 1,200 troops who were part of the regiment, 285 died in battle and 586 were injured, many crippled for life. Undoubtedly, the men were ill-prepared to face the grim nature of their journey. The townsfolk who sent the volunteers off didn't realize that 70 percent of their fathers, brothers, and sons would be injured or killed during the rebellion.

Seventy-Third Ohio Voluntary Infantry, Chillicothe, Ohio, 1862.

1862.4

The War Must Be Prosecuted with More Vigor

From J.A. Gurley, *The War Must Be Prosecuted With More Vigor*, a speech delivered in House of Representatives, January 29, 1862. Washington, DC: McGill and Witherow, 1862.

John Addison Gurley was born in Connecticut on December 9, 1813. He moved to Cincinnati, Ohio, in 1838 and became owner and editor of the *Star and Sentinel*, and also served as a pastor. This speech reflects a theme of many wars—an information gap between upper command and the soldiers at the front. Lincoln's replacement of the Secretary of War was a recognition that the war needed to be fought more aggressively. While Gurley thought the superiority of the Union troops would prevail in a swift victory, the Confederate forces proved to be as able and tenacious as Northern volunteers.

Speech of Hon. J. A. Gurley, of Ohio
Delivered in the House of Representatives,
January 29, 1862

[Excerpts]

I do not rise for the purpose of making a long speech, but simply to offer a few suggestions in reference to that great struggle in which our Government is engaged, having for its object the suppression of treason and rebellion, and the preservation of a nation's honor and life. Sir, it is useless, in my judgment, to attempt to disguise a fact now almost everywhere recognized, that we must have a more active and practical war policy in this House, in the Cabinet, but more especially in the field, or we may prepare for a war of several years' duration, both domestic and foreign. As we have been going on, and as we are now proceeding in the military campaign, when a few more months have gone by, it would be no strange thing if the southern confederacy should be acknowledged by foreign Powers; and when that takes place, if ever, our Government will stand before the civilized world not only humiliated, but utterly disgraced.

But what means this long delay in attacking the rebellious forces? Sir, our army has long been ready and anxious to fight; our soldiers are burning with a desire to strike at the traitors—the madmen who have risen up against the best Government in the world—and our subordinate officers are chafing and panting for the battle-field; but what avails all this? They have earnestly cast about for a bold and daring leader, ready for the great contest; but where is he? Sir, echo answers in the far distance—where is he? It is painful to confess the real truth on this subject at this late day. Thus far they and the country have looked in vain for a commanding general—a commander-in-chief. I mean—who has exhibited the will and the requisite enterprise and genius to lead our forces on to victory. But why not fight? What lion is that which stands in the way? Is it feared that if we do fight somebody will get hurt? Or is the ghost of Bull Run still hovering about and haunting the minds of our commanding generals? Sir, we have lost more men in camp by ordinary disease and sickness during the last five months than we should have lost, in all human probability, in a half dozen general engagements in the field. . . .

We must now fight or be disgraced! Yes, sir, fight as only men can who are on the side of justice, right, and human freedom—otherwise our people will become discouraged and disgusted, the Treasury bankrupt, and the Government be brought into utter contempt. . . .

This war has reached a point where kid gloves, pleasant words, and gilded promises are of no further use. The exigencies of the hour demand hard words and still harder blows; for remember, this contest must close, either in the ruin of a Republic that has filled the eyes of the best men of the world with admiration, and possibly the destruction of civil and religious freedom in America, or in the more perfect supremacy of law and order, and the renewed stability of our cherished institutions. I have firm faith in the latter result, for I long since learned that great revolutions move the world forward, but backward never. . . .

Sir, I wish just in this place to notice one remarkable fact connected with this war. Eight out of ten of the subordinate officers and soldiers in our army, the very men who are to bare their breasts before the fire of the enemy, the very men who must receive the shock of battle and the rain of bullets, are precisely those who complain most, because they are not permitted to go forward and fight. Those upon the ground, and who see and know the danger, and realize the strength of the rebels, ought to be able to form a correct judgment as to whether they can whip them or not. Leave the question to them, and ten out of twelve would vote that there has been no necessity for the delay of the last four months. . . .

Why should the great army of the Union remain idle when the people everywhere, soldiers and civilians, are imploring for and demanding active movements against the rebels in the South? Sir, the people of East Tennessee, for example, have long been asking for ten thousand men to save their part of the State from the desolating hand of the rebels, and their wives and children and families from insult, persecution, and starvation. How have their prayers been answered? By an announcement that we have no troops that can be spared from the great army; yet there are absent from the Potomac—or were a few days ago, and this is about the average at all times—on business or pleasure or other objects, nearly one thousand officers and over seven thousand privates, a great army of themselves, and as many as were required to save Tennessee, and for the lack of which large numbers of citizens have been imprisoned, shot, and hung; and still larger numbers driven from their homes and hunted like the wild beasts of the forest. Why were not eight or ten thousand men from this great army sent at an early day on an errand so important, and which would have secured the great railroad over which the rebels carry their troops and supplies? Why, in these times of peril, give leave of absence to eight thousand soldiers, and yet plead the want of men in reply to a people who chose to sacrifice all they had in this world rather than desert the flag of the Union? Unlike us, they were in the power of the infuriated confederates; in the very jaws of the lion, but boldly dared them to do their worst; and yet we have left these loyal people to suffer, to hide in the caves and the mountains, and even starve, under the plea that we have no army to send to their rescue, when some two hundred thousand well fed troops in this neighborhood have been three or four months begging and pleading to be led against the enemy rather than pine away in camp. . . .

Mr. Chairman, I am very sure that the Commander-in-Chief, the President, is as anxious as any man in the country that the war shall be prosecuted with vigor but from necessity he must rely mainly upon the judgment of the first military officer in its management. While I know that he is behind none in zeal for forward movements, I presume that he does not feel justified in setting up his judgment as the standard for military operations; and his multiplied duties leave him little time to study the plans of battles. No man in the nation, however, is more anxious for the speedy suppression of the rebellion, and he will second, I have no doubt, every daring and wise effort to accomplish that object.

Mr. Chairman, no one can dislike more than I do to criticize in terms of severity the conduct of this war; I would rather a thousand times praise every act of the commanding general; but this is no time and this is no place for flattering and deceitful words. Sir, it is a serious question with many honest minds whether this Congress, this Government, and this great nation are not to-day sleeping upon a volcano. Murmurs, deep and strong, are everywhere coming up from the people against the inaction of the army; they are amazed and grieved that the most intelligent body of soldiers in the world are restrained by a single hand from vindicating the honor of our flag upon the battle-field. Meanwhile, the public Treasury is being drained for their support; the fleets of three powerful nations are nearing our shores, and if our military do not rouse themselves to speedy action, and strike quick, sharp, and heavy blows, some fine morning those fleets may make a visit to our southern coast, politely announce to us that cotton is an absolute necessity in Europe, and the blockade must continue no longer. All this is not only possible, but in the contingency of continued inactivity, and the standing menace of the rebel army against this capital, almost at its very gates, highly probable.

But I see at last a streak of daylight ahead. I see it resting upon the chair of the new Secretary of War [Edwin Stanton, born in Steubenville, Ohio and a graduate of Kenyon College], a man who, if report speaks truly, is like brave Ben Wade of Ohio [a U.S. Senator from Ohio and abolitionist]—a good combination of Old Hickory [Andrew Jackson, 7th President of the United States] and Zack Taylor [12th President of the United States]. He certainly appears to have a mind of his own, a brain to plan, and an iron will to execute; and if I am not greatly mistake, he will push on this war with all the vigor that characterized the people in raising so vast, so mighty an army. Let us thank God and take courage, and unite all our energies with those of the new Secretary, as well as the Chief Magistrate's, that we may bring it to a speedy and glorious termination.

1862.5

Supplying the Troops

From "Sutlers in the Army," J. Res., Ohio Leg., Feb. 21, 1862.

As the war turned from adventure to business, federal and local governments began to create resolutions, laws, and other legal devices to codify procedures. The military had its rules of engagement and political entities had rules of enforcement. The following document, concerning sutlers, was one of many resolutions passed during 1862, in an attempt to have Ohio's congressional delegation introduce laws at the federal level.

Sutlers followed the army and sold supplies to soldiers from makeshift tents. Without any competition, sutlers were often accused of selling items at exorbitant prices. Sutlers responded that soldiers stole sutlers' goods and forced them to escalate prices.

Sutlers in the Army

—

Joint Resolutions
of
The Ohio Legislature,
Relative to

The protection of our soldiers from the imposition of sutlers in the army.

—

February 21, 1862
Laid on the table, and ordered to be printed.

—

Resolution

relative to the protection of our soldiers from the imposition of sutlers in the army.

Whereas the privileges allowed by the general government to sutlers have been greatly abused, and as the result thereof soldiers have been cheated and defrauded of their money, and have paid large sums to sutlers without any adequate consideration therefor:

Therefore be it—

Resolved by the general assembly of the State of Ohio, That our senators in Congress be, and they are hereby, instructed, and our representatives requested, to use their best endeavors to procure the passage of a law abolishing the office of sutlers in the army, and providing that all necessaries be furnished our soldiers through the commissaries of the army.

Be it further resolved, That the governor of Ohio be, and is hereby, requested to forward copies of these resolutions to our senators and representatives in Congress.

James R. Hubbell, *Speaker of the House of Representatives.*

B. Stanton, *President of the Senate.*

Passed February 7, 1862.

A Nation at War

On February 25, Union forces take control of Nashville, Tennessee, the first Confederate state capital to fall to Northern troops.

1862.6

A Missouri Hermit

From Charles Wright, *Experiences in the Ranks of Company C, 81st Ohio Volunteer Infantry, during the War for the Maintenance of the Union, 1861–1864*, Philadelphia: James Beale, 1887.

During the war, newspapers reported almost daily on particular skirmishes, battles and other happenings. Letters were sent home by soldiers, and soldiers' families wrote back. Although the system wasn't foolproof, information spread at a brisk pace. This particular story is remarkable, not only because of the actions of George Bowman, but because he had become a local icon. In many ways, a visit to Bowman was a nice respite from reality.

While at Danville, two comrades—Lieut. W. H. Chamberlin and myself—visited the cave of a hermit who was located in the side of a ravine about two miles from Danville. Under directions we followed a path through the woods until we came to a ravine, and, following down the same until we noticed smoke issuing from the rocks above our heads, we clambered up the side until we came to the mouth of the den or cave. Hearing a noise down in the bowels of the earth, and a sepulchral voice saying "Come in, fill up the hole," we made our way down into the apartment of this lover of solitude. He was engaged in making a cup of red-pepper tea. We took rude seats that he pointed out for us. Lieutenant Chamberlin engaged him in conversation. His name was George Bowman. He stated that he was born in Ohio, and came to this part of the country several years ago. Had been a dweller in this cave eleven years; was engaged in digging for money, of which a great many thousand dollars had been deposited under the rocks a certain number of feet. A portion of the money, gold and silver, had been placed there three thousand years ago by the "ancients." He showed us one place where he had dug through the rock to the depth of thirty feet. By digging four feet further he said he would come to four bushels of gold! Taking us under a ledge of rocks close to the mouth of his den, he pointed out several places where by digging down a certain number of feet a certain amount of gold and silver already coined could be found. On any other subject but money this strange man talked with ordinary intelligence. In regard to the war he was "non-committal." We suppose that he reasoned that for his business it did not matter which triumphed, the Union or the Confederacy. We bade him adieu at the mouth or entrance of his subterranean mansion to repair to our camp and hold ourselves in readiness for the behests of Uncle Sam, and he to follow his profession of digging for gold deposited under the rocks in that ravine by the ancients. (circa February, 1862)

1862.7

Combating Waste and Seeking Retribution

From "Fraud and Corruption by Agents and Officers of the Government," J. Res., Ohio Leg., Feb. 21, 1862.

The following two resolutions, passed in February and March of 1862, are indicative of how public opinion shapes the enterprise of war. The first resolution is concerned with waste and fraud that comes with supplying armies with needed equipment. During war, oversight falls behind the speed of war itself. The second resolution brings home the reality of war. People suffer during the fighting, and those who have caused the war must pay, in this case with their lives. If "war is hell," then according to the Ohio legislature, the Confederate instigators had to end up there.

FRAUD AND CORRUPTION BY AGENTS AND OFFICERS OF THE GOVERNMENT.

—

RESOLUTIONS
OF
THE LEGISLATURE OF OHIO,
IN RELATION TO

FRAUD AND CORRUPTION BY AGENTS AND OFFICERS OF THE GOVERNMENT.

—

FEBRUARY 21, 1862.
LAID ON THE TABLE, AND ORDERED TO BE PRINTED.

—

RESOLUTION
RELATIVE TO REQUESTING CONGRESS TO PASS SUCH LAWS AS WILL PREVENT FRAUD AND CORRUPTION BY THE AGENTS AND OFFICERS OF THE GOVERNMENT.

Whereas we regard with surprise, anxious alarm, pain, and regret the evidences that have reached us, and the disclosures that have been made in Congress of wastefulness, fraud, and peculation based upon deep corruption among the subordinate agents of our national government in connexion with supplies for the army of the United States; and whereas these frauds largely increase the public expenditure, the burden of a loyal people, bring scandal upon our free institutions, and poison the people's confidence in their government in short, strike a death blow at the cause of freedom; and whereas, especially at this time, an abiding faith and firm confidence in the integrity of our public officers is indispensable for the public good, the successful overthrow of the rebellion, and the nation's credit at home and abroad: Therefore—

Be it resolved by the general assembly of the State of Ohio, That Congress be, and hereby is, respectfully asked to provide suitable and effective laws, with proper penalties attached, for all manner of fraud practiced by any person in any contract with the national government, and especially in those made in conformity with appropriations for the supply and pay of our army and navy, exposing the names of all that are found guilty of such violations.

Resolved, That the governor be requested to forward copies of the foregoing preamble and resolution to our senators and members in Congress.

James R. Hubbell, *Speaker of the House of Representatives.*

B. Stanton, *President of the Senate.*

Passed February 11, 1862.

From "Execution of Leading Rebels," J. Res., Ohio Leg., March 24, 1862.

Execution of Leading Rebels.

—

Joint Resolutions
of the
Ohio Legislature,
Expressive

Of their views as to the treatment of the leading rebels.

—

March 24, 1862.
Laid on the table, and ordered to be printed.

—

Joint Resolution

RELATIVE TO THE EXECUTION OF LEADING REBELS

Whereas wicked and ambitious traitors have, without cause, plunged our nation into civil war, disregarding all fraternal obligations, falsifying the most sacred injunctions that can be applied to the conscience—their solemn oaths; forcing upon its an expense of millions of money and incalculable loss in the prostration of business, and untold miseries in the sacrifice of human life; and

Whereas recent developments manifest a disposition on the part of some of the leaders of the rebellion to ask terms and sue for peace therefore, be it

Resolved, by the general assembly of the State of Ohio, That, in view of the loss of loyal blood and treasure, our government cannot, without loss of character and injustice to the noble dead that have fallen in defence of its authority and the rights of humanity, accept less than an unconditional submission to the supremacy of the Constitution and the laws,

Resolved, That the future peace of the United States and the permanency of the government, as well as the best interests of humanity throughout the world, demand the speedy trial and summary execution of all leading conspirators in the attempt to destroy the government; and in the name of the people of Ohio, who have given their money and lives without stint for the preservation of our liberties, we protest against the entertainment of any proposition for settlement other than unconditional submission to rightful authority and the condign punishment of the authors of the rebellion.

Resolved, That the governor be requested to transmit a copy of the foregoing to the President and to each member of the cabinet, and to each of our senators and representatives in Congress.

James R. Hubbell, *Speaker of the House of Representatives.*

B. Stanton, *President of the Senate.*
March 14, 1862.

A Nation at War

On March 9, the *Monitor* and *Merrimac*, ironclad vessels, engage off the coast of Hampton Roads, Virginia, completely revolutionizing naval warfare.

1862.8

Captured in the Lap of Luxury

From *The Athens Messenger*, "Letter from Columbus," April 10, 1862.

During the early days of the Civil War, captured Confederate officers were free to live in Columbus, Ohio, with their promises not to escape. Union and Confederate officers intermingled quite regularly at local cafes. The freedom given to the enemy outraged a great majority of the general public and volunteers in the Northern army. The following two letters rail against the benevolent treatment granted to the Confederate officers while Ohioans were dying on the battlefield. The Ohio Legislature finally reacted to the public outcry by passing a resolution in April 1862 (see 1862.10).

Columbus
March 31, 1862

Editor Messenger—In my last letter to your spicy paper I aimed to give your readers a faint idea of the character of some of the innumerable and pestilent dens that abide in this Capitol city. Of late a new kind of institution has sprung into being that has become a mortal stench in the nostrils of all patriotic and loyal people. Little did I think when, come weeks ago I had the exquisite pleasure to behold eight hundred thorough bred Southern rebels direct from the "sacred soil" of Tennessee unloaded from the cars at the Columbus depot and take their places betwixt two files of Uncle Sam's sturdy troops and marched to the prison at Camp Chase, that any of their butternut crew [Butternut was a term given to a Confederate soldier or an individual disloyal to the Union. Bark from the butternut was used to dye Confederate trousers.] would so soon be reproduced in the shape of toadies and favorites among the codfish aristocracy [the new-moneyed class] here who would gladly rule the public sentiment of the day. But nevertheless we are daily compelled to meet at the hotels, public offices of the city quite a number of those chivalrous warriors who unconditionally surrendered to "Northern mudgills" at Fort Donelson, and who now in return for the kindness they received by parole of honor at the hands of the Government, are boldly and defiantly promulgating their hellish secession doctrines in open day, and I am sorry to say there are members upon this floor that not only apologize for, but indorse their conduct and applaud their audacity. One of the members from Franklin county, in discussing resolutions offered by Judge

Myers, looking into these outrages, declared in his place there were as good and true men in the prison at Camp Chase as were on this floor. Every loyal member cheerfully indorsed the sentiment so far as the gentleman from Franklin was concerned but unfortunately for the country, he only gave utterance to what is pent up in the hearts of more than twenty honorable gentlemen who are sent here to represent in part a State that has sent eighty thousand of her noble men to the field to fight for God, humanity, and the right. Could these gentlemen stand by the road side and see themselves go by, it might improve their manners, for treason has always been at a discount in this country since the days of Arnold [Benedict Arnold was a traitor during the Revolutionary War.]. But a traitorous heart is the most effectually purged by the application of a few inches of cold steel or the end of a stout rope. This sympathy is not confined to men alone, but there are she traitors also. The wife of one of our ex-Supreme Judges of the State has been out to Camp Chase offering sympathy and condolence to those much abused rebels, and even indicated her preference for the society of rebel, over that of Federal officers. If the fiery ordeal of civil war is not sufficient to purge Northern dough faces [Northerners sympathetic to the South] of their inate [sic] desire to eat dirt, then indeed will it take a stronger prescription than we have yet found in the books; and I would recommend all such to the tender mercies of those barbarian devils who applied the scalping knife to our dead and wounded soldiers who bravely fell at the bloody battle of Pea Ridge. [Evidence surfaced that Confederate troops employed Native Americans during the battle.]

When Southern chivaliery [sic] marched out to Camp Chase with Col. Moody's [commandant at Camp Chase] men acting as convoy, I noticed some seventy or eighty of the sons of Ham [A name given to slaves due to the fact that according to the Bible, one son of Noah, Ham and his descendents peopled much of Africa.] bending beneath loads of old dirty quilts, comforts, pieces of carpets, and many other traps too tedious to mention. I heard the question repeatedly asked at the time are these negroes slaves, or are they rebels taken with arms in their hands? This question is now settled by the report of a Senate committee who have visited Camp Chase for the purpose of investigating the whole subject, the result of which proves what many had predicted. Out of eighty-four negroes in prison, none of which can legally be considered rebels, fifty are slaves, fed and cared for by the General Government but for what purpose I am at a loss to know. Mighty events bring out strange developments, and people of Ohio are startled with the announcement that rebel officers imperiously demand the right to call the roll of their slaves, not "at the foot of Bunker Hill Monument [Revolutionary War monument located in Charlestown, Massachusetts]," but in cannon shot of our own Capitol where the laws of freedom for a free people are being enacted. Some one is responsible for this state of things which is in direct conflict with the fundamental laws of the land. Secesh stoutly protest against any interference with the present status—refusing peremtorialy [sic] to allow their slaves to be detailed to wait on the sick in hospital—claiming them as body servants, no doubt much prefering [sic] the use of black hands to their own bloody ones.

B.

From *The Athens Messenger*, "Letter from Camp Chase," April 10. 1862.

Camp Chase, Ohio,
April 2, 1862

Mr. T. F. Wilkes—Sir: I again take the liberty of writing to you a few lines to let you know where we are. We are still guarding prisoners, and I think this will be our occupation all this spring and summer. New companies of them arrive almost daily, and new prisons are still going up, the old ones being full. Several of the officers are allowed the liberty of the camp on parole, and last week two of them availed themselves of the liberty thus granted them and made themselves scarce, and have not been heard of since. I think this will put a stop to paroles.—Last night the camp was in a state of high excitement. Between eleven and twelve o'clock the bugle sounded, and almost simultaneous with it came the long roll, and the word was passed through the camp, "The prisoners are breaking out of the upper prison." In a few minutes the prison was surrounded by three regiments with loaded guns and fixed bayonets, when it was ascertained that the alarm was occasioned by a soldier who attempted to pass the brigade guard and was fired on—the ball passed between the arm and body. The prisoners are still dying off, but not as fast as at first; they do not average more than four per week. A man belonging to our regiment was poisoned last night. It seems that a boy from Columbus was in one of the prisons selling apples, and as he came out one of the guard bought some of them and after eating them was taken with convulsions and died this morning. A post mortem examination of the body takes place this evening. It is supposed the apples were poisoned while in the prison by some one. The rebels here are furnished with the best of liquors when they come to the city, and at file camp, the government keeps a force of nearly a hundred negroes, mostly slaves, for the benevolent purpose of blacking the boots and doing other little choice for the Southern lords. If their quarters are to be cleaned, hands are hired for the purpose, or else the soldiers have to do it, while if our camp wants any cleaning up, we have to do it ourselves. The rebels are furnished with nice large cooking-stoves while we have to cook in a dirty, smoking kitchen, with our kettles hung on a pole, while at Louisville three paroled prisoners are boarding at a first class hotel in that city, at an expense to the government of $2 per day. The work seems to be going on bravely in the South. All praise and honor to the brave commanders there and in the west. . . .

I have nothing more of interest to write now.

Yours respectfully,

John Bougher

[Possibly a member of the 40th Iowa Volunteer Infantry stationed at Camp Chase.]

A Nation at War

On April 6 and 7, the bloody Battle of Shiloh, a Union victory, is fought near Pittsburg Landing, Tennessee.

On May 8, Confederate General Thomas J. "Stonewall" Jackson begins his Shenandoah Valley campaign with a victory at the Battle of McDowell in Virginia.

1862.9

Is there a Doctor in the House?

From "Relative to Authorizing the Governor to Accept the Volunteer Services of Surgeons," J. Res., Ohio Leg., April 8, 1862.

Sometimes the technology of weapons progresses faster than the tactics of war. The group charge, like Picket's at Gettysburg, was a common part of many Civil War battles. However, the Minnie ball and canisters used in cannons provided an advance that leveled the charging soldiers with devastating consequences. The Minnie ball, invented by a French officer, Claude Etienne Minnie, allowed for improved targeting at a longer distance. On impact, the ball left a gaping wound and shattered bones. Surgeons were left little choice but to amputate limbs. The modern canon round was a thin metal container loaded with layers of lead and iron ball usually packed in sawdust. On firing, the canister disintegrated and the balls exited the canon's muzzle mowing down soldiers within a 400-yard range.

The following resolution calls for surgeons (a similar one called for nurses, too) to aid the increasing number of soldiers wounded during the early stages of the war. Medicine, as a science, had not caught up with the breadth of injuries the new weapons wrought. Most doctors, moreover, had little formal training, often two years or less with little clinical practice.

JOINT RESOLUTION,

RELATIVE TO AUTHORIZING THE GOVERNOR TO ACCEPT THE VOLUNTEER SERVICES OF SURGEONS.

WHEREAS, It is a melancholy fact that, in the extensive engagements of our troops with rebellion, many of our brave soldiers have suffered and died for the want of that immediate care which, from the circumstances of battle and the smallness of the regular medical and surgical force, it was impossible to extend to them; and

WHEREAS, It is suggested that many eminent surgeons and physicians, through motives of patriotism and humanity, propose to go and render their services without compensation in the hospitals and upon the battle-field, in affording relief to the diseased and wounded, wherever the governor may direct, upon condition that transportation and subsistence be furnished them at the expense of the state; therefore,

Resolved by the General Assembly of the State of Ohio, That the governor be and he is hereby authorized to accept the volunteer services of such number of competent physicians and surgeons, upon the conditions aforesaid, as he may deem proper, who are willing to go where the governor may direct, without compensation, upon being furnished transportation and subsistence.

Resolved. That provision be made in the general appropriation bill to carry this resolution into effect.

JAMES R. HUBBEL, *Speaker of the House of Representatives.*

B. STANTON, *President of the Senate.*

April 9, 1862.

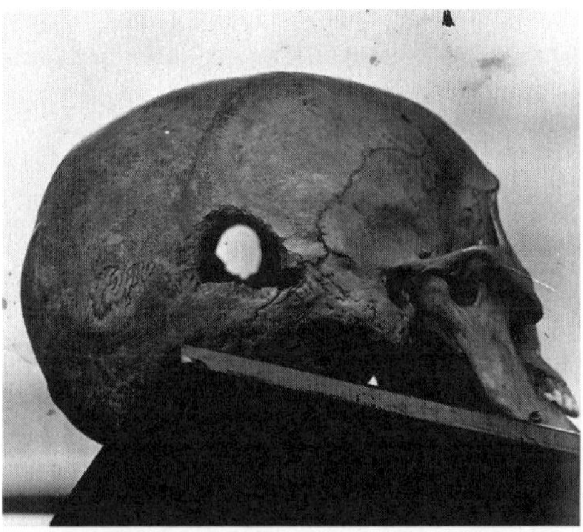

Skull of Edward Volck with bullet hole. Volck was a private in Company D of the 55th Ohio Volunteer Infantry, and died from wounds suffered at the Battle of Bull Run, 1862. From Library of Congress.

1862.10

A Grieving Mass of Bleeding Flesh

From James A. Garfield to Augustus Williams, April 16, 1862; The James A. Garfield Collection; Western Reserve Eclectic Institute; Hiram College Archives. Courtesy Hiram College Archives, Hiram, Ohio.

This letter is from James A. Garfield to Frederick Augustus Williams, a colleague at Hiram College. Garfield describes his route to the battle of Corinth, Mississippi, which took place on October 3–4, 1862. The city was the base for the Confederate army that fought at the Battle of Shiloh (April 1862). After Shiloh, Corinth, a vital rail crossing, was occupied by Union troops. Southern forces led by Generals Earl Van Dorn and Sterling Price failed in the attempt to retake the city. Although counts vary, the Union losses were 355 killed, 1,841 wounded, and 324 missing. The Confederate side saw 1,423 killed, 5,692 wounded and 2,268 missing.

HEAD QUARTERS 20TH REG.
ARMY OF THE OHIO BATTLEFIELD
OF SHILOH NEAR PITTSBURGH PA

APRIL 16, 1862

My Dear Augustus:

It was very hard for me to leave you at Cin. [Cincinnati] as sick as you were, but necessity compelled me to do so. When I reached Louisville on Tuesday evening, I found a dispatch for Gen. Buell ordering me to join him immediately at Nashville and take command of a fighting column that was hastening forward to the great battle near Corinth, Miss. To be—separated thus suddenly—and finally from my dear boys, was the severest trial that I have suffered since the war began. I would much prefer to have remained Col. of the 42nd than to have been promoted to any position away from there. I, of course, appreciated the compliment which Gen. Buell designed to bestow on me in thus choosing me to go with him but, it seemed like leaving all in the army that I loved or that loved me. The thought also of taking command of nearly 4,000 men who had never been tried in battle, who were strangers to me and I did not know what officers I could rely on in an emergency made the future a gloomy one. Especially as men were in immediate expectation of a great battle. I received the order about nine o'clock in the evening of my arrival at Louisville. I could not bear to meet our boys and so I sat up all night at the Galt House preparing to leave. Early next morning I took the Cars and reached Nashville that night.

Gen. Buell had gone on. Next morning I took [the] train toward Columbia, and by cars, wagon and on foot I reached that place late in the afternoon. Gen Buell had gone on and I obtained a horse and a cavalry escort and rode all that night. At 3 o'clock in the morning I reached the Gen's Head Quarters. In an hour the army was on the March and a West Point Col. who had been commanding the 20th Brigade had introduced me to the Brigade—and delivered up the command—it was a dreary morning, the rain pouring down in turrets and the mud very deep. Thus we marched on till Sunday afternoon, when we came in hearing of the guns on the Tennessee—About which we received orders to take three day's rations in haversacks—leave our trains, knapsacks, and all our baggage and hurry forward to the fight. We marched all night and at 11 o'clock reached the river at Savannah. Thousands of wounded now were being brought down from the field. The boats were waiting to take us forward—(I met Henry Johnson [mustered out of the army in 1866; moved to Columbus, Ohio, and started a chair manufacturing enterprise] at the Landing—380 of the 41st went into the fight and 147 were killed or wounded—) We embarked and steamed up to the Pittsburgh Landing, landed and immediately, set the column in march to the field. We marched five miles over the muddy hum[an] carnage that any American battlefield ever presented. We reached the front about 3 o'clock and were greeted by a shower of shot and shell—For an hour and a half, [unknown word] were bursting all around me, but none struck me—One went whizzing past my head and struck a mounted officer a little ways beyond me. Both horse and rider fell a grieving mass of bleeding flesh. But the enemy was making his last stand. He stood under arms all that night. The extreme [unknown word] and next day made a reconnaissance of six miles—and a fight with the enemy's cavalry (Texan [Rangers] among them.) and lost 20 killed and 41 wounded. Our cavalry here are a disgrace to the service—We have slept with tents now for 8 days on the Battlefield which covers 36 square miles—A letter from Mr. Owens tells me you are better. I hope this will find you at home. I have not heard from Col. Sheldon or Major Pardee [both subordinates to Garfield when he commanded the 42nd O.V.I.]. [Sentence not legible.] I address you as usual—Do write to me. Give my love to your Father and the family—address me as Comd. 20th Brigade 6th Div. Army of the Ohio [unclear word–possibly "at"] Tenn. River.

Ever Your Friend and Brother

J.A. Garfield

1862.11

The Ohio Legislature Acts

From "Rebel Officers in Columbus and Camp Chase Prison," J. Res., Ohio Leg., April 25, 1862.

The treatment of prisoners during the Civil War was governed by International Law and the "laws of war." In short, once captured, a prisoner was no longer a combatant and was afforded honorable and humane protection. Prisoners weren't always treated with dignity, especially as supplies and food became extremely scarce during the latter part of the war. As public opinion crystallized against the extremely benevolent treatment of Confederate prisoners in Ohio, the legislature reacted by passing the following resolution.

RESOLUTIONS OF THE LEGISLATURE OF OHIO,

RELATIVE TO REBEL OFFICERS IN COLUMBUS AND CAMP CHASE PRISON

—

APRIL 25, 1862.

ORDERED TO LIE ON THE TABLE AND BE PRINTED.

—

JOINT RESOLUTION

RELATIVE TO REBEL OFFICERS IN COLUMBUS AND CAMP CHASE PRISON.

Whereas, the feelings of the loyal people of Ohio have been outraged by the appearance in the streets of their capital of rebel officers in rebel uniforms, released on parole, and by the fact that rebel prisoners in Camp Chase prison have been permitted to retain and use their former slaves as servants, thus practically nullifying our State constitution by allowing slavery in Ohio; and,

Whereas, said matters are not under the control of the governor or State authorities; therefore,

Resolved by the general assembly of the State of Ohio, That in the name of the people of Ohio, who have freely given their treasure and their blood to sustain the government and the Union, we do most solemnly protest against this mistaken clemency to the guilty, and this outrage upon the feelings of the loyal people of Ohio.

Resolved, That a copy hereof, together with a copy of the report of said select committee, be forwarded by the governor to the President of the United States, the Secretary of War, and our senators and representatives in Congress.

James R. Hubbell, *Speaker of the House of Representatives.*

James Monroe, *President pro tem. of the Senate.*

Passed April 8, 1862.

EXECUTIVE CHAMBER.

—

In communicating the above resolutions it is due to Colonel Moody, the commander of Camp Chase, that I state that the legislature labored under a mistake in supposing that the rebel prisoners were permitted to retain and use their former slaves as servants. It is also due that I add that, by a vote of 41 to 26, the house of representatives in form reconsidered their action.

David Tod, *Governor of Ohio.*

—

Report of Select Committee

Mr. Gunckel, on leave, submitted the following report:

The select committee to whom was referred S. R. No. —, relative to the rebel prisoners at Camp Chase, together with the special message of the governor in relation thereto, beg leave to report:

That, finding the reply of the governor to the senate inquiries less full and explicit than was desirable, they waited upon him and were favored with a long and satisfactory interview, and also with passes to Camp Chase prisons, and such other facilities for investigation as it was possible for him to afford.

Subsequently your committee visited Camp Chase, and by the worthy commandant of the post, Colonel Granville Moody, were shown through the three prisons, and kindly allowed all the liberties necessary to further the object of their visit.

Your committee found some thirteen hundred persons confined in the three prisons, mostly from Tennessee, Kentucky, Missouri, and Mississippi. Their quarters were in all respects as good and in some a little better than those of the soldiers outside, and your committee were assured that the rations distributed were the same in quantity and quality as those given to our own men. No complaint was made as to any of these things, but there was a general expression of satisfaction therewith.

Your committee found seventy-four negroes in the prisons, mostly taken at Fort Donelson. Of these, from what they could learn, a few were free when taken, having been hired by officers as cooks and servants. The remainder, perhaps fifty in number, were slaves in attendance upon their masters, and while so employed were taken along with their masters. None of them were in arms, all of them having been retained for menial service merely. Since their capture they have travelled [sic] with their masters, attending and serving them as before. On their arrival at Columbus they took charge of and carried the baggage of their former masters from time depot to Camp Chase, the men having no servants being compelled to carry their own, as our soldiers do on similar occasions. Arrived at the camp, the privates were, as far as possible, separated from the officers, and, for obvious reasons, placed in different prisons; but the negroes were placed in the same prisons with the officers who were their former masters. Why, unless that they might continue to attend and serve their former masters? And they have ever since done so, cooking, washing, waiting upon, and serving them just as before their capture, the relation of master and slave being as rigorously maintained by the master, and as fully recognized by the negroes and the other inmates of the prison, as it ever was in the State of Tennessee!

But why were these slaves taken at all? They were not and had not been in arms against the government; their presence at Fort Donelson was not even voluntary. Why are they retained in prison? They have done no wrong, they deserve no punishment. Is it to furnish rebel officers with servants? And was it for this they were transported at the expense of the government, and are now subsisted at her cost? Is our constitutional provision thus to be made a nullity, and slavery practically established in Ohio? And this under the protection and at the expense of the federal government?

As to rebel officers released on parole your committee could not get much definite information other than that, with few exceptions, these paroles were granted by order of General Halleck. That the clemency so shown was mistaken the following facts as to the conduct of these officers while in Columbus will show. They came wearing their side arms stopped at the principal hotels, registering their names as "Colonel," "Major," or "Captain," with the significant letters "C.S.A." added; appearing from day to day in rebel uniforms (some of them gaudy, all of them noticeable) in the offices and parlors and at the public tables of these hotels and in the streets and drives of the city; frequenting the theatre and other places of public amusement, and visiting the senate and house chambers, where, with marked consideration they have been invited to privileged seats within the bar; at all these places and on all these occasions giving expression to sentiments of confirmed adherence to the rebel cause, and of bitter hostility to the government and people of the United States.

While prominent officers are thus enjoying the freedom of the city and the luxuries of hotel life, hundreds of poor and ignorant privates—some of them impressed and all of them deceived into the rebel service penitent for the wrongs they have done, ready, willing, and anxious to take the oath of allegiance—are kept confined in the prisons at Camp Chase. This is a matter of complaint among the prisoners themselves. They argued to file committee—and with much force, it must be admitted—that of the two, they were the less guilty and the less dangerous, and if the sympathy of the people and the clemency of the executive should be exerted at all, it ought to be in their behalf.

Your committee are satisfied that many of these privates and officers of lower grade could be safely, and with advantage to the cause, released. But they are equally satisfied that too much clemency has already been shown to the higher officers, both in and out of the prison. They and their like are the men who have instigated this most wicked rebellion and inaugurated this inhuman war, and who are responsible before God for all the misery, suffering, and bloodshed which have followed. Is it a wonder that the loyal people of Ohio, both in the field and at home, knowing all these things, and remembering how our prisoners were confined in loathsome slave pens and tobacco sheds, and the bodies of our dead barbarously desecrated by the rebels, should feel outraged by this misguided sympathy, this mistaken clemency towards the perpetrators of all these foul wrongs?

But who is to blame? Your committee are satisfied that Colonel Moody has done his whole duty in the premises. They are equally satisfied that the governor has endeavored to discharge his duties honestly, faithfully, and impartially. His position has been one of great delicacy, his control over the camp and prisons being by courtesy of the federal authorities and not by any right as governor of Ohio. He has probably done all he well could in the premises. The responsibility, then, rests with the federal authorities, and our only remedy is by protest to the President. Your committee therefore recommend the adoption of the preamble and resolution herewith reported.

Lewis B. Gunckel

T.H. Whetstone

J.P. Robison

1862.12

Across the Picket Line in Mississippi

From Frank Moore, ed., *The Civil War in Song and Story 1860–1865*, New York: P.F. Collier, 1889.

The esprit de corps that many soldiers felt during battle, according to a University of California, Los Angeles study of Civil War veterans, helped them later in life. If a unit was cohesive, its soldiers were far less likely to die of heart attacks in their 50s and 60s. Camaraderie extended across the lines, too, especially during the early stages of the war. Soldiers on both sides were facing enemies who had been their countrymen. The following account serves as an example of camaraderie between combatants. Considering when the Union captured New Orleans, this encounter can be dated to sometime shortly after April 25, 1862.

A private of the Sixth Ohio regiment gave the following lively sketch of campaigning life:

I must record a little adventure, pleasing and interesting, I had day before yesterday near Corinth [Mississippi]. I last spoke about the continued firing between pickets. To such an extent was it carried, so incessant the firing day and night, that nothing short of a battle would alarm the camp, whereas a single gun should be the signal for the long-roll. But within the last three or four days a change for the better has taken place.

On Monday our regiment was sent to the fortifications. It is the custom for the various battalions to take their turn in staying at the breastworks for twenty-four hours, forming a sort of reserve picket; and from each regiment so stationed two companies are sent to the outposts. It fell to our lot to go out. The company we relieved informed us that the rebels were disposed to be friendly; and with instructions from the field-officer not to fire unless fired upon, or the enemy attempted to advance, we set to work to watch the movements of our neighbors. The enemy's pickets were in the edge of a wood about two hundred yards from us, and my post—one of the best for observation—similarly situated in another wood, with a level between us. For some time we looked closely without being able to see any of them, as they were disposed to be shy. We, on the contrary, exposed ourselves to their view, which had the effect of making them bolder; and occasionally a rebel passed from one tree to another and leveled a field-glass at us.

I waved a handkerchief, which was answered from the other side, and tacitly understood to mean no firing. An hour later one of our Southern friends waved a handkerchief and shouted: "Meet me half-way." "All right;" and arming myself with a newspaper profusely illustrated with pictures incidental to the capture of New Orleans, I started out. A rebel surgeon of the Third Tennessee was the individual who met me. He was dressed in a citizen's suit of black, with military buttons, and the rank of captain designated, not by shoulder-straps, but by marks on the collar. After shaking hands and exchanging the customary salutations, we proceeded to talk about the war. He was at Fort Donelson [along the Cumberland River near Dover, Tennessee], and made his escape the night before the surrender; spoke of the battle of Shiloh, at which he assisted; said it was their intention to have made the attack on Saturday instead of Sunday, but on account of a misunderstanding between their generals the plan failed. The number of deserters from his side appeared to have a prominent place in his mind, which he vainly endeavored to conceal. "Do you have many deserters from your ranks?" he commenced. I told him of only two cases which had come under my notice for more than a year, taking care to add that they ran home. He wanted to know if many of their men came over to us. I answered rather equivocally: "A few." "How many?"

Fearful now that if I told him the great number that actually did come to us, the rebel leaders would increase their vigilance, I merely said that I had seen six, the number I had personally beheld. "I guess they go the other way," he replied, thereby acknowledging they suffered much from desertion. Mr. Tennessee wanted to know why we did not make the attack; they were anxiously waiting for us, and confident of victory. I said that they could not be more eager for the battle, or more sure of success, than ourselves; that to us everything appeared to be ready; but we were not supposed to know Gen. Halleck's plans.

We talked together some fifteen minutes, both of us very wary about giving contraband information. He was a gentlemanly, well-educated man, apparently under thirty years of age, and from Maury County, Tennessee. I gave him the pictorial, and asked for a Memphis paper. He had none, but promised to send me over one, if he could procure it during the day. Before parting, I remarked that it would be well to make some agreement about picket firing, and learned that they had received orders precisely like ours.

Gen. Garfield, who had the supervision of the outposts, called me in; so we again shook hands and separated, leaving many things unsaid that we would like to have spoken about. Garfield questioned me closely as to our conversation, and seemed satisfied that it was all right. However, being fearful that the rebels might learn something from us if such intercourse was allowed, he ordered us not to go out again, but to let any rebel that wished it to come over all the way. I had reason to regret this very much, as in the afternoon my friend, the doctor, came half way with the promised paper. We gave him to understand that it was against our orders to leave the post, and if he would come all the way we would do him no harm. He said he had a very late paper, but could not be induced to come further than the neutral ground, and returned, much to our disappointment.

After the interview of the morning all apprehension of danger from bullets from either side was at an end, and the sentinels on both sides paced their beats without so much as thinking to seek cover.

General James A. Garfield. From Library of Congress.

1862.13

A Hero Dismissed

From *The Cleveland Daily Herald*, "Col. DeVilliers Dismissed from Service," June 2, 1862.

Charles De Villiers' (see 1861.11) reputation plummeted in the span of six months. Renowned for escaping from the enemy, his fame obviously went to his head. He began to use his position to profit from the rebellion. The following is the list of charges brought against De Villiers that led to his ouster from the Union army. All is not fair in love and war.

During the war, the Judge-Advocate General's office was in charge of court-martial procedures. Common offenses included desertion, spying, aiding the enemy, or compelling a commander to surrender. Desertion was by far the most prevalent charge. Estimates put the number of Union deserters at over 199,000 and Confederate deserters at about 104,500.

Our readers will remember that Col. Charles A. DeVilliers, the "dashing Zouave" whose military and other exploits in this city, in Richmond, and in Western Virginia, have kept him before the public eye for some time, finally got himself into trouble in Western Virginia by his high handed method of "confiscating" property, imprisoning citizens, and setting the authority of the U. S. Court at defiance. He was recently arrested and tried by Court Martial for "conduct unbecoming a gentleman and an officer in the U. S. Army." Among the specications [sic] of the charge were the following:

On the 17th day of November A. D. 1861, the said Charles A. DeVilliers, Colonel aforesaid, did take, seize and drive into camp at Gauley Bridge aforesaid seven head of cattle not declared contraband of war by any Court of Judicature, and sold the same to Quartermaster E. H. Rice, of said 11th Regiment, for the sum of one hundred dollars, which sum be appropriated to his own use.

On or about the last day of December, 1861 the said Colonel Charles A. DeVilliers did arrest one James H. Lewis, a citizen of Mason county, Va. and the said Colonel Charles A. DeVilliers did refuse to release the said Lewis until he (the said Lewis) paid the said Col. DeVilliers the sum of eleven dollars and fifty cents; the said Col. DeVilliers did also arrest, about the same time aforesaid, two negroes said to be slaves, one supposed to belong to Williams P. Hawkins, the other to John S. Lewis, both citizens of Mason county, Va., and the said Colonel DeVilliers did refuse to release the two negroes until he was paid the sum of twenty dollars:—the above sums were paid to Col. Charles A. DeVilliers aforesaid, and the money was appropriated to his own individual use.

On or about the 10th day of December A.D. 1861, and divers other times to wit: Between the 10th day of December and the 24th day of said month, 1861, the said Colonel Charles A. DeVilliers entered the house of Henry J. Fisher, a citizen of Point Pleasant, Virginia, took possession of and appropriated to himself, in currency, the sum of between two and three hundred dollars, and a quantity of bonds, notes, mortgages, &c, property of said Fisher: also, bed clothes and bedding, queensware, silverware, knives, forks, table cloths, towels, napkins, and other household goods.

The Colonel was found guilty. The following is the sentence.

And the Court did "therefore sentence him, the prisoner, Colonel Charles A. DeVilliers of 11th Reg. O.V.I.," "To be dismissed the service of the United States, and forfeit all pay and allowances. And the Court orders his property to be seized by the Commanding Officer of his post, and held, subject to future legal disposition."

Sentence approved, except as to the forfeiture and seizure of his property. That is respectfully referred to the U. S. District Attorney for action.

A Nation at War

On June 9, Thomas J. "Stonewall" Jackson's troops defeat Union forces at The Battle of Port Republic, Virginia.

On July 1, Confederate Commander Robert E. Lee attacks Union troops at Malvern Hill, Virginia, and is defeated.

1862.14

Getting the Measles and Being Discovered

From *The Athens Messenger*, "Female Teamster," June 12, 1862.

In order to fund the war, Congress passed the Revenue Act of 1862. The act created the position of commissioner of Internal Revenue and enacted an income tax. The monthly pay of Union privates in 1861 was $12 for the cavalry and $11 for the artillery and infantry. Confederate privates in the cavalry and light batteries received $12 per month and those in the artillery and infantry $11 per month. The following account is of a female teamster, and perhaps highlights the financial benefits for joining up, rather than working as a laborer back home.

The Nashville Dispatch of the 31st ult. says:

"Yesterday one of the soldiers, or rather a teamster to the teams of horses attached to one of the Ohio regiments, and who has been confined at the hospital for a few days with the measles, was discovered to be a woman. She hails from the vicinity of Gallipolis, O., and first joined the regular army, when her sex was discovered and she was rejected. She was then employed as a house servant at seventy-five cents per week, when she engaged as a teamster to an Ohio regiment at twenty-five dollars per month. She is represented as about eighteen years old, and made rather a handsome boy. She has three brothers in the army, but not in the regiment to which she was attached."

Sketch depicting women's roles during the War. From Library of Congress.

1862.15

Orations on the War

From Twelfth Commencement Program of Western Reserve Eclectic Institute, June 12, 1862; Hiram College History; Commencement Programs; Hiram College Archives. Courtesy Hiram College Archives, Hiram, Ohio.

On June 12, 1862, the commencement exercise for the Western Reserve Eclectic Institute (WREI) took place. The war decreased the number of students at institutions of higher learning, but some students still received their diplomas. James Garfield, the president of WREI, went off to fight in the Civil War and with him went 100 of his pupils. The document is of interest for the subject of many of the orations, and the discussion topic "Should the war continue until the ultimate emancipation of the slaves is ensured."

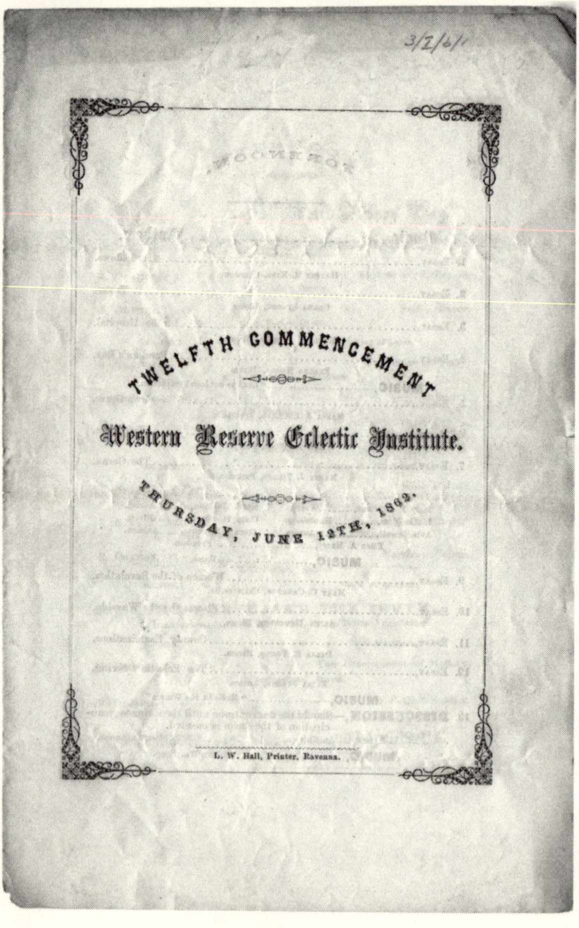

TWELFTH COMMENCEMENT

Western Reserve Eclectic Institute.

THURSDAY, JUNE 12TH, 1862.

L. W. Hall, Printer, Ravenna.

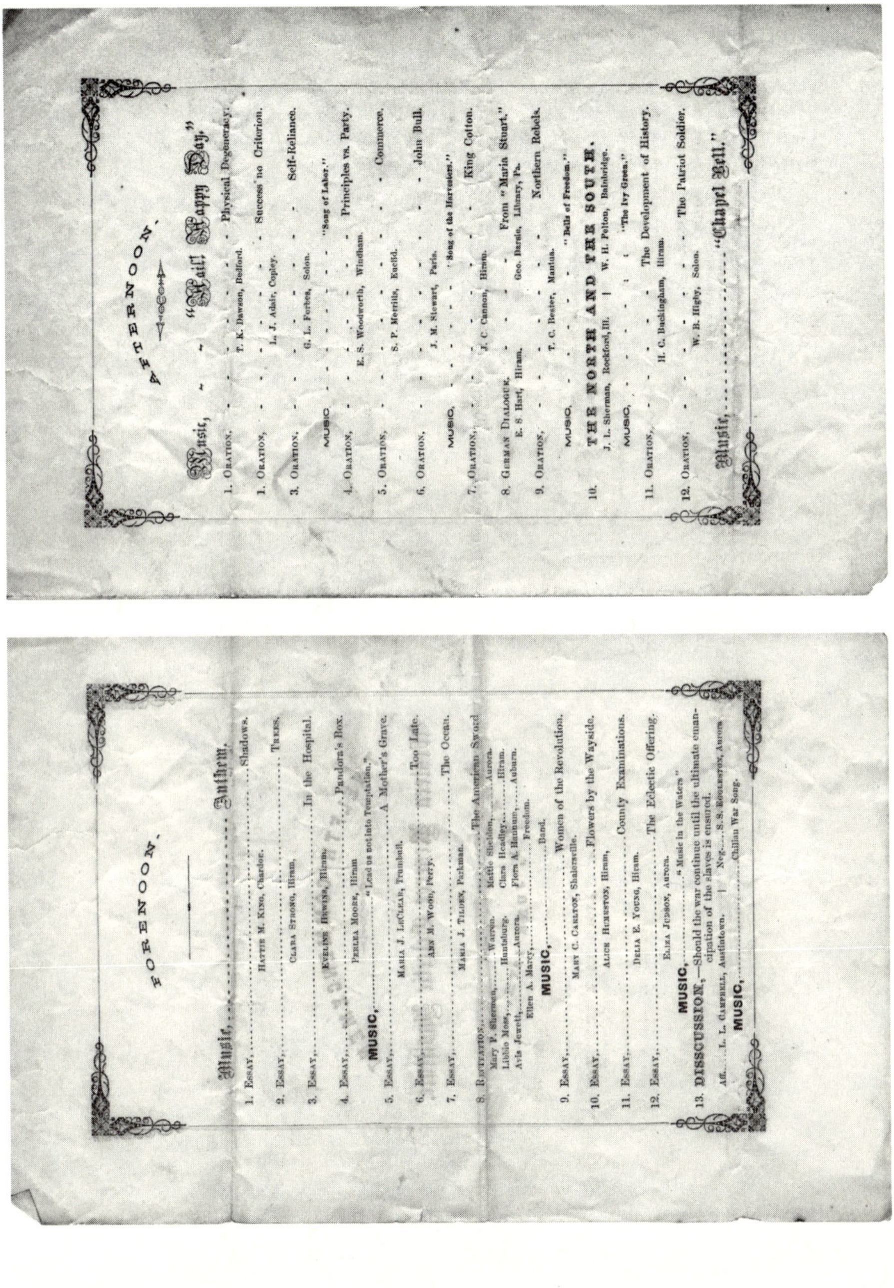

FORENOON.

Music,........................ Anthem.

1. Essay,........................Shadows.
Hattie M. King, Chardon.

2. Essay,........................Trees.
Clara Strong, Hiram,

3. Essay,........................In the Hospital.
Eveline Hewins, Hiram.

4. Essay,........................Pandora's Box.
Perlea Moore, Hiram

MUSIC,........................"Lead us not into Temptation."

5. Essay,........................A Mother's Grave.
Maria J. LeClear, Trumbull.

6. Essay,........................Too Late.
Ann M. Wood, Perry.

7. Essay,........................The Ocean.
Maria J. Tilden, Parkman.

8. Recitation,........................The American Sword
Mary F. Sherman,........Warren. Mattie Sheldon,........Aurora.
Libbie Moss,........Huntsburg. Clara Headley,........Hiram.
Avis Jewett,........Aurora. Flora A. Hannum,........Auburn.
Ellen A. Marcy,........Freedom.

MUSIC,........................Band.

9. Essay,........................Women of the Revolution.
Mary C. Carlton, Shalersville.

10. Essay,........................Flowers by the Wayside.
Alice Humeston, Hiram,

11. Essay,........................County Examinations.
Delia E. Young, Hiram.

12. Essay,........................The Eclectic Offering.
Eliza Judson, Aurora.

MUSIC,........................"Music in the Waters"

13. DISSCUSSION,—Should the war continue until the ultimate emancipation of the slaves is ensured.
Aff.....L. L. Campbell, Austintown. | Neg.....S. S. Eggleston, Aurora

MUSIC,........................Chilian War Song.

AFTERNOON.

Music, - - "Hail! Happy Day."

1. Oration, - - - - - - - - Physical Degeneracy.
T. K. Dawson, Bedford.

1. Oration, - - - - - - - - Success no Criterion.
L. J. Adair, Copley.

3. Oration, - - - - - - - - Self-Reliance.
G. L. Forbes, Solon.

MUSIC - - - - - - - - "Song of Labor."

4. Oration, - - - - - - - - Principles vs. Party.
E. S. Woodworth, Windham.

5. Oration, - - - - - - - - Commerce.
S. P. Merrills, Euclid.

6. Oration, - - - - - - - - John Bull.
J. M. Stewart, Paris.

MUSIC, - - - - - - "Song of the Harvesters."

7. Oration, - - - - - - - - King Cotton.
J. C. Cannon, Hiram.

8. German Dialogue, - - - - From "Maria Stuart."
E. S. Hart, Hiram. Geo. Darsie, Library, Pa.

9. Oration, - - - - - - - - Northern Rebels.
T. C. Bester, Mantua.

MUSIC, - - - - - - "Bells of Freedom."

10. THE NORTH AND THE SOUTH.
J. L. Sherman, Rockford, Ill. | W. H. Pelton, Bainbridge.

MUSIC, - - - - : : "The Ivy Green."

11. Oration, - - - - - - The Development of History.
H. C. Buckingham, Hiram.

12. Oration, - - - - - - - - The Patriot Soldier.
W. B. Higby, Solon.

Music,........................"Chapel Bell."

1862.16

Giving a Soldier His Due

From Charles A. Poland, *Army Register of Ohio Volunteers in the Service of the United States*, Columbus, OH: Ohio State Journal Printing Company, 1862.

In times of necessity, businesses spring up to serve new customer populations. The advertisement from T.W. Tallmadge & Company extends an offer to help individuals remedy claims against federal and state governments concerning reimbursement for a variety of services, including back pay. Many soldiers complained of not being paid or of the slowness of the payroll system. To persuade potential customers of Tallmadge's reputation, an Ohioan, West Point graduate, and leading general of the war, W.S. Rosecrans and the former Governor of the state, William Dennison, provided endorsements.

ATTENTION, SOLDIERS!

T. W. TALLMADGE & CO.'S

OHIO AGENCY,

FOR PROCURING

Bounty Money, Back Pay, and Pensions for Soldiers, their Widows and Heirs.

FEE ONLY $5, IN EACH CASE.

OUR OFFICES

Are at COLUMBUS, OHIO, and WASHINGTON CITY, D. C.

☞ *See Our Advertisement on the Cover of this Book—(Outside.)*

ALSO COLLECT ALL MILITARY CLAIMS.

Many persons hold valid claims against the Government of the United States, or State of Ohio. Some have claims for expenses in recruiting, others for subsistence, others for damages, etc.

COMMISSIONERS

Are appointed to adjust and allow such claims. By sending them to us, it will insure their prompt presentation and collection.

READ THE FOLLOWING:

COLUMBUS, OHIO, March 24th, 1862.

Capt. T. W. TALLMADGE has been in the service of the United States, and of the State of Ohio, almost constantly since the commencement of the present war, having served upon the staff of Gen. Rosecrans and acted as Assistant Quartermaster of Ohio. He now proposes to retire from the service and engage in another business, in which he hopes to advance the interests of the soldiers. In every capacity in which Capt. TALLMADGE has acted for the Government, he has proved to be a man of good business habits, and his honesty and integrity of purpose have been evident in all his transactions with the Government. We cordially recommend him as a man entirely worthy of confidence, and one who will honestly carry out whatever he proposes to do. Having been a soldier himself, he is peculiarly adapted to the business in which he is now engaged, and to which he proposes to devote his time and energies.

W. S. ROSECRANS, Brig. Gen., U, S. A.
WM. DENNISON.
C. P. BUCKINGHAM, Adj. Gen. of Ohio.
C. DELANO, Com. Gen. of Ohio.
GEO. B. WRIGHT, Q. M. Gen. of Ohio.

1862.17

The Boys Go to War; Send Money

From Sarah Merion to her sister, September 4, 1862; Oberlin Students; Sarah M. Merion, 1858–65; Oberlin College Archives. Courtesy Oberlin College Archives, Oberlin, Ohio.

Sarah Maretta Merion (Mrs. Vincent) was a student at Oberlin College during 1862 and 1863. She came from nearby Elyria, Ohio. Writing to one of her sisters at the beginning of the semester in 1862, she describes the situation at the college in light of the defeat of Union troops at Richmond, Kentucky, in late August. Governor Tod issued a proclamation for all loyal men of Ohio to join the militia for "a few days" due to the threat of a Confederate invasion. In early September, martial law was declared in Cincinnati so that all citizens could defend the city. One thing hasn't changed, though, about college students—their need for cash.

OBERLIN, SEP. 4TH 1862

Respected Sister:

I am here at last and having got pretty well settled so that I can begins to taste of study once more, I thought I would write you a few lines. I am well, but very anxious since the call of our Governor. This morning, for every man that could shoulder a gun to hasten to Cincinnati, for fear that David [likely Sarah's father] will go now for sure. I want you to let me know immediately. Will Weet has gone to war: he went before I returned. Alsina [married Will Weet in 1858] feels very badly, is alone now. Oberlin sends 100 men all armed with guns tonight, with 5 days rations, all raised since the news came in this morning. We have very exciting times here as a natural consequence of the war.

I found my folks willing to do all that I can ask, but money is very hard to get. If they can sell some of their stock they would help me to all the money I need, but as they can not now, I would like three or five dollars next week Wednesday or as soon as convenient for you to send it, don't send much at a time for fear it will get lost, or the rebels will get it, for we think this place is not out of danger. Yesterday the rebels captured a train of cars only twelve miles from Cincintati [sic]. My expenses are more than I expected, on account of having to get all new books, and they are very high endeed [sic], excuse this, for I am in a great hurry. My love to you all, and a kiss for Suella, be sure and write the first of the week. Direct to S.M. Vincent, Oberlin O.

Yours affectionately,

S.M.V.,

Has Uncle come yet? Tell the girls and Father I am well and want them to write.

1862.18

Squirrel Hunter's Discharge

From "The Squirrel Hunter's Discharge," William McKinley Presidential Library and Museum Archive Collection. Courtesy William McKinley Presidential Library and Museum, Canton, Ohio.

The Squirrel Hunters were civilians who were called in late 1862 to assist against a possible Confederate attack on Cincinnati, Ohio. Confederate forces had captured Lexington, Kentucky, and the threat to Cincinnati seemed imminent. Governor Tod appealed to the citizens of the state and over 15,000 men reported, many with their own shotguns. So many men showed up that several national publications remarked that hunting had to be the primary occupation of Ohio men.

The invasion never came. The regular army had no need for the additional troops, and the squirrel hunters were discharged. The Ohio legislature formally thanked them and with the Governor, gave them official papers for services rendered. The following document was awarded to John Whitmer.

THE SQUIRREL HUNTER'S DISCHARGE.

Our Southern Border was menaced by the enemies of our Union David Tod Governor of Ohio called on the Minute Men of the State and the Squirrel Hunters came by thousands to the rescue. You John Whitmer were one of them and this is your Honorable Discharge.

September 1862

Approved by
DAVID TOD.
Governor

Chas W Hill
Adjt. Genl of Ohio

Malcolm McDowell
Major & A.D.C.

THE GREAT SEAL OF THE STATE OF OHIO 1803

A Nation at War

On August 30, Union forces were routed at the Second Battle of Bull Run (Manassas).

1862.19

A Fine Wine

From Charles Wright, *Experiences in the Ranks of Company C, 81st Ohio Volunteer Infantry, during the War for the Maintenance of the Union, 1861–1864*, Philadelphia: James Beale, 1887.

While most soldiers went to fight for a justifiable cause, alcohol consumption and abuse followed, much of it resulting from the brutality of battles and pitiful camp life. Union soldiers had better access to liquor since they were stationed around larger cities, and drinking was an acceptable form of entertainment. Other substances led to cases of "soldier's disease" or "army disease," an affliction that came from drug withdrawal. The hypodermic syringe was developed during this period and injections of morphine increased. Union forces received approximately 10 million opium pills and 2.8 million ounces of opium powders and tinctures. The following story reflects a "warmer" view of alcohol and soldiering—food and drink aplenty.

As we have before stated, our stay at Hamburg [Tennessee] was rather uneventful. No doubt many things transpired worthy of record, but I do not recall anything exciting or sensational. One thing may be added which is really of the utmost importance in a soldier's life, and that was—we had a variety of things to eat, and in abundance.

Quite a large amount of blackberry wine or cordial was confiscated and taken possession of by the provost-marshal, and I believe a quantity of it was distributed to each company in the regiment, and limited quantities issued to the men. About thirty bottles were placed upstairs above the office of the provost marshal—not for his use, for he was a man that never touched anything of the kind; it was intended for hospital use. After the cordial was located upstairs our office, a comrade of Company C visited me often. He manifested his friendship and affection for the provost marshal and his clerk to such an extent that he would often call twice each day; and the steps of the stairway being broad and comfortable, he preferred to sit on a step instead of a camp stool. The native Tennesseans coming in on business often occupied the attention of the provost-marshal and clerk. Our comrade would tire of sitting on the step, and as there was a window upstairs from which an excellent view of the Tennessee River could be had, he would quietly ascend the stairs and take—a view of the Tennessee?

Of course we felt flattered at the assiduous attentions of our comrade, coming regularly and helping to relieve the tedium of a provost-marshal's office;

and it was doubtless gratifying to him to be able once each day, and sometimes twice, to relieve the monotony of camp life by coming to the office, ascending the stairs, and taking a satisfying view of the winding Tennessee! Orders came suddenly for the regiment to march to Corinth. The clerk was directed by the provost marshal to pack two or three bottles of the cordial in the officers' camp-chest, which the clerk did, placing an extra one there for himself. Our comrade came while I was engaged, for the purpose of taking a last view of the Tennessee. I found that the artistic way to view the Tennessee was to uncork a bottle of the cordial, swallow its contents, and then there was no trouble in taking in all its beauties at a single glance. There had been so many views taken that there were only four bottles left. I placed them in the chest, assisted by our obliging comrade, who would not stand by and see me perform all this labor without lending a helping hand. The chest was placed in the headquarters' wagon, and I saw no more of it until we reached Corinth, and in unloading I reached in the chest to get out my bottle of cordial, but alas it was not there! In fact there was no cordial in that chest for anybody! As there were no hills or high ground on the road from Hamburg to Corinth from which a good view of the Tennessee could be had, our comrade could not be suspected, and the disappearance of those four bottles of cordial remains a mystery to this day.
September 1862

A Nation at War

On September 17, Confederate and Union armies confront each other at the Battle of Antietam in Sharpsburg, Maryland.

On October 8, Confederate troops are defeated at the Battle of Perryville, Kentucky.

On November 7, Lincoln removes McClellan from command of the Army of the Potomac and replaces him with Ambrose Burnside.

On December 11–15, the Battle of Fredericksburg, Virginia, is fought, resulting in 12,600 Union casualties and 5,300 Confederate casualties.

1862.20

Searching for Sons and the Truth

From James A. Garfield to J. Henry, Dec. 11, 1862; The James A. Garfield Collection; Western Reserve Eclectic Institute; Hiram College Archives. Courtesy Hiram College Archives, Hiram, Ohio.

The following response is from James Garfield to John Henry of Bainbridge, Ohio, regarding an inquiry into the whereabouts of his son, Edward. Edward was a student at the Western Reserve Eclectic Institute at Hiram, where James A. Garfield was the principal. On April 23, 1861, Edward became one of the first two students from the institute to enlist, was wounded at Antietam (September 17, 1862), and was for several months an inmate of Libby prison. At the close of the war, he returned and resumed his studies and graduated from the Western Reserve College, in Hudson, Ohio. At the time of this response, Garfield was participating in the court martial of General Porter, who was accused of failing to follow orders at the Second Battle of Manassas, fought on August 28–30, 1862. Porter was found guilty.

WASHINGTON, DEC. 11TH 1862

J. Henry

Dear Sir,

Your letter, making inquiries concerning Edward, was duly received. After a full investigation here at the War Dept, I have only been able to trace him to Annapolis where you last heard from him, but the Department wrote yesterday a letter of inquiry to the proper authority and promised to let me know the result as soon as they heard which will not be many days. When I learn, I will immediately communicate it to you. I have every reason to be proud of your two noble sons [Edward and Charles, mustered out on December 2, 1864] who have done such good service for the country in its hour of peril. I am very sorry I could not have stayed with the 42nd. I have yet to see a regiment in the army that all things considered is its equal. I am on the Court-Marshal for the trial of Gen. T. J. Porter and hope to get into the field again as soon as it is over. Hoping to be able to send you good news from Edward soon.

I am Very Truly Your Friend,

J. A. Garfield

1863

". . . to our inexperienced and susceptible youth, there are on all sides exhibited dishonesty, corruption, envy, jealousy, persecution, cruelty, murder; man arrayed against his country, against order and progress, against humanity and civilization."

Professor William Chauvenet,
Washington University, St. Louis

1863.1

The Bounds of Disloyalty

From various sources.

With the 1863 Ohio gubernatorial election, in which John Brough ran against Clement Vallandigham, some uncertainty existed about the future of Ohio's involvement in the Union effort. While rifles and cannons fired in the south, in Akron, Ohio, the war was fought with the printed word. The *Summit County Beacon* (a pro-Union paper) had an open rivalry with the *Akron Democrat* (considering the reference to J. Hays Webb as the paper's editor, the title of the newspaper might have actually been the *Free Democrat* or *True Democrat*), as seen in these excerpts from articles published in the *Beacon* between January 1 and November 23, 1863.

From *The Summit County Beacon*, "The Assassination of the President Recommended by the Akron Democrat," January 1, 1863.

If any thing were before lacking to demonstrate the disloyality [sic] and utter devilishness of the conductor, or conductors, of the *Akron Democrat*, the contents of the last week's issue of that treasonable sheet has dispelled all doubts upon the subject. Not only the articles selected from the *New York World*, *Stark County Democrat* and other secession organs, and a muddled re-hash purporting to be a communication, over the signature of "Thoron," but its "editorials," also, are calculated to poison the minds of its readers against the Administration, and to give direct encouragement to the enemies of the Government.

In the first paragraph of its leading editorial, entitled "The Fredericksburg Slaughter," after repeating the officially contradicted statement of secession reporters that "fifteen thousand soldiers were slaughtered needlessly and criminally, in direct opposition to the protest of our best military men," the writer of the article in question, exclaims in *holy horror* "*And if the entire Administration, with the President at its head, is accountable for the murder, we pray for a second Orsini* [Felice Orsini attempted to assassinate Napoleon III] *to deliver the people from its hands.*"

And who was the *first* Orsini, for a duplicate of where this *loyal* and *pious* editor so devoutly prays? No less a personage than an Italian desperado, who was detected in an attempt to assassinate the present French Emperor a few years since; and we know of no more suitable person, to execute such a commission than the utterer of that prayer. Like a sneaking assassin, he has, for over a year, under the guise of Unionism, been secretly plotting with its enemies, until, emboldened by the leniency of the Administration towards the particular class of traitors to which he belongs, he has, recently, thrown off his mask, and now openly proposes to effect a change of Administration by the assassination of the President and his Constitutional advisers.

We would say or do nothing to curtail, in the slightest degree the liberty of speech, or the freedom of the press in time of peace; but we believe we speak the sentiment of every loyal man, who has perused the last number of that paper, when we say that it should be immediately suppressed by the Government—When the Nation is struggling with a rebellion inaugurated under, and fostered by, a Democratic Administration, it most certainly ought to protect itself against the evil influences of that portion of the Democratic conspirators within its control. Within the rebel lines, a paper that would utter a single sentence adverse to the interests of the rebel government, would not be tolerated for one hour. Nor should a paper that will continually falsify and misrepresent the legitimate Government, and persistently endeavor to disaffect its loyal subjects and create a sympathy for those who are seeking its overthrown, be permitted to circulate among the people. Were the Democratic party still in power, and grappling with the monstrous rebellion that the Republican party now is, the utterance of language half as treasonable, by the *Beacon* as that to be found in last week's *Democrat* would have subjected us to immediate arrest and imprisonment, if not a speedy trial by Court Martial, and a hempen cravat [noose]; and it would have served us right, too.

We learn however, that some of his political friends—whether authoritatively or not we cannot say—fearing probably, that an indignant and outraged people would summarily squelch the traitorous concern, have attempted to excuse the ostensible on the ground that he copied the article in question from some other paper. That idea, however, is *preposterous*; for did not the *truthful* editor of that paper positively asseverate a few weeks ago, that not one line ever appeared, as editorial, in its columns, *but what was written by himself.* But, admitting that he did thus copy it without giving credit for it, as he did the article which we detected him in purloining from the *Cincinnati Commercial*, it only augments his turpitude by adding the crime of larceny to those of falsehood and treason in the publication of the article referred to.

From *The Summit County Beacon*, "Listen to the Traitor," February 19, 1863.

That such of our readers as do not patronize, or have not had *forced* upon them the little dirty rebel rag, known as the *Akron Democrat*, may have an inkling of its traitorous character, we give the following extract from one of the "editorials" of last week, upon the subject of Gen. McClellan's dismissed from the command of the army of the Potomac by the President. After a total perversion of the facts as to the non-success of McClellan and the support given to him by the Administration, the *Democrat* says:

"We believe that the radicals have completely won the weak man whom we call President, and that sooner or later the war will be conducted upon the avowed radical basis. If this surmise is correct, and we certainly have the best reason for believing it so, THE COUNTRY IS DOOMED—ITS DESTRUCTION IS ONLY A QUESTION OF TIME—AND THE SOONER THE CONSUMMATION IS REACHED, THE BETTER."

That is to say, if the plan pursued by the President and Commander-in-chief of the Army and Navy, for subduing the rebellion, don't tally with the political notions of J. Hays Webb and the real editors of the *Democrat*, so far as they and their fellow tories [Americans during the American Revolution who favored the British side] are concerned, the destruction of the Government is "a consummation most devoutly to be wished." What an outrage upon the loyal sentiment of the people of Summit County!

From *The Summit County Beacon*, "The Democratic Party and its Organs," February 26, 1863.

Friend Lane:—I have seen some half a dozen of the late issues of the *Akron Democrat*, and for what purpose the editor circulates that paper, (except it be for treasonable purposes.) I can not for the life of me understand. Can it be possible that a man can be found in Summit County, so lost to every *patriotic principle*, as it seems the man of the *Democrat* must be, to persist in sending week after week, a paper far and wide, filled with the rankest kind of treasonable sayings, (saving and excepting an unusual large amount of advertisements.) and lay any claim to loyalty? Does that paper, in the least, pretend to be a loyal paper? If so, I must think the evidence cannot be found upon its pages. If loyal, why so much at variance with its Democratic brethren? . . .

From *The Summit County Beacon*, "From the 107th—What the German Soldiers think of the *Akron Democrat* and its disloyal Editor," March 19, 1863.

CAMP NEAR BROOKS' STATION, VA.
MARCH 3RD, 1863

Friend Lane:—The arrival of our much looked for friend, (the *Beacon* of last week,) this day, reminds me that I ought to inform you and our numerous friends of Summit county, where we are, how we fare.

We are encamped but one mile from Brook's Station [a respite between the battles of Fredericksburg and Chancellorsville], with a fair prospect of staying here some time, at any rate some five or six weeks. The boys have built good substantial log huts, which are quite comfortable in comparison with our late shelter tents pinned to the ground; and as to how we fare, why, we have plenty to eat and drink; crackers in abundance, and what is still more valuable, the army of the Potomac enjoys good health, and is in very good spirits. It would be still more so if we could have a *good deal less secesh sympathy*, and a little more "Union" feeling in the North to back us up; but it seems that there are some men that must always be a-croaking, regardless of how injurious it may prove to our just cause and their own interests. Among other newspapers your worthy (?) neighbor, the *Akron Democrat*, has found its way to our camp. I wish its editor could have witnessed how scornfully its pages were perused; but Oh! the "cruel soldiers," they seem to be bent on destruction, for the poor *Democrat* was "*doomed*," and with contempt torn to shreds, upon which Captain Feederle [resigned May 12, 1863] remarked, "its editor deserves the same fate." I will not argue this case much, but this I must say, that the soldiers are subject to the severest hardships and privations while in defense of our Country; it is therefore the most sacred duty of those at home, to encourage them in their noble work. But pray, what does the editor of the *Democrat* and all those of his caliber do? While our true and loyal ladies from Summit county (*God bless their dear little hearts,*) send box after box stuffed full of all the good things imaginable to aid our sick, and for the encouragement of those in the field, there lurks one in Summit that would sow the seed of discontent among the soldiers, and then cry, "the army of the Potomac is going down;" "numberless deserters," &c. &c. Men!

if such you are, stop and think what is your duty, your sacred duty? How will you, with your actions thus far, give an account to the 100,000 men, which you have sent from their bright homes in Ohio? Did they not go forth to fight your battles as well as their own? Have not thousands of them laid down their lives, a sacrifice to your welfare? Stop and think; consider the facts; to advocate disunion, would be demoralizing the army; it would hurl down a "curse" upon the whole nation, (the proudest of the world,) while a "united" effort of the North, would crown us with victory. Let us be united, and this rebellion, *must* and *will* speedily be crushed from the face of our glorious land; so let it be "*United we stand.*" . . .

Yours,

George Billau [Billow, mustered out on July 10, 1865]

Lieut. Col. 107th Regt. O.V.I.

From *The Summit County Beacon*, "Double-distilled Treason," July 9, 1863.

If any doubts have existed heretofore as to the traitorous proclivities of the *Akron Democrat* those doubts were dispelled by its last week's issue. Upon the outside are over four columns of the slimiest kind of treason, purporting to be a speech delivered by the Rev. (!) J. Hamilton, in Copley, on the 20th day of June, and one of the most unblushing tissues of falsehood and misrepresentation against the Administration ever issued by that well known organ of secession in the North, the *New York Day Book* [the newspaper advertised itself as a "wool-dyed Democratic weekly journal" and a "white man's paper"], while upon the inside the Vallandigham [see also, 1861.1, 1863.6] banner is unblushingly flung to the rankest treason and blasphemy that can be found either in or out of rebeldom.

We do not wonder that its loyal subscribers who had been inveigled into its support under false pretenses are returning to it by scores.

—•—

CERTAINLY.

—

"The *people* throughout the North are anxious to know why it is, that after two years of patient waiting for the overthrow of this rebellion, frantic appeals came from the Administration for militia to save the National Capitol, and protect Northern States from invasion."—*Akron Democrat*

For the purpose, probably, of preventing the South from being reinforced by the Northern wing of the rebel army.

"They [the people] desire to know why the immense sacrifice of life and money, which they have sustained, has not produced results at least measurably commensurate with the outlay."—*Akron Democrat*

Because of the factious opposition of just such traitors as the writer of the above, and the aid and encouragement which they have given to the enemy.

"They [the people] would like to be informed of the cause of the disasters which of late almost invariably attend our armies when in conflict with those of the Rebel Government."—*Akron Democrat*

For the reason that the rebel Government have been enabled to obtain information of our strength, position, and intentions, through a set of pimps and spies in our midst, calling themselves "Democrats."

"And further, they [the people] desire to know how long they are expected to continue their present expenditure of life and money without a reasonable prospect of victory."—*Akron Democrat*

For answer read the glorious news from Pennsylvania, Tennessee, and Vicksburg, in today's paper. The miserable pettifogging sneak, who gave utterance to the above mean and traitorous flings at the Administration and the Union Army, will now probably make a great flourish of trumpets about "our" glorious Union victories—the great energy displayed by "our" noble President—the matchless skill of "our" Generals, and the unsurpassed gallantry of "our" soldiers in achieving such signal triumphs over "our" enemies.—Out upon the traitors!

From *The Summit County Beacon*, "Too true, Alas! too true," November 12, 1863.

The "painful rumor" to which we alluded, some two or three weeks since, that the *Akron Democrat* is about to depart from us, has finally culminated in a "sad reality," the proprietor thereof baying in his last week's issue, declared "the causes which compel him" to skedaddle. This manifesto is as great a curiosity in a literary point of view as its putative author is in the natural history lineage. As a rich treat to our readers, and for the purpose of bringing the "blush of shame"—if there's any shame-facedness about them—to the brows of the "Loyal Leaguers" who won't give the poor butternut a place to lay his head, we give the document entire and bespeak for it a careful and "tearful" perusal. It is as follows:

—

To the Democrats of Summit County.

—

We are sorry to announce to our Democratic friends in Summit county that there is considerable uncertainty regarding the further publication of the *Democrat* in Akron. This announcement, we know, will surprise our readers, particularly those who are acquainted with the present prosperous condition of the paper, and we assure them that such a step would not be taken if it could possibly be avoided.

The necessity to which we refer is simply this: we are unable to procure rooms in which to longer publish the paper. Our lease for the buildings which we now occupy expired several months ago and can no longer be had for our purpose. There are but one or two other suitable places in town, and they, being the property of "Loyal Leaguers," cannot be had for money for "Copperhead" purposes.

This is precisely the situation—what can we do? We have stood by the Democracy of this county during the "reign of terror" which characterized politics during the late campaign, always receiving the lion's share of abuse; we have been threatened with personal calamities of every imaginable variety. Our office has been threatened with destruction by mobs, and on three different occasions the time was fixed for the destruction of our property. And even since the election our establishment has twice been guarded at night when it was known that a conspiracy was on foot to destroy it;—the first time by a detachment of the Akron Guard, and the second by the mayor, city marshal, and captain of the Guards. These are a few of the trials through which we have passed, and it now seems to us that the other party, finding that we cannot be frightened into a suspension of the *Democrat*, have adopted the policy above indicated, in order to rid themselves of an obnoxious paper. . . .

A Nation at War

On January 1, President Lincoln issues the Emancipation Proclamation, declaring that all slaves in areas still in rebellion are free in the eyes of the federal government.

On February 27, the Confederate steamer *Nashville* is destroyed by the Union Navy near Fort McAllister, Georgia.

1863.2

Taking Up Our Beds

Source: *The Athens Messenger*, "Letter from the Thirty-sixth," March 26, 1863.

George Crook was born on September 23, 1829, in Montgomery County, Ohio. In 1848, Crook enrolled at West Point. He graduated in 1852 and served as a second lieutenant in the Fourth United States Infantry. In early 1863, Crook joined the Army of the Cumberland and served under the command of General William Rosecrans. In February 1864, Crook assumed command of the Third Division, known as the Kanawha Division, of the Department of West Virginia. He was mustered out of the volunteer army on January 15, 1866.

The following letter from a soldier in the 36th Ohio Volunteer Infantry during the early months of 1863 recounts a number of skirmishes with Confederates forces in and around the city of Carthage. While the writer mistakenly reports that Vicksburg had been taken by Union forces, he does capture the bane of the infantry—marching. The letter also highlights the scourge of disease. Of the Union and Confederate soldiers who died in the war, over 63 percent perished from disease.

CROOK'S DIVISION [11th, 36th, and 92nd Ohio and the 18th Kentucky]
CAMP NEAR CARTHAGE, TENN.,
MARCH 9TH, 1863.

Mr. Editor:—You will see by the heading of my letter, if you have not learned it before, that we have changed our homes—"taken up our beds and walked;" but this is a part of soldiering. The prime injunction for the soldier is, "Be ye also ready, for in such an hour as you think not, the order shall come to march."

We left Charleston, West Va., Jan. 25th, and arrived at Nashville, Tenn., Feb. 7th—went into camp within three miles of the city on the pike leading to Franklin, where we remained till the 22nd February, when we came by boats to this place. We reached Carthage on the 26th. The 11th, 36th, 89th, and 92nd O. V. I., and the 13th and 24th Ky. are here.

Carthage is an almost deserted little town, fifty miles above Nashville by land, and 140 by water. We were the first troops with boats who have been here for a year. What citizens are left were quite surprised to see so many boats. We are using some of the buildings for hospital purposes. Carthage is the county seat of Smith county, I believe.

The health of this command is not very good at present, among the new regiments especially. The small-pox is in the Kentucky regiments, but I believe in no other, and but few cases even there; but this is true, that old troops have less sickness than new ones. The health of the 36th is very good. We have had rain nearly every other day since we came here.

On the night of the 2nd inst. our outside pickets were attacked, and all hands were ready for a trial of their strength, but nothing more occurred to disturb us. Next day, while on drill, a squad of rebel cavalry made a dash on some of our boys who were out on passes. We saw them just in time to drive a off the impudent pups and rescue our boys; but they succeeded in taking a few of the boys prisoners the same day further out from camp. We have to be wide awake. There are large parties of rebel cavalry prowling around camp among the hills, in order to take our boys, whether on passes or picket, and forage parties.

On the evening of the 4th, the 36th and 11th O. V. I. started on a scout to Rome, with three days' rations, taking different roads. Our object in going was to capture a force of rebels reported there. The 11th reached there first, having only a little over half the distance to travel the 36th had. They found some rebel cavalry there, drove them out and captured a number of prisoners. The 36th also took several prisoners, one of whom was an officer. We hid in ambush, and set every trap possible to catch some of these guerrillas, but failed in every attempt. It is almost impossible to do anything with the enemy's cavalry with nothing but infantry. We could run upon them, or meet them, and see them on the hills around, but they were able to get out of our way in most every case. If we only had a good, true regiment of cavalry here these squads of rebels might soon be driven out. We have been promised cavalry ever since we came here.

Yesterday a foraging party of some eighteen teams with about fifty guards from the 11th regiment were captured but a short distance from camp. At all events they were attacked and have not been seen since. Co. C. of the 36th was ordered the day before to go out with the train as guards, but the order was countermanded on account of Capt. Beckley [resigned November 23, 1863] of that company being field officer of the day. Several companies went out as soon as the news came, but nothing was to be seen. We could hear the firing in camp. There was a heavy volley, a few scattering shots, and then a death like stillness in contrast. There was a terrible shout in the charge; so I suppose a few more of our brave boys are captives of that foe they often fought.

March 10.—I was obliged, in the midst of my letter, to break off, as our company and three others from the 36th were ordered out on a visit to the place where our wounded boys are who were with the train day before yesterday when it was taken. There are two of the 11th wounded left at a good place. The train was taken about five miles from camp.

There are a great many good and true Union men in this part of the State, and not a few of them are willing to volunteer when opportunity is offered.

We are building a gunboat here for our own use. The "Orient" is being changed for that purpose. You know these gunboats are "a terror to evil doers"—*Secesh.*

We have the report now that Vicksburg has fallen, but we know not how much to believe of these rumors. We get but few papers, and very little news, but from all indications we feel quite encouraged with the prospect of the war. Let the good work go on till the word "secesh" or "sympathizer," shall be the synonym for all that is detestable. Now is the time for the true hearted to rally, and come up to the rescue! The country needs mass meetings, such as the late one in Cincinnati, all over the North, till public opinion shall frown down on all treason, or false prophets who cry "Peace! peace!" when there is no peace!

Yours for the Union.

F.H.D.

A Nation at War

On March 3, President Lincoln signs the Enrollment Act, initiating the first military draft in the United States.

1863.3

Laughing Away the Sorrow

From Alf Burnett, *Incidents of the War: Humorous, Pathetic, and Descriptive,* Cincinnati: Rickey & Carroll Publishers, 1863.

The 123rd Ohio Voluntary Infantry was organized at Camp Monroeville in Huron County. Company B of the 123rd was mustered into service on September 24, 1862. At times, humor is the only way to overcome the misery of war. The following listing, undoubtedly a parody of biblical writing, points out the inequities of the soldiering life, but also the interactions that result in a great deal of camaraderie.

Fun in the 123d Ohio

One of the boys furnished me with a copy of his experiences of camp, entitled *"Ye Chronicles of ye One Hundred and Twenty-third Regiment."*

1st. Man that is born of women, and enlisteth as a soldier in the One Hundred and Twenty-third Ohio, is few of days and short of rations.

2d. He cometh forth at reveille, is present also at retreat, yea, even at tattoo, and retireth, apparently, at taps.

3d. He draweth his rations from the commissary, and devoureth the same. He striketh his teeth against much hard tack [a very hard cracker or biscuit], and is satisfied. He fileth his canteen with apple-jack [alcoholic cider], and clappeth the mouth thereof upon the bung [stopper] of a whiskey-barrel, and after a little while goeth away, rejoicing in his strategy.

4d. Much soldiering has made him sharp; yea, even the seat of his breeches is in danger of being cut through.

5th. He covenaneth with the credulous farmer for many turkeys and chickens; also, at the same time, for much milk and honey, to be paid for promptly at the end of ten days; and lo! his regiment moveth on the ninth day to another post.

6th. His tent is filled with potatoes, cabbage, turnips, krout [sic], and other delicate morsels of delicious taste, which abound not in Commissary Department;

7th. And many other things not in the "returns" and which never will return; yet, of a truth, it must be said of the soldier of the One Hundred and Twenty-third, that he taketh nothing he can not reach.

8th. He fireth his Austrian rifle at midnight, and the whole camp is aroused and formed in a line of battle, when lo! his mess come bearing a nice porker, which he solemnly declareth so resembled a Secesh that he was compelled to pull the trigger.

9th. He giveth the provost-marshal much trouble, often capturing his guard, and posseth himself of the city.

10th. At such times "lager" and pretzels flow like milk and honey from his generous hand. He giveth without stint to his own comrades; yea, and withholdeth not from the One Hundred and Sixteenth Ohio Volunteer Infantry, or from the lean, lank, expectant Hoosier of the Eighty-seventh Indiana [part of the same brigade as the 123rd].

11th. He stretcheth forth his hand to deliver his fellow-soldiers of the One Hundredth and Sixteenth from the power of the enemy; yea, starteth at early dawn from Petersburg [Virginia; in December of 1862], even on a "double-quick" doth he go, and toileth on through much heat, suffering, privation, and much "vexation of spirit," until they are delivered. Verily I say unto you, after that he suffereth for want of tents and camp-kettles. Yea, on the highs of Moorefield [West Virginia; it was here the 123rd relieved the 116th O.V.I.] his voice may be heard proclaiming loudly for "hard tack and coffee," yet he murmureth not.

12th. But the grunt of a pig or the crowing of a cock awaketh him from soundest sleep, and he goeth forth until halted by the guard, when he instantly clappeth his hands upon his "bread-basket," and the guard, in commiseration, alloweth him to pass to the rear.

13th. No sooner hath he passed the sentry's beat than he striketh a "bee-line" for the nearest hen-roost, and, seizing a pair of plump pullets, returneth, soliloquizing: "The noise of a goose saved Rome; how much more the flesh of chickens preserveth the soldier!" [The roman historian, Livy tells of how the cackling of geese saved Rome from the Gauls.]

14th. He even playeth at euchrer [sic] with the parson, to see whether or not there shall be preaching in camp on the following Sabbath; and by dexterously drawing from the bottom a Jack, goeth away rejoicing that the service is postponed.

15th. And many other things doeth he; and lo! are they not recorded in the "morning reports" of Company B? Yea, verily.

1863.4

A View from the Front Lines

From *The Athens Messenger*, "Letter from the Seventy-Fourth," March 26, 1863.

The 74th Ohio Voluntary Infantry was organized in Xenia, Ohio, and trained at Camp Chase. The unit mustered into service in September 1862. The following letter was written after six months of active duty.

The writer makes two complaints that were echoed by many soldiers: some unpatriotic Northerners were trying to derail the war effort and the Army's upper echelon's decision-making left much to be desired. The writer also makes note of Confederate troops of color.

There has been a running dispute as to the contribution blacks made to the Southern war effort. Most accounts indicate that blacks were no more than a labor force to build fortifications. Some evidence exists that points to "free blacks" taking part in the actual fighting on the Confederate side, but the Confederate Congress did not pass an act to arm blacks until March 1865.

ARMY OF THE CUMBERLAND,
MURFEESBORO, TENN. MARCH 12, 1863.

Messrs. Editors:—Again I resume my pen to let you know how the time passes here in this dirty rebel town.—Severe skirmishing has been going on for the last week or ten days, and it is rumored that the rebs are advancing their lines in this direction, but I guess it is an idle tale. Be it so or not, the rebels are getting singularly bold, and frequently dash upon our pickets in small squads, but they are generally repulsed without any loss on our side.

Another of those calamities which so often have befallen our arms, took place last week in the vicinity of Franklin [Tennessee]. An expedition was sent out against the rebels near that town, was attacked by an overwhelming force of rebels, and for six hours these devoted men fought until they were literally cut to pieces. Our force consisted of four regiments of infantry and two or three batteries of artillery. Our men succeeded in bringing off their artillery. The rebels had two negro regiments in the fight, and they fought like tigers, it is said. The whole affair took place in hearing of our forces at Franklin, and they could easily have been reinforced if the General commanding had seen proper. Why it was not done is a mystery to me. Hardly a day passes but the roar of artillery can be heard.

A large forage train, which was sent out on the Lebanon pike the 27th ult., was attacked in returning by a force of three or four hundred guerillas at the Stone River crossing. There was two or three regiments of our infantry along with the train, who immediately opened upon the rebels, and after a brisk skirmish for a few minutes, succeeded in driving them off, killing eight and wounding twenty.—Among the rebel slain was one commissioned officer, a Captain I believe. Another expedition, sent out the 2nd inst., routed a rebel camp, captured all their camp equipage, stores, etc., and sixty prisoners. The rebs were completely surprised, and thought the advance of our army was upon them.

The circulations of the *Cincinnati Enquirer* and *Chicago Times* have been forbidden in the Army of the Cumberland. Our Northern copperhead friends will find that they cannot always send their treasonous editions in our midst.

We are rejoiced to hear the conscription act has passed; it is just the thing for the times. [The Enrollment Act of 1863 basically instituted a federal-level draft to populate the Union army. In reaction, the New York draft riots took place from July 13 to 15.] Those who are at home, trying to get the soldier to desert his post, will now have a chance to try it themselves. The way they fix deserters down here now is to shave their heads, brand them on the left cheek with the letter D, and then drum them out of camp at the point of the bayonet. Serves them right. If we had a few of the copperheads down here we would send them home in such a condition that they would not need the three hundred dollar exemption law. [An individual could avoid the draft by paying three hundred dollars.]

Some indications of a move are discernible at present and I hope it will take place ere long.

Yours in bonds of peace,

Seventy Fourth.

1863.5

Meeting the Enemy

From Charles Wright, *Experiences in the Ranks of Company C, 81st Ohio Volunteer Infantry, during the War for the Maintenance of the Union, 1861–1864*, Philadelphia: James Beale, 1887.

The two-day Battle of Shiloh in April 1862 was the engagement that illustrated completely how gruesome the war would turn out to be. *The Defiance* [Ohio] *Democrat's* headline of the time read—"40,000 to 50,000 on Both Sides Killed, Wounded, or Missing." The paper called the battle one of the greatest and bloodiest of modern day. As a Captain of the Iowa infantry later recalled, the battlefield was where "a hundred thousand human souls [were] pitted against each other, bringing to bear every possible resource for supremacy in a death-struggle; where the brotherhood of man was forgotten and a revelry of carnage reign[ed] supreme; where human sympathy congeal[ed] and mock[ed] at Death." The following excerpt describes a portion of the battle.

We then moved across an open field bordered by a thick woods on the southwest, towards which we were marching. Our skirmishers, a short distance in advance of the main line, gave evidence as soon as they reached the edge of the timber that we were close upon the enemy. As soon as we reached the edge of the timber we were saluted with a shower of musket-balls.

Some of our men drop on their knees and commence firing; others take trees and logs for cover, and we send them bullets as fast as we can load and fire. We have marched too fast, and are close on their line and in advance of our own on the left, and it is soon made evident that we cannot maintain our advanced position. The rebels had thrown up a breastwork of logs, from behind which they could shoot and be very well protected from musketry.

The comrades of the 81st know that this was a fierce fight, kept up I cannot say how long; we were too busily engaged to note the flight of time. To make matters worse for us, the rebels had a flanking fire on our line, and amid the rattle of musketry the order was given for the regiment to retire. The order was not heard by a great many, and the men went back in a disconnected manner, which was the very way they should have been ordered to do; for if we had gone back in line the regiment would have been mown down like grass. That open field was swept by a storm of grape [an antipersonnel weapon consisting of a cluster of small iron balls shot from a cannon] and canister [a metallic cylinder packed with shot and used as ammunition in a firearm] which would have made terrible gaps in a solid line. The writer of this remembers with what alacrity he sped for two hundred yards, and how the infernal missiles hissed and screeched, tearing up the ground and dashing the dirt in his eyes, until reaching a rallying-point in the same field, just over an elevation, where we reformed and moved to the left into the timber.

We crossed a ravine where the dead of both armies lay thick; a place no doubt where many had crawled to get water, and had died there. Moving at a "left oblique," and keeping under cover of the timber, we came upon nearly the same line that we had occupied under fire, but farther to the left. We moved slowly and cautiously, knowing the enemy were close at hand, but whom the density of the undergrowth through which we were passing prevented its from seeing.

A Nation at War

On April 27, General Burnside is relieved of command of the Army of the Potomac and replaced by General Joseph Hooker.

1863.6

Trying a "Traitor"

From "The Trial of Vallandigham," Artist Unknown, 1863. From the Library of Congress.

During a speech in early May at Mount Vernon, Ohio, Clement L. Vallandigham indicated that the war was not waged for the preservation of the Union, but was waged for the purpose of crushing out liberty and erecting a despotism. He continued, saying "the Government of the United States was about to appoint military marshals in every district, to restrain the people of their liberties, to deprive them of their rights and privileges." These words violated General Order No. 38, issued in April 1863, by General Burnside, head of command of the Department of the Ohio, composed of the states of Ohio, Kentucky, Indiana, Illinois, and Michigan, with headquarters in Cincinnati. To combat against Copperheads, the Order in part stated that those in the "habit of declaring sympathies for the enemy will not be allowed" and persons committing such offenses "will be at once arrested, with a view to being tried . . . or sent beyond our lines into the lines of their friends."

Tried and convicted, Vallandigham was banished to the South as "a war measure." From the South, he ran the Union blockade and took up residence on the Canadian side of Niagara Falls. In the same year, he ran to become Governor of Ohio, but was defeated, ending his political career. He died at Lebanon, Ohio, June 17, 1871, from the accidental discharge of a pistol. Some contended that he committed suicide, but the evidence doesn't support the assertion.

This cartoon drawing, in three scenes, shows the trial of Clement L. Vallandigham and the aftermath. In scene one, Vallandigham, seated before the judge in military court, General R.R. Potter, demands a jury trial. Samuel S. Cox, a congressman from Ohio and later New York, testifies for Vallandigham in the second scene, while George H. Pendleton, a Democratic congressman from Ohio and the future vice-presidential candidate on the McClellan ticket in 1864, encourages George Pugh, a former U.S. Senator from Ohio and a Democrat. Pendleton and Pugh were co-counselors for Vallandigham. In the third scene, Vallandigham is dragged off to Tortugas, an island 70 miles west of Key West, Florida, with a chain around his neck, while Pendleton runs toward George Pugh, candidate for lieutenant governor, warning him that "No. 38 is coming," in reference to Burnside's general order.

[Cartoon on following page.]

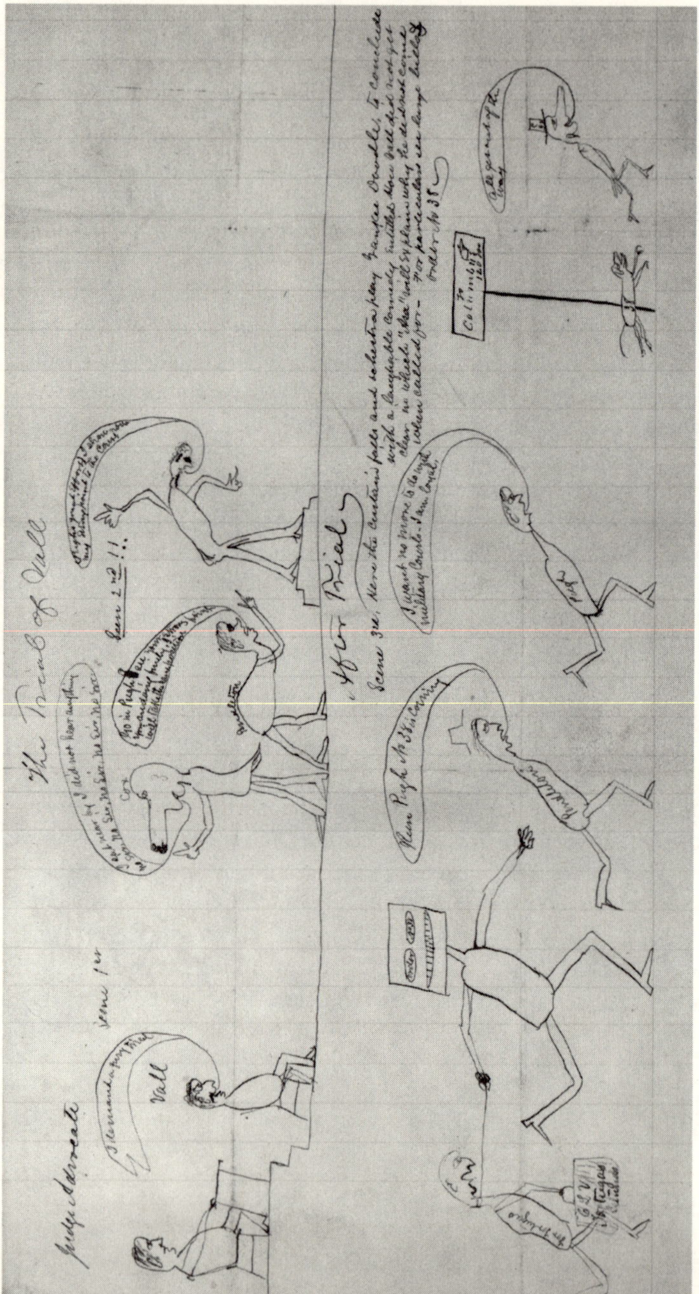
The Trial of Vall
Judge Advocate
Scene 1st
Vall
Scene 2nd !!
After Trial

1863.7

1863.7

Little Johnny Clem

From Frank Moore, ed., *The Civil War in Song and Story 1860–1865*, New York: P.F. Collier, 1889.

Drummer boys, many who were too young to enlist as regular soldiers, joined up and aided the armies by providing a means of communication in camp and on the battlefield. Johnny Clem was born on August 13, 1851, in Newark, Ohio. He left his school classes when he was ten years old to drill with the Third Ohio Volunteer Infantry Regiment. Although there is some uncertainty, Clem probably became a drummer boy in the Twenty-Fourth Ohio Volunteer Infantry and later in the Twenty-Second Michigan Infantry.

The story of the little hero who brought down a Confederate officer was an inspiration. Modern scholars now contend that Northern reporters enhanced Clem's exploits to help promote the war effort. Following the Civil War, President Ulysses S. Grant nominated Clem to become a student at the United States Military Academy at West Point. Clem repeatedly failed to pass the entrance exam, but was eventually commissioned as a lieutenant.

Of course you remember the story of Little Johnny Clem, the motherless atom of a drummer boy, "aged ten," who strayed away from Newark, Ohio; and the first we knew of him, though small enough to live in a drum, was beating the long roll for the Twenty-second Michigan. At Chickamauga he filled the office of "marker," carrying the guidon [a small flag or banner] whereby they form the lines—a duty having its counterpart in the surveyor's more peaceful calling; in the flag-man, who flutters the red signal along the metes [parcel of land] and bounds. On the Sunday of the battle, the little fellow's occupation gone, he picked up a gun that had fallen from some dying hand, provided himself with ammunition, and began putting in the periods quite on his own account, blazing away close to the ground, like a fire-fly in the grass. Late in the waning day, the waif left almost alone in the whirl of the battle, a rebel Colonel dashed up, and looking down at him, ordered him to surrender. "Surrender!" he shouted, "you little d—d son of a —!" The words were hardly out of his mouth, when Johnny brought his piece to "order arms," and as his hand slipped down to the hammer, he pressed it back, swung up the gun to the position of "charge bayonet;" and as the officer raised his sabre to strike the piece aside, the glancing barrel lifted into range, and the proud Colonel tumbled from his horse, his lips fresh-stained with the syllable of vile reproach he had flung on a mother's grave in the hearing of her child!

A few swift moments ticked on by musket-shots, and the tiny gunner was swept up at a rebel swoop, and borne away a prisoner. Soldiers, bigger but not better, were taken with him, only to be washed back again by a surge of Federal troopers, and the prisoner of thirty minutes was again John Clem "of ours;" and Gen. Rosecrans made him a Sergeant, and the stripes of rank covered him all over, like a mouse in a harness; and the daughter of Mr. Secretary Chase presented him a sifter medal, appropriately inscribed, which he worthily wears—a royal order of honor—upon his left breast.

Union drummer boy, Johnny Clem, at Point Lookout, Tennessee. From the Library of Congress.

1863.8

Marching with the Band

From F.A. Eileman, "Dress Parade." Publisher unknown (but probably J. Church, Cincinnati, Ohio), circa 1863.

If "music can soothe the savage beast," music can surely help the downtrodden soldier raise his spirits. In the North a very noted war hymn was Mrs. Julia Ward Howe's "Battle Hymn of the Republic." The most noted writer of war lyrics was George F. Root, of Chicago; among whose most widely known productions were "Just Before the Battle," "Mother," and "Tramp, Tramp, Tramp, the Boys Are Marching." "The Battle Cry of Freedom" and "O, Wrap the Flag around Me, Boys," were also very popular war lyrics. Other war songs were "John Brown's Song" and "Marching through Georgia." The most noted Confederate war songs were "Hurrah, Hurrah for the Bonnie Blue Flag" and "My Maryland, My Maryland." "Dixie" was also a popular Southern song, written a few years before the Civil War.

The 105th Ohio Volunteer Infantry was made up of recruits from Ashtabula, Geauga, Lake, Mahoning, and Trumbull counties. The regiment mustered into service on August 20 and 21, 1862, at Camp Taylor. The "Dress Parade" of the 105th O.V.I., is reproduced below (the cover was originally in full color). The piece, as the title implies, was for a parade in full dress uniform. F.A. Eileman, the musical director of the 7th Ohio Volunteer Infantry, composed other pieces including "Lieutenant General Grant's Grand March" and "Col. E.B. Tyler's [Colonel, 7th Ohio Volunteer Infantry] Patriotic March."

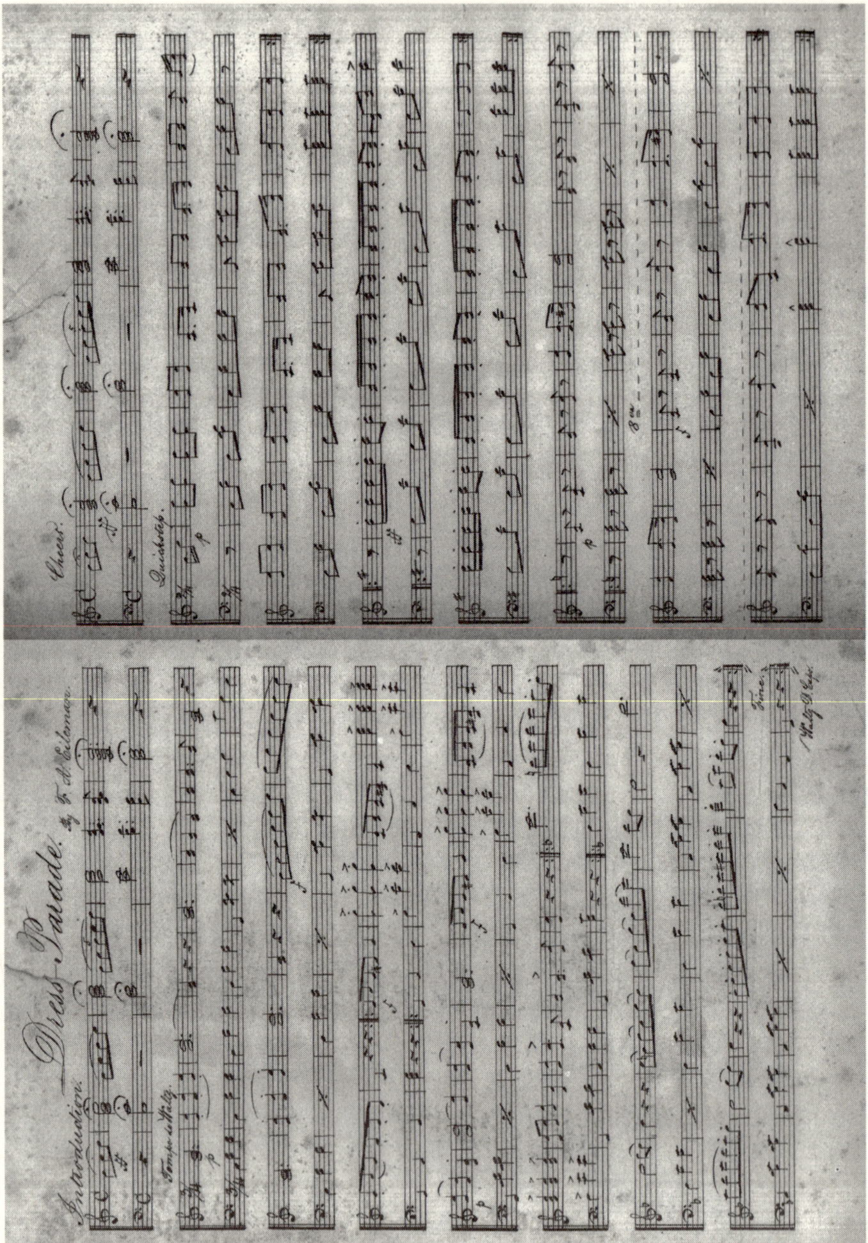
Dress-Parade.
Introduction.
Tempo di Waltz
Quickstep.
Chorus.
Fine.

1863.7

1863.9

Keeping the Troops in Line

From Charles B. Smith papers, 1858–1867, Manuscripts, Western Reserve Historical Society Archives. Courtesy Western Reserve Historical Society, Cleveland, Ohio.

Charles B. Smith was a Lieutenant with the 61st Illinois Volunteer Infantry, serving as a Judge Advocate General at Camp Dennison, Ohio, through most of 1863. The following two documents represent a view of the conflict outside the battle lines. While the disposition of these cases is not known, the punishment in both instances did not result in discharges for the accused. Both Wilson and VanBuren mustered out after fulfilling the terms of their enlistments. Wilson's victim, Phillip Johnson survived his wounds and mustered out, too.

Charges and specifications against Samuel Wilson Private of the 2nd Ohio Vol. Heavy Artillery.

Charge 1st
Assault
Specification 1st

In this that the said Samuel Willson a private of the 2nd Ohio Volunteer Heavy Artillery did on or about the 14th day of August 1863 take a rock, or stone, proceed to the bunk or bed of one Phillip Johnson and did while said Johnson was asleep inflict severe blows with said rock or stone upon the person of said Phillip Johnson so as to badly wound him. All this at Camp Dennison Ohio.

Charge 2nd
Conduct prejudicial to good order and military discipline
Specification 1st

In this that the said Samuel Wilson—a private of the 2nd Ohio Volunteer Heavy Artillery did on or about the 14th day of August 1863 while in custody on his way to the guard house use the following violent and threatening language respecting said Phillip Johnson to wit:—"God damn him, the matter is not ended yet; I will fix him worse than I have done," or words to that effect. All this at Camp Dennison Ohio.

Wm. S. Irwin Capt.

Witnesses
Mahlon Brooks
Samuel Wiley
Lieut. Chas. O. Baker

2nd O V H A

Charges and Specifications against
Private William H. Vanburen Company B 22nd Regt. Ill.
Volunteer Infantry

Charge 1st

Drunkenness

Specification

In this that the said Private William H. VanBuren Company B. 22nd Ill. Vol. Infantry did on or about Sept. 2. 1863 at or near Camp Dennison Ohio become intoxicated.

Charge 2nd

Conduct prejudicial to good order and military discipline

Specification 1st

In this that the said Private William H. van Buren Company B. 22nd Regt Ill. Volunteer Infantry did on or about Sept. 12. 1863 at or near Camp Dennison, Ohio insult and abuse Mrs. Farmer and Daughter by offering money and by using other means endeavor to induce them to have illicit intercourse with him.

Camp Dennison O.
Sept. 18th 1863
Francis C. Russell
Capt. Company C. Fifth Independent Battalion O.V.C.

Witnesses

Capt. Francis C. Russell
Sergt. Orlando Crows
Private Jasper M. Whaley

1863.10

A Rebel in My Boots

From J.W. Chamberlain, "Scenes in Libby Prison," in *Sketches of War History: 1861–1865*, ed. by R. Hunter, Cincinnati, OH: Clarke, 1888.

During the Civil War, roughly 270,000 Union soldiers and 220,000 Confederate soldiers were held as prisoners of war. Of those numbers, approximately 22,570 Union soldiers and 26,436 Confederate soldiers died while imprisoned. Initial conditions in the prisons of both sides were tolerable, but as the war continued, conditions deteriorated rapidly. By war's end, prisoners at Libby Prison, which is described below, were allocated a floor space of only ten feet by two feet. Within this average space the prisoners had to cook, eat, wash, sleep, and take exercise. After prisoner exchanges between the sides ceased, Union prisons filled up rapidly, and the number of deaths in prisons rose.

BY J. W. CHAMBERLAIN,
LATE CAPTAIN AND BREVET MAJOR ONE HUNDRED AND TWENTY-THIRD O. V. I.

The One Hundred and Twenty-third Regiment Ohio Volunteer Infantry was organized at Monroeville, Ohio, in the month of September, 1862, composed of men recruited in the counties of Seneca, Huron, Erie, Crawford and Wyandot.

About the middle of October, the regiment was sent to Parkersburg, Va., thence to Clarksburg, Buckhannon, Beverly, Webster, New Creek, Burlington, Romney, finally reaching Winchester in March, 1863. During the month of May, and part of June, the writer was detailed as a member of a general court-martial, though at same time he was quartered with his regiment. On the 13th of June, on going to camp for dinner, found the tents standing, but entirely deserted. Hearing occasional musket shots to the south of town, made my way in that direction, and soon found the One Hundred and Twenty-third in line for their first real battle. As it afterward appeared, the enemy in our front was the advanceguard of Lee's army, on their march to Pennsylvania [Gettysburg Campaign], although at this time our commanding officer was not aware that the rebels were in such force until some time later. In a very short time, we were brought into action, and although a number were killed and wounded, our regiment behaved nobly under their first fire, and were complimented for their bearing and bravery by General Milroy.

Toward evening, we fell back into the edge of town, and remained the larger part of the night, standing under arms in a drenching rain. At daylight, our command was marched into one of the forts, where we remained nearly all day Sunday. The enemy now advancing on our flanks, and still pressing us in front, and their large superiority in numbers becoming known, our commander decided to evacuate Winchester; and the movement began at one o'clock in the morning of June 15th. Our brigade being in advance, when about four miles from town, struck the enemy, and were wheeled off to one side to hold the enemy in check while the remainder of our troops escaped. Three times our regiment charged on the enemy's artillery, and the last time, just as the last man was killed at their guns, reinforcements reached them, and we were compelled to fall back; and as we turned our faces to the rear, saw a white flag displayed nearly a half mile back of us, indicating that we had been surrendered; this done by the officer then in command of our brigade. A few minutes after, we found ourselves with a new commander, in the person of Brigadier General [James A.] Walker, commanding the "Old Stonewall Brigade" [a noted Confederate combat unit formed by Thomas "Stonewall" Jackson]. We were then taken back to the fort. Next day the officers were separated from the men, and taken to the courthouse in Winchester. Not having had any thing to eat for thirty-six hours, I succeeded, through the intervention of Surgeon [Orrin] Ferris, of our regiment, who was permitted to go outside of our immediate guard line, in sending a line to a loyal family, whose acquaintance I had made some time previous. As soon as they could get the necessary pass from the rebel provost marshal, the old gentleman, some seventy-five years old, and his daughter, appeared with a supply of bread, meat, and coffee, which I assure you proved very acceptable. The next morning they came again, bringing a towel and some soap—by the way, the only towel three of us had for several months.

A few days previous, thinking it essential that I should have a pair of very high military boots, I purchased a pair of the boots, finding them high in price, as well as in cut, and, as a matter of course, felt very proud of them. When captured, did not have them on, and one day, while a prisoner in the courthouse, saw a rebel officer marching by with them on, and from his appearance, should judge he was just as proud of them as I had been. Afternoon of Thursday, June 18th, 108 commissioned officers, including 20 from our regiment, were started on their march to Richmond, in charge of Captain Winfield's company of the Fifty-eighth Virginia, C.S.A.

Our march to Staunton, some eighty miles, occupied a little over four days, nothing of any special moment occurring on the way, excepting sore feet and fleas. The latter were found in great abundance, in an old barn in which we were quartered our first night out, and finding our blood in good condition, stayed by us for several days, to our great discomfort. From Staunton we were taken by railroad, to Richmond, reaching there Tuesday, June 23d, and were immediately introduced to our quarters in the "Hotel de Libby," first being pretty thoroughly searched, ostensibly for money, but really for any thing they could use or thought they wanted. Nearly all succeeded, however, in secreting the bulk of the money they had. I remember a rebel officer taking from me several sheets of paper—which, being white, was a great rarity with them, they only having brown paper—and placed it in the rear pocket of a frock coat he was wearing. While he continued his search, another of our officers noticed it, and, adroitly removing it, returned it to me.

A brief description of the prison building may be necessary to a full understanding of some incidents that afterward occurred there. Before the war, it was occupied by Libby & Son, ship chandlers and grocers, from which fact it took its name of Libby Prison. It was of brick, 150 feet front by 105 feet deep, fronting on Cary Street, and extending back to Canal Street, just beyond which was the canal, and then James River. The building was three stories high, with floors, but no ceilings, much resembling a grain warehouse inside; window frames, but no glass, instead of which, at first, there were wooden bars, leaving apertures about the size of common glass. Consequently we had plenty of ventilation, especially during the winter. No bunks of any description; no seats, excepting one or two benches. A small kitchen, partitioned off, in which were three old brokendown cooking stoves and a few broken kettles. Each story was divided in three rooms. The lower room of first tier was occupied by the various officers employed in control of the prison. Lower middle room only occasionally occupied; lower third tier, as hospital; and the balance of building for prisoners. The basement was used by a few darkies, who did the rough work in prison. There were also two or three cells, dungeon like, in the basement. Castle Thunder was about a square distant; Belle Isle about two miles [two other prisons located in Richmond].

When I entered Libby, we found about fifty prisoners there, composed of the officers of Colonel A. D. Straight's [51st Indiana Infantry] command. Before I left, the number was increased to more than eleven hundred. The rebel officials directly in charge of the prison were Captain Thos. P. Turner [A West Point cadet prior to the war. Escaped to Cuba after the war.], commandant of prison, subsequently promoted to major; Adjutant Latouche [Died on October 4, 1890, in Richmond, Virginia]; R. R. Turner [Became a successful lumber dealer after the war. Died on December 5, 1901.], familiarly called "Dick Turner," inspector of prisons; E. W. Ross [died in the Spottswood House hotel fire of 1873], clerk. For the first month, we were compelled to subsist on the rations doled out to us, as Milroy's thieves [Robert H. Milroy, Commander of the Union Mountain Department, West Virginia. A $100,000 reward was authorized by Jefferson Davis for Milroy, dead or alive, due to tactics Milroy used to fight Confederate guerrillas. If guerillas confiscated property or killed loyalists, retribution was required or Milroy retaliated by killing Confederates or burning their property.], as we were insultingly styled, were not permitted to make any purchases outside. We were given just about half enough of sour soft bread, small red beans, poor slabby beef, with an occasional taste of very poor sweet potatoes. Each man's rations were doled out to him very exactly, and the crumbs that fell to the floor were closely looked after, and when found, promptly appropriated. As soon as we were put on the same footing as prisoners from other commands, and permitted to purchase articles, we fared better. The kitchen, in one corner, was about eight by twenty feet in size, and contained three wornout stoves and a few broken utensils. The prisoners were divided into messes of from four to twenty in size, and the cooking for several hundred men was done in this little room. The kitchen, crowded full of occupants about meal time, was a lively place, I assure you. Green pine wood for fuel, and any of you who have ever used it know what a nice fire it makes; every available spot on the stoves covered with cooking utensils of every imaginable shape and kind, each cook watching his own particular pot or pan; and woe betide the man who stepped out of the room for a minute on his return, he would be sure to find his own pan removed, and some one else's in its place. Then came the fun; like little children, their angry passions would rise, and, although they did not exactly scratch out each others' eyes, on more than one occasion these disputes came very near having a serious ending, demonstrating thoroughly that starvation would bring to the surface all the animal there is in man. I well remember a captain in our regiment, a large, powerful man, very slow and deliberate in action, washing the ration of meat for our mess of twenty—a piece weighing probably three pounds—at the water faucet, when a young lieutenant in the regular army suddenly thrust his cup under the faucet, pushing away the meat, when the captain slowly raised his eyes, and seeing in the lieutenant's face a look of contempt, like a flash he raised the meat, and the lieutenant received a "sockdolager" [a heavy blow] back of the ear with it, that struck him like a solid shot, followed by a lively little scrimmage. In it all, you may be sure, the meat was carefully looked after and applied to its intended use.

Our wheat bread rations continued for two months, when a change was made to solid corn bread, made out of corn, ground cob and all, and mixed with cold water, baked solid, supplying us with a *very substantial* article of diet. The supply of meat soon became very uncertain; sometimes a whole week would elapse without any; and on three occasions, to my own personal knowledge, mule meat was issued to us, and, as a matter of course, it was not a very fat mule either, for they did not kill that kind—they had better use for them; and in fact we had serious doubts whether they had been killed, or only died a natural death. The officers in hospital, at one time, were forty-eight hours without any rations. On one occasion, meat was issued to us only once in sixteen days; at another time, once in two weeks. The rations furnished officers were always uncooked, but those given to the enlisted men were cooked, and consisted of weak soup—as it was called; better say weak water—in old dirty pails, and about six ounces of poor bread to a man. When complaint was made to the prison officials, as to quantity and quality of food furnished, their reply would be that it was the best they could do, and I presume there was possibly a grain of truth in that. The daily papers of Richmond were constantly complaining about their government feeding so many Yankees there, and even one paper advised the authorities to confiscate boxes of clothing and provisions sent us by our friends in the North. As soon as we became satisfied that immediate exchange was very uncertain, we began to order provisions and clothing from our Northern friends. At first, these supplies were delivered to us quite promptly, but they soon suspected us of smuggling in letters and money in this way, and they had good cause to. The many different ways used to conceal these articles, exhibited the ingenuity of our friends at home. As all letters sent to us in the regular way were read by the rebel officials before delivery to us, we did not know where to look for the concealed articles, and sometimes they were not found for weeks. The writer, on one occasion, received money which had been placed in a small vial, and concealed in a jar of canned fruit; on another occasion, in a package of ground coffee; and again, in a loaf of bread, where it had been placed before baking. Other parties found such articles in a roll of butter, deftly inserted in a plug of tobacco, or laid between two leaves of a book and the edges neatly pasted together. The result of this suspicion on the part of the officials was, that great delay ensued in the delivery of packages. They were ruthlessly torn open, bread and cakes cut up in small pieces, cans of fruit opened, and we received the contents of our boxes in a terribly mangled condition. This continued to grow worse, until it became almost impossible to get boxes sent you, and finally delivery was often refused in any shape. As soon as we were permitted to do so, we began to send out orders for provisions, to be bought in the markets at Richmond. This had to be done through a prison official, and you can rest assured that the commission he retained was no small one. We could only purchase certain articles, and those usually of very inferior quality. I recollect that I had been a prisoner five months before I succeeded in purchasing any butter in this way. In mentioning the attaches of the prison I neglected to name two that we saw more frequently than any of the others. George Stansil (a sergeant) who was used to communicate orders to the prisoners, and "General Johnson," a gentleman of color, who was a prisoner as well as ourselves. His duty consisted in supplying us with smoke for fumigating purposes, which he did every morning, carrying a large skillet, filled with tar and coals, through all the rooms of the prison, crying out: *"Here is your nice smoke, without money and without price. Only one more smoke and then."* He also gathered up the dirty clothes once a week, which he was permitted to take out to be washed, returning them Sunday mornings, at the small charge of three pieces for one dollar. He also for some time monopolized the shaving and hair cutting, which operations he performed at the moderate price of twenty-five cents for the former and seventy-five for the latter, but he was finally superseded by a German lieutenant, which compelled him to abandon his calling and turn bootblack. The old man was a regular fixture in Libby, having been in the prison almost two years. He was also an old soldier, having accompanied a Pennsylvania regiment through the Mexican war. Every morning at nine o'clock George made his appearance, and with a peculiar intonation, of voice calling out, *"Fall in, sick, and go down."* At this command, those who desired to be prescribed for huddled together, and went down to the first floor, where they were examined by the rebel surgeon—who was always spoken of as a kind and attentive physician—who, after making a minute of their cases, sent them back to their quarters, excepting those whom it was deemed necessary to send to the hospital. In the course of two or three hours, the medicine would be brought up and distributed to the sick. And, while speaking of the sick, I wish to say that our enlisted men, prisoners, who were so unfortunate as to become sick, were treated outrageously. They were often allowed to lie on the wet or frozen ground on Belle Isle until the last moment, when they would be brought to the hospitals in the city to breathe their last. Out of sixteen brought over in one day, I have known four to be taken out dead the next morning.

The prison guards were usually quartered near by, and when on duty walked their beats, on the curbstone of the sidewalks around the building, and during the night calling out the hours: *"Nine o'clock." "Lights out." " One o'clock and all's well,"* sometimes varied to suit the exigencies of the occasion. I remember one cold morning the cry was: *"Six o'clock, and cold as h—l."* There were usually no guards in the building, except one or two stationed at the foot of the stairways leading to second floor. The guards employed were city troops, whose treatment of us was in great contrast with that received from Captain Wingfield's [A schoolteacher before the war, he became a professor at Randolph-Macon College after the fighting ceased] company, 58th C. S. A., who brought us to Richmond. When with the latter we fared in every respect just as well as they did. They had been in active service, and knew something of the horrors of war, while the city militia seemed to take delight in adding to our sufferings, if possible. On several occasions, prisoners were fired at, on the slightest provocation, or even none at all; one prisoner, in his anxiety to see what was going on in the street, stuck his head out of the window, and without any warning a guard fired, and a ball whistled very close to the poor fellow's head. On another occasion, a prisoner while in the closet, and infringing no rules, had the tip of his ear shot off.

Everything in the line of reading matter was eagerly sought after. A portion of the time an old darky was permitted to bring in the Richmond daily papers for sale. Twenty-five cents apiece, printed on a very small sheet of inferior quality of wrapping paper! To get a Northern paper of a late date was a prize indeed. A case of "Harper's Select Library" of novels, sent to a prisoner by his Northern friends, had a large circulation. Letterwriting was carried on to some extent, until the prison officials got so tired of reading so many before starting them north, that an order was issued by Major Turner, that no Federal officer would be permitted to write letters of more than six lines each, to the *socalled* United States, and not more than one letter per week, and that to be handed to the sergeant on Monday mornings. The one universal thought that predominated in a prisoner's mind, from the time he entered *"Hotel de Libby"* —as the boys facetiously termed it—until his release, was: "How soon will we be exchanged." When we first made our advent into that highly popular institution, it was certainly thought that we would not possibly remain longer than ten days or two weeks—at the end of that time we were still there, and remained there for nearly nine months before any officers were exchanged, excepting chaplains and surgeons. Who was to blame for this, to us unaccountable delay, we could not tell, situated as we were. The rebels continually said it was the fault of the federal authorities. Exchange rumors were very abundant. The slightest foundation sufficed for the most extravagant reports. One day our hopes would be raised to the highest point, the next they would be away below zero . . . To keep the mind off this subject, all imaginable plans were devised to employ the time either beneficially or for amusement. Classes were organized in a variety of branches. Capable teachers were readily found. Those who were skillful with the knife and file employed their time in carving trinkets out of bones taken from the meat furnished us, and some very handsome specimens were the result of their labors. Card playing was an almost universal pastime, and many became very proficient at it. While the chaplains remained with us, prayer meetings were regularly held. The writer has seen a prayer meeting and two or three faro [card game] tables in operation at the same time, in one of the large rooms. Some very fine chess players among the prisoners. One lieutenant became so proficient that he could play two, and even three games at the same time, blindfolded. Amateur theatricals were indulged in to some extent performers blacked as minstrels, under the name of "Libby Burlesque Troupe," and their entertainments became so interesting on some occasions, that even the rebel officials and their friends came in as spectators. . . .

On the Fourth of July an attempt was made to get up a little impromptu celebration. A flag was constructed by tearing up some shirts of the proper colors, and when completed, we fastened it up in the ceiling of thirdstory room, and commenced our speeches. Rebels soon detected what was going on, and sent up an officer, with orders to us to take the flag down, but not a prisoner touched it, and he was compelled to take it down himself.

October 13, 1863, the officers from Ohio, one hundred and sixty-five in number, held an election. One hundred and sixty-two votes were cast for Brough [John Brough, Ohio Governor, 1864–1865] and one for Jewett, two not voting. It was an exciting day, as much so as an election day at home could have been.

New prisoners were brought in every few days, until the number in Libby reached nearly twelve hundred. The new arrivals were designated as "Fresh Fish," and a great deal of sport was had at their expense, until they became thoroughly naturalized.

Notwithstanding all the privations endured, an unflinching loyalty to the old flag was maintained. One officer, suspected of disloyalty, was arrested, tried by an informally organized drumhead court martial, plead guilty, and was sentenced, but clemency was exercised and sentence suspended. Some ten or twelve negroes were kept in the basement, to do police work in the different rooms; they were not permitted to go outside the guards around the prison. During the night of July 24, 1863, those of us on second floor were aroused by the cries for mercy of a poor darky being whipped. As we afterward learned, a barrel was laid on the floor, he was stretched over it, and received on his bare back two hundred and fifty lashes by actual count. This was done, as we supposed, for exchanging money, but the negroes said for attempting to escape. Soon after the writer became an inmate of Libby, he found it necessary to exchange our "greenbacks" for Confederate money, to enable him to purchase any thing in Richmond. It was a criminal offense for a citizen of the Confederacy to sell any thing and take his pay in greenbacks.

The blockade runners were very anxious to get the greenbacks to make their purchases with, and this led to an exchange system, carried on through the rebel guards. My first attempt resulted in an exchange of two dollars Confederate, for one dollar Federal money. Succeeding pretty well in my attempts in this line, others brought me their money, as they needed it for use, and I would sometimes have several hundred dollars to exchange at one time. My plan of operation was to station myself at the head of the stairs leading to first floor, and when the right man was pacing his beat at the foot of the stairs, signal to him, and as he walked along with his gun on his shoulder, bayonet fixed, he would move the bayonet along on the wall above his head, writing the number of dollars he would give for one. If satisfactory, would roll up my money in as small a wad as possible, and quietly drop it near his feet, where he could pick it up without stopping his walk. If he made the exchange speedily, he would toss a little roll up when he came on his beat again. Sometimes it would be a day or two before the trade was consummated, but in not a single instance did they betray the trust we were compelled to place in them. Greenbacks soon began to increase in value; or perhaps, more properly speaking, Confederate money began to decline, so that before I was released, we could get fourteen for one. For a while the exchanges were effected through the sentinel on guard at the stairway, but two or three having been caught at it, and arrested, put a stop to that manner of procuring it, and another, but less dangerous plan, was adopted. A hundred dollars would be raised in greenbacks and sent out by one of the negro boys belonging to the establishment, who would exchange it with some citizen and bring us back the Confederate rags. We had occasional lectures on different topics, one or two on medicine, that I recall, two on temperance, by Brigadier General Neal Dow [a famous Prohibitionist from the 13th Maine Volunteers], which we thoroughly appreciated, for we were then living in the strongest prohibition locality we had ever been in. Until the chaplains were exchanged, we had frequent religious services. After their departure, several prominent rebel divines officiated for our benefit, but this occasioned one or two mass meetings, to decide whether we would have loyal preachers or none. They were finally permitted to continue their services, but the attendance was not very large, nor very enthusiastic. On one occasion we were all marched into one room, while the other rooms were thoroughly searched for money, hatchets, knives, saws and files, we having accumulated a quantity of the three latter, to use in the manufacture of bone work. [See 1863.11] We had received an intimation of the proposed search some days before, and I had concealed a gold watch, that I then had, in the bottom of a large wooden spittoon, that was filled with sawdust, where it remained for more than a week. My money, at this time, I carried concealed between the outside leather and stiffening of a pair of old government brogans [a heavy, ankle-high work shoe] I was wearing. July 6, 1863, occurred one of the most dramatic scenes I ever witnessed or participated in. Although more than twenty years have elapsed, I believe that today I would rather take the risk of the most severe battle I ever saw, than to go through with the same ordeal again. All the Federal captains in the prison, seventy-five in number, were ordered to fall in line, marched down stairs, and into a large vacant room, where we were formed in one rank in a hollow square, and remained there for some moments before we knew what was to take place. A table was brought in and placed in the center, and a box similar to an ordinary ballotbox placed on it. An order was then read from General Winder, commanding Department of Richmond, addressed to Commandant of Prisons, in substance as follows: "You are ordered to select at once, by lot, from among the Federal captains in your charge, two for immediate execution." Seventy-five slips of paper, each having on it the name of one officer, were deposited in the box. We were then informed that we could select one of our own number, or one of the chaplains up stairs, to draw out two of the slips. Father Gray, a chaplain, was chosen. He made a short prayer, after which he closed his eyes, and with tears streaming down his cheeks, he drew out two slips, and handed them to the rebel officer in charge, who read the names aloud. The officers selected were Captains Sawyer, of the First New Jersey Cavalry, and Flinn, of the Fifty-First Indiana Volunteer Infantry. We were marched back to our quarters, and the two captains were taken to General Winder's headquarters. This scene was one of the most trying ones of my life, the few moments it occupied seemed like years, and I do not think there was a single one of the seventy-five, but what would have gladly preferred to have met the enemy face to face in battle a dozen times in preference to once drawing lots in this manner for his life.

Fortunately for the two captains, they were not immediately executed, but were placed in dungeons in the basement of Libby, where they were kept about two weeks. During this delay, our government, being notified of the action of the rebel authorities, at once had General W. H. Lee, a nephew of General Robert Lee, and Captain Winder, a son of General Winder, placed in close confinement, with instructions to the officer in charge to execute them at once, on receipt of official notification that Captains Flinn and Sawyer had been executed. This prompt action on the part of the Federal authorities brought the rebels to time, and after about two weeks close confinement, Sawyer and Flinn were restored to their old quarters with the other prisoners. . . .

October 28th, "George," a prison policeman, without any provocation, drew a revolver on one of the prisoners, when Lieutenant Reed, Third Ohio, a wounded officer, told him he must not attempt that there; for this offense, the lieutenant was taken down to the cell, and kept there three days, the first night without any blanket. At one time, a cage about six feet by ten was constructed in one of the lower rooms, and four officers—white men—of colored regiments, were confined in there with several negro soldiers, as an extra punishment, for being guilty of commanding negro troops.

Occasionally an officer would escape from the prison. Major Huston, who had been in the hospital—then in lower east room—for some time, and was a tailor by trade, was employed by a rebel surgeon to make a uniform for him, which he did; but when completed, instead of giving it to the surgeon, donned the uniform himself, and about dusk one evening walked out as "the surgeon," and succeeded in passing the guards without any difficulty. This escape so alarmed the rebels that they took possession of the lower east room, locating the hospital in the room above, nailing up the door between that and the other upper rooms; then gave us the lower middle room, after taking the precaution to nail up the windows in the rooms and double the guard on the outside of the building . . . During the winter, plans were made to tunnel out; but a number of difficulties presented themselves. The prison building extended from one street to another only one hundred and five feet, and another street ran along one of the sides; on the fourth side there was a vacant space of about forty feet in width, then a high board fence inclosing a lot on which stood a building used for the storage of private boxes sent there for prisoners. A large portion of the time the officers were confined entirely on second and third floors; but being crowded very much for room, we were finally permitted to use what was called the lower middle room for cooking and promenading, but not for sleeping purposes. In this room there was a fireplace, only used to pile wood in, to be used in the cookstove that stood directly in front. A board in the floor in the fireplace was taken up, and thus access was gained to that portion of the basement, a few feet in depth, and not occupied for any purpose. Once there, it was necessary to get an opening through the division foundation wall into the basement under the outside tier of rooms. Fortunately, the only portion of the basement in use was at the other end of the building. Then an opening had to be made through the outside foundation wall, from which point the tunnel had to be excavated some fifty feet to a place inside of the enclosure before mentioned. The appliances for doing this work were limited. Knives and an old hatchet or two were used. A wooden spittoon was used as a car to transport the dirt as it was dug from the person working back into the basement; a string attached to two sides of it enabling it to be pulled back and forth. Work progressed slowly. Once, thinking they had got far enough, they carefully made a small opening to the surface, when, finding they were directly under the beat of the prison guard, it was hastily closed and the tunnel extended.

February 9th, it was understood by those in the secret, that all was ready for the escape. It had been arranged that a certain number should go out each night for three nights in succession—that being as long as we could probably keep the roll call all right.

At roll call each day, the men were formed in four ranks and the files counted—this in each of the three rooms on second floor. They were counted in the first room by a rebel sergeant, who then went down stairs, and up into second room and counted there, and then into third room. Doors between rooms were supposed to be closed, but in fact there was an opening in them, concealed by shelving, through which enough men could pass to keep the count in the aggregate all right. About nine P. M., the first attempt was made to pass out. It being discovered by many who were not in the secret, they became so excited that a crowd was gathered around the starting point. Soon the cry was raised that the rebels had discovered it and were coming in, and the prisoners scattered to their quarters. After all had quieted down, a number more succeeded in getting out; but the original plans having all been broken up, we were unable to tell how many had escaped, and consequently our plans for keeping count all right were frustrated, and at the morning roll call the prison officers discovered there had been quite an exodus during the night. One hundred and nine succeeded in getting out. Of this number about one-half reached our lines. The others were recaptured, singly and in squads, and returned to Libby. The rebels, after discovering the opening to the tunnel, sent a darky boy to crawl through before they were able to find where the outlet was located. One of the prisoners, who was a very large man, in attempting to crawl through, came very near sticking fast, and it was only by the exertions of those in front and rear of him that he succeeded in getting through. This escape caused the rebels to redouble their vigilance, and we hardly dared look out the windows for fear of being shot at; and it was nothing strange to have roll call by name, which was a very slow and tedious affair, occupying several hours. Not long after, when the Federal troops, on one or two occasions, came very near reaching Richmond, and the rebels feared an uprising among the prisoners, one of the prison officials very coolly informed one of the prisoners that one thousand pounds of powder had been placed under Libby, and in case any attempt was made to break out, the prison would be blown up. At this time there were over eleven hundred officers confined in Libby.

November 12th it was announced that the surgeons had been exchanged. Every body at once went to work writing long letters—to be secreted on the persons of the fortunate doctors, and in that way smuggled through the lines. Finally, on the 24th, the surgeons were notified to be ready to leave in a few moments, as the rebel surgeons had arrived. They were told to disgorge the letters they had concealed about their persons, and a few did so. They were searched below, but with what success those remaining did not know. Letters were concealed in a variety of ways—in the lining of hats, coats, pants, boots, under shoulderstraps, bandaged around sore legs, twisted up in small wads and carried loosely in the pockets, concealed in plugs of tobacco, loaves of bread, and so on.

January 22d. It is five days since we received any rations, except one half of a loaf of corn bread per day to a man, and two weeks since we have had any meat. The issue of meat occurs now only semioccasionally, like a great many other things the "*rebs*" are in the habit of performing. The supply of wood was often very limited, and the wooden partitions, tables, and every thing that would burn, suffered accordingly. . . .

. . . It is simply impossible to describe the sufferings we witnessed. Men, dying from starvation, begging for something to eat; others with the extremities frozen by exposure; and others swarmed with vermin, too weak to keep them hunted down. Thank God! those days of suffering are over. Wounds and death on the battlefield were far preferable to those months of starvation and suffering, and in so many cases, finally, death, followed by a burial among that large army of graves marked "unknown." . . .

During the afternoon of Sunday, March 6, 1864, a few paroled rebel officers, and quite a number of private soldiers, were brought up from City Point. As they marched past the prison, fat and hearty, and well clothed, no further evidence was necessary to convince those who saw them of the striking difference in the manner in which prisoners were cared for North and South. The following morning was an exciting one in Libby. Different rebel officers had notified a number of the prisoners that their names were on the list to go, myself being among the number; but, when the list was called, only a few were taken. A few days later, I was sent for by Inspector Turner for a private interview, it had been currently reported for a day or two that several officers had secured their exchange by bribing one of the rebel officials. Turner knew that I had a gold watch that I had managed to retain, and I strongly suspected it would secure my release, but I hated to part with it; and, although he was very courteous, informing me that he had intended I should go on the first boat, but had been unable to so arrange it, but now assured me I should go in the next party. The interview terminated, and I and my watch went back to our quarters together, and when the second list was called, in a few days, for the next party, my name was not there. About this time, it became the rage to secure autographs of as many of the prisoners as possible, and many promises were made to exchange photographs when released.

March 21, 1864, 62 Federal officers were selected for exchange, myself among the number, and were marched down to the landing, and placed on the gunboat "Schultz," and 925 enlisted men on the steamboat "Allison," and started for City Point. Before leaving the prison, the officers were searched for letters they were supposed to have concealed about their persons, from prisoners left behind to their friends in the North. The officers were kept below deck until we had passed Drury's Bluff that we might not see the fortifications about Richmond.

About 11 P. M., at City Point, we were transferred to the Federal steamer "New York." When all were on board, rousing cheers were given for the "Old Flag," that once more floated over us, realizing the fact that we were again in "God's country."

An hour or two later, with full stomachs once again, and with thankful hearts, we laid down to rest among friends.

A Nation at War

From May 1–6, the Battle of Chancellorsville (Virginia) is fought and won by Confederate troops.

On June 28, General Hooker resigns and is replaced by General Meade as commander of the Army of the Potomac.

1863.11

The Bone Dust Trade

From Lawrence Wilson, ed., *Itinerary of the Seventh Ohio Volunteer Infantry: 1861–1864,* New York: Neale, 1907.

As other documents in this collection show, unique economies developed within Confederate prisoner of war camps. This written account by Leroy Warren, held in New Orleans' Parish Prison (used by the city from 1834 until 1894), explains the particulars of the "bone-dust trade," a system that involved the production and selling of trinkets and ornaments made of bone. Many of these pieces, some meticulously detailed, have survived and are a key part of displays and exhibits concerning the war. Warren was discharged on July 22, 1862, on a surgeon's certificate of disability.

BY LEROY WARREN OF COMPANY C.

The branch of industry chiefly followed by the war-prisoners in New Orleans was the so-called "bone-dust trade." It consisted of the manufacture of all manner of bone trinkets, such as rings, toothpicks, bodkins, crosses, Bibles, and ornamental pins. This business grew up gradually until it came to be the all-engrossing employment of most of the prisoners.

It was natural that those of us who had been able to retain our pocket-knives should take to whittling. At first the whittlers made elaborately carved wooden boxes, fingerrings from knots and pieces of hard coal, little baskets from almond shells and peach pits. In the growing scarcity of other materials some genius whittled a bone into something useful or ornamental; and it soon became apparent that bone was of more value for the purposes of art than any other material we could obtain. Bone, too, was plentiful, owing to the highly osseous character of our Texas beef. Indeed, the bone came to be the most valuable part of the ration. A fine shinbone was sometimes sold to makers of bone works for twenty-five cents, a sum of far more importance to one of us prisoners than five dollars under ordinary circumstances. It was discovered that raw bone was clearer and tougher, and would take a better polish than after it had been boiled; so the bone was taken out before boiling.

The rascals who dealt out beef to us, finding how much value was attached to bones, stole the bones and sold them to the men. The manufacturers gradually attained great skill. There were professional engravers and watch-makers who did the finer work, and employed others to saw and do the coarser work.

Some of the chased rings and embossed pins were really elegant. Red, blue, and green sealing wax were used in lettering and in the insertion of figured work and flowers. The making of bone work would not have become so all-absorbing nor have attained such perfection had it not been a paying occupation, and the only means by which money could be earned. The citizens of New Orleans who came to visit us bought rings and other articles of bone-work, as mementoes of the Yankees. It got into the papers that we were making a variety of fanciful and ingenious articles, and the demand for bone work increased. Men came into the prison to buy on speculation or to fill little commissions for female friends. The guards who were placed over us at night, though forbidden to hold any communication with us, traded for bone work with eagerness. The sentry would order a ring to be made and engraved with his sweetheart's name or his own initials, or he would buy a quantity to sell again outside.

Our boys did not hesitate to engrave on their work the Confederate flag or the legend "C. S. A." The rings representing a good "poker" hand were, however, more in demand than those engraved with the rebel flag. Saws and files and other forbidden tools were brought in by the sentries.

The men contrived lathes and drills and made the most ingenious use of the tools they possessed. The bone business became the great business of the prison. Many men worked incessantly at this money-making and time-killing employment. Bone rings sold at various prices from twelve and a half cents to two dollars, according to quality of material and beauty of workmanship. A beautifully wrought penholder sold for two dollars. The currency received for these articles, and the only currency circulated in the prison, was shin plasters of various sorts, chiefly omnibus tickets on the various city lines.

These tickets passed for five cents and constituted the small change of New Orleans. Gold and silver passed out of circulation in rebeldom much sooner than among us. The scarcity of silver was one of the standing editorial jokes among Southern newspapers that winter.

I regret that I have few statistics of the amount of bone-work made by the prisoners. One man sold forty dollars' worth in prison, besides a still larger quantity which he kept to bring home and to sell on the road.

Sixteen men in one of the smaller cells sold bone work to the value of over two hundred dollars. With the currency received for the work, the men bought bread, cornmeal, potatoes, onions, oranges, tobacco, and molasses. Molasses was used by all the prisoners in large quantities. It was found to be the cheapest article of food we could buy. The finest golden syrup could be bought for twenty-eight cents per gallon, and a good article of molasses for twenty cents. A bone ring of ordinary pretensions was thus worth a gallon of molasses. Many of the men ate molasses at the rate of a pint a day; the majority, however, did not use more than one-half of this quantity.

I have no doubt that this free use of molasses contributed to prevent fevers and scurvy. It was certainly of great service in eking out our scanty rations. Sometimes three or four barrels of molasses would be bought by various men in the prison in a single day. I think that toward the latter part of our stay in New Orleans we did not use less than a barrel daily.

General Palfrey [the Provost Marshall of the city] was kind enough to act as our agent, expending our money advantageously and sending the molasses in to us. He also made efforts at one time to establish a market in the city for bone work, but with little success the demand for bone work having subsided. . . .

A Nation at War

On July 1–3, Lee's northern advance is stopped at the Battle of Gettysburg (Pennsylvania), the bloodiest battle of the war.

1863.12

Enclosed with Patriotism

From "Outside of envelope containing letter to Susannah McKeever," William McKinley Presidential Library and Museum Archive Collection. Courtesy William McKinley Presidential Library and Museum, Canton, Ohio.

Letters from soldiers to their loved ones were the primary communications vehicle during the war. To facilitate the demand, publishers and printers offered the public over 15,000 different envelopes, most of them supporting the Union cause. The envelopes were a ready-made public relations tool. Some of the images were sarcastic, some patriotic, and some romantic. Envelopes depicted camp life scenes, prominent war figures, and political cartoons. Among the sayings on the envelope were slogans like "If I cannot fight, I will feed those who do;" "Southern rights will be defended by southern men;" and "Death to traitors."

This particular envelope was sent by John McKeever to his wife, Susannah. At the time, McKeever, who was 48 years old and the father of seven children, was training at Camp Tiffin, near Wooster, Ohio, as part of the 16th Ohio Volunteer Infantry. McKeever would not make it back home, dying aboard a hospital steamer on August 15, 1863. Mrs. McKeever would be awarded a pension amounting to $8 per month for the services rendered by her late husband.

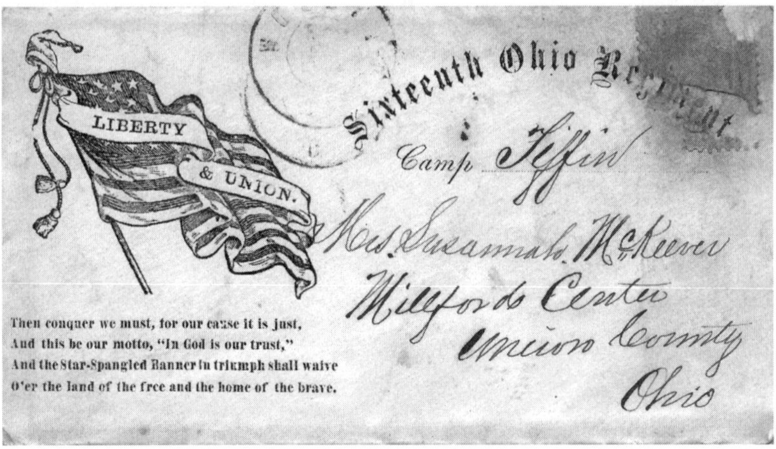

A Nation at War

On August 21, Quantrill's Raiders attack Lawrence, Kansas, a stronghold of pro-Union support, and kill 183 men and boys.

1863.13

A Ticket to Ride to the Front

From "Sergeant Hamilton Transportation Order;" Charles B. Smith papers, 1858–1867; Camp Dennison; Western Reserve Historical Society Archives. Courtesy Western Reserve Historical Society, Cleveland, Ohio.

The Little Miami Railroad Co. was chartered by the Legislature of Ohio, during the session of 1835–1836. The railroad ran from Cincinnati to Springfield, Ohio, a distance of eighty-three and a half miles. During the war, transportation by train and boat was an invaluable way to move troops and supplies to the front lines.

The Fourth Independent Cavalry Battalion was organized at Georgetown, Ohio, on the July 9, 1861. Each man furnished his own horse and horse equipments, and was armed with a saber and carbine. The Fourth was sent to Camp Dennison for further training. Sergeant Hamilton, the ticket's holder, joined the battalion on July 13, 1863, and mustered out on March 12, 1864. The saddler in the battalion was his son, Octavius.

As of May 1862, railroads that transported Union troops, including a baggage allotment of up to 80 pounds per troop, received two cents per man per mile. M.C. Meigs, the Quartermaster General of the Union Army, estimated that the total cost for transportation of troops and supplies between 1861 and 1862 would amount to over $16 million. The image below is of an order allowing Sergeant Hamilton to travel to Cincinnati, Ohio, a departure point, for in all probability, the Cumberland Gap area of Kentucky.

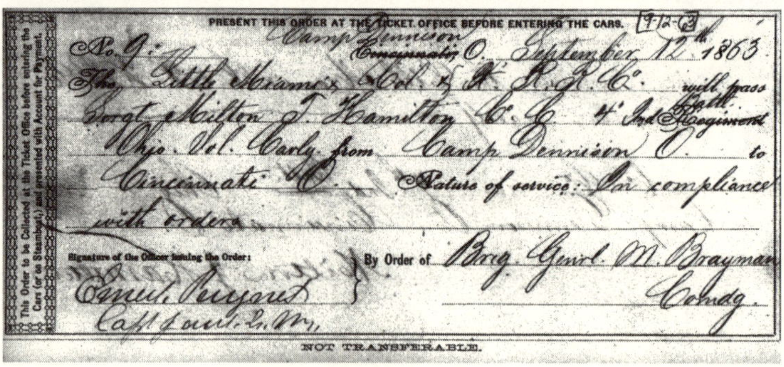

PRESENT THIS ORDER AT THE TICKET OFFICE BEFORE ENTERING THE CARS. 9-12-63

No. 9 Camp Dennison ~~Cincinnati~~ O. September 12th 1863

The Little Miami & Col. & X. R.R. Co. will pass

Sergt. Milton T. Hamilton C. C. 4th Ind. Batt. ~~Regiment~~

Ohio Vol. Cavly. from Camp Dennison O. to

Cincinnati O. Nature of service: In compliance

with orders.

Signature of the Officer issuing the Order: [illegible] Capt [illegible]

By Order of Brig. Genl. M. Brayman Comdg.

This Order to be Collected at the Ticket Office before entering the Cars (or on Steamboat), and presented with Account for Payment.

NOT TRANSFERABLE.

1863.14

The Elevation of the Black Race

From *The Oberlin News,* reprinted in *The Daily Cleveland Herald,* "The 5th Regiment Colored U.S. Troops," October 2, 1863.

The following letter highlights the somewhat contradictory nature of praise for black regiments during the war. Hidden within the admiration are hints of subtle racism—these blacks aren't lazy; these black aren't dirty; these blacks can sure play sweet music. The author of the letter is likely Henry Everard Peck, a faculty member at Oberlin College. Peck was an anti-slavery supporter who played a key role in the Oberlin-Wellington slave rescue affair, denying the return of a fugitive slave to Kentucky. Peck's descriptions of the 5th Regiment need to be viewed in that light.

After the July 17, 1862 passage of the Second Confiscation and Militia Act, freeing slaves who had masters in the Confederate Army and the January 1, 1863 Emancipation Proclamation that freed all slaves in the rebellious states, the recruitment of black troops for the Union army accelerated. By the end of the Civil War, roughly 179,000 black men (10 percent of the Union Army) served as soldiers in the U.S. Army and another 19,000 served in the Navy. Nearly 40,000 black soldiers died over the course of the war—30,000 of infection or disease.

I spent Sunday and part of Monday of this week at Camp Delaware, where the regiment named above is lying.

What I saw and heard during the visit interested me beyond measure. A paragraph or two of the notes which I took may interest the public.

The regiment now numbers two field officers (Lieutenant Colonel and Major,) seventeen line officers and six hundred and ninety-four enlisted men. The officers are picked men. They have passed a rigid examination before a Board of regular army officers and have been appointed by Gov. Tod only after it has been made to appear to him that they have special fitness for their place. The majority of them are liberally educated men and all of them are gentlemen. All but one or two have learned the art of war in the field itself. The appearance of the companies shows that they know how to care for their men and how to drill them.

The enlisted men are, on the whole, a capital body of troops. Of course some of them are slouching and stupid. Slavery has left its ineffacable [sic] blight upon them. But the most of the men are intelligent and wide awake, and their manner in drill and on parade proves that they would not have had more military enthusiasm or capacity for arms if their faces had had the Caucassian [sic] hue. They are, with some exceptions, tractable and apt to learn, and the respect they show their officers is such as we never see in a camp of white men. The last remark, however, must not be misunderstood. The men are not crouching and servile, as haters of the colored race think they would be. The uniform and the musket have inspired their self-respect. They obey the scripture injunction in calling "no man master." Their deference to their officers is not that of the slave, but that of the man—of the man who feels that he is rising and is thankful to the superior who helps him rise.

The camp itself, its streets and parade ground, is as neat as a parlor.

The tents of the men and their clothing are moderately well kept. Their food and tables are tidier far than those of ordinary white regiments.

On drill and parade the men appear uncommonly well. Excepting a few incorrigible slouches, they all "get right up" and put on the best soldier style.

The field music in the regiment is good. I never heard a drum corps play so well as theirs but once and that was in a battallion [sic] of regulars.

I spent a good share of Sunday in private and public labor among them. I found them accessible and seemingly grateful for kind words even when they were joined with plain talk.

I found them, as a rule, happy. "Which is the most unhappy man in this mess, boys? I want to talk with him," said I to a dozen men in one of the tents. They looked at each other significantly for a minute and then a waggish fellow drily replied, "He don't stay in this tent, you'll find him down the street."

Still the poor fellows have their griefs. Uncle sam [sic] gives them only ten dollars [white soldiers received greater pay] a mouth and no bounty. Some of them have families which are suffering for the necessaries of life. Lieut. Col. Shurtleff [Giles W. Shurtleff, see 1861.12 and 1861.13] told me that the men often come for furloughs and to enforce their petitions, show letters from home, which are heart-rending. Wives write that they and their children are actually starving, that their neighbors will not help them, and that the County Commissioners say that the relief fund is "not for niggers," and that their husbands must come and bring help. "We have to refuse them all," the Colonel added, "but it is heart-rending to do so."

There were sixty men in the hospital. Many of them were very sick. The quarters were narrow and inadequate and there were no conveniences. There is as yet no surgeon regularly attached to the regiment and no hospital stores can be drawn. How my heart ached at what I saw in that miserable hospital! In the name of mercy, I implore the people of Ohio to remember the wretches and to make instant supply of all needed conveniences and comforts for the sick. Bedding, fruits and vegetables are much wanted. The supplies can be sent through the Cleveland Soldiers' Aid Society.

The officers of the regiment and the people in the neighborhood spoke in the highest terms of the conduct of the men. "We had," said the gentleman with whom I lodged, "two white regiments here last year, and the men stole almost every pig and chicken. There was nothing safe against them. When we heard there was another regiment coming and that it was to be made up of colored men, we thought we might as well give up. But, as a matter of fact, we have not lost anything by these soldiers: they act like gentlemen."

I wish people who are interested in the elevation of the black race would visit the 5th. Their hopes and labor would certainly be encouraged. It would even do haters of the "nigger" good to go and see what the black man can be when he has a chance.

And now I solemnly beg all people to consider whether the government does justice when it invites the black man to enlist, and then gives him, for pay, a pittance which will only little more than clothe him and leave nothing for his starving family at home. To drive a hard bargain with a poor wretch, who has been under the heel all his days, is in a sort of policy which man ought to despise, and which God will condemn.

Countrymen, cry out to the government in behalf the men who at Port Hudson [in Louisiana; Union siege began on May 23, 1863, Confederate troops ultimately surrendered on July 9, 1863] and Fort Wagner [in South Carolina; siege began July 18, 1863, and resulted in a Union defeat. The incident is depicted in the film, "Glory" (1989)] have nobly fought our hottest battles.

H. E. Peck.

A Nation at War

On September 19–20, the Battle of Chickamauga, Tennessee temporarily halts Northern incursion into the South.

On October 14, the Army of Northern Virginia and the Army of the Potomac engage for the first time since Gettysburg, resulting in a nominal Union victory.

1863.15

Presenting the Stars and Stripes

From John Mercer Langston, *The Virginia Plantation to the National Capitol: The First and Only Negro Representative in the Congress from the Old Dominion,* Hartford, CT: American Publishing Company, 1894.

In the summer of 1863, Ohio Governor Tod instructed Captain McCoy to begin the process of recruiting a colored regiment at Camp Delaware. After several attempts, a regiment was mustered as the Fifth Colored U.S. Infantry.

The image below depicts the presenting of the flag to the Fifth Colored Infantry at Camp Delaware. At the ceremony, Tod remarked, "My boys, sons of the State, go forth now as you are called to fight for our country and its government! Let your conduct be that of brave, intelligent, devoted American citizens! If such shall be your course, if spared and I can reach you no otherwise, on your return I will come upon my hands and knees to meet and greet you!"

1863.16

The War Rides into Ohio

From *The Athens Messenger*, "A Young Hero," July 7, 1863.

Brigadier-General John Hunt Morgan led the only major attack by Southern forces in the State of Ohio during the Civil War. The attack took place during the summer of 1863, and spread across Ohio from the Indiana border. Union troops chased Morgan to Buffington Island and further up the Ohio River. Morgan and his troops were surrounded at Salineville, in Columbiana County and most were captured.

The following newspaper story details the bravery of two young boys during the raid. Undoubtedly, the story has to be viewed with a large grain of salt—records could not be found of Joe Pickering's enlistment with the Third Ohio Volunteer Infantry. Perhaps there is truth to the newspaper account, but creating boy heroes who could whip the Southern scalawags helped sell papers.

Joe Pickering, of Athens, O., though not yet 17 has already won a name as a daring soldier such as few gain in a lifetime. He enlisted in the three months' service under Capt. McVay, and cried with bitter vexation when compelled to surrender at Harper's Ferry just before the battle of Antietam. He had two brothers, who enlisted in the 3rd O. V. I. on the fall of Fort Sumpter, though neither 18 years of age.—One of these noble fellows, a great whole souled boy, who seems never to have felt fear, was instantly killed at Perryville, and young Joe has held the thought of revenge nearer than his own life. [Levi Pickering was killed in Kentucky on October 8, 1862. William Pickering left the Third Ohio Volunteer infantry to join the Fifth Tennessee Cavalry in 1862.]

Morgan's Raid furnished the opportunity, and rubbing up an old flintlock pistol, and taking a shot-gun, he was off to find the rebels. On Saturday, he was beside Major D.H. Moore [of the 125th Ohio Volunteer Infantry. He was wounded in Georgia on May 5, 1864 and resigned his commission on September 20, 1864.] at Rutland, when Morgan entered the place, and the Major fired at the rebel, who was dashing up toward them with the intent to capture them. He admired the coolness with which he held his revolver, and the skillful shot that grazed his foeman's neck, and that was only avoided by a side spring of a well trained horse and a drop behind him for protection.

The rebel looked at them only a moment, and wheeled his horse, and shortly a host of rebels came pouring into the village with drawn revolvers and loud imprecations against "the two Yankees." In the meantime, the Major had withdrawn, and Joe had thrown aside his blouse, and came out of a house wearing a large palm hat in his shirt-sleeves, an interested spectator of their mad ravings and indiscriminate plunder. One rebel not receiving a satisfactory reply to his question, Where is that d—d yankee that was with the officer? replied, "your [sic] a d—d liar" and drew his revolver, but could not find it in his heart to shoot the peaceful farmer's boy that Joe seemed to be. After taking all they wanted including even women's and children's shoes, the marauders moved on. Joe sought his horse and musket, where they had lain in the bushes unobserved by the horse-hunters, and came back to our forces. The next day he and young Charley Finsterwald [Likely 17 years old at the time. Joined the 125 Ohio Volunteer Infantry in January of 1864 and was discharged in September of 1865.] had joined the Union forces in the chase. They took five prisoners of which Charlie took one alone and Joe three. The other was a joint capture.

These were stragglers from Morgan's gang, and one of them begged most lustily for his life as they came up to them. Another then surrendered to Joe alone, trembled violently, and was very pale. He said, he was glad to get with our men. After these prisoners were reported to the rear, the boys set out again to the front of the column, and as soon as skirmishes began there, they galloped forward.

A Rebel volley was fired from a hill a little ahead, and a ball whistling rather close to Joe's ears, he sent one in reply from his carbine and followed their retreat. The boys were now well supplied with arms from their recent captures, and when on the hill they heard the firing down in the hollow below Joe struck his horse and dashed down the road to take part in the engagement. A squad of rebels had left their horses behind a large barn and come back up the road to a barn, built of logs, and opened out a perfect volley on our advance. These immediately dismounted and returned the fire. Joe fired twice and stepped out from behind his horse for a fairer shot, when a ball passed through his right thigh inflicting a severe, though not dangerous wound.

Fearing they might strike a more vital part next time, he stepped to a large sycamore and fired three other shots with deadly effect when the rebels skedaddled in a hurry; but there were several empty saddles as the horses came into the road. The woman of the house said that when the boy by the sycamore fired, one man fell, and as he passed the house he was quite bloody, and on following the trail the evidence of a fearful revenge was fully apparent. Charley, who saw the whole fight, is confident that three of Joe's shots were fatal.

The bravery of these boys attracted the attention of Col. Shackleford [Brigadier General of the 1st Brigade, 2nd Division of 23rd Army Corps], who inquired their names, and directed the Military Committee to make them suitable presents of the captured arms. Joe's wound is doing fine.

A Nation at War

On November 19, Abraham Lincoln delivers his address at the dedication of the Soldiers' National Cemetery at Gettysburg.

On December 8, President Lincoln issues a general proclamation of amnesty and reconstruction, granting to the majority of Secessionists, upon taking a prescribed oath of allegiance, pardon and restoration of many rights.

1863.17

The Death of Ohio Copperheads

From "Deaths," William McKinley Presidential Library and Museum Archive Collection. Courtesy William McKinley Presidential Library and Museum, Canton, Ohio.

One Ohio newspaper declared "Ohio Is Saved by Her Citizens" after the results of the 1863 gubernatorial election were confirmed. The race pitted the anti-war candidate and exile, Clement Vallandigham, against the pro-Union Republican, John Brough. Running on a campaign emphasizing patriotism, Brough won by more than 100,000 votes—the largest victory margin of any governor of Ohio and the largest pre-Civil War victory margin of any governor of any state.

The following piece, written sometime after the election, is a repudiation of Vallandigham and his Copperhead followers. The author is brutal in his description of, in most cases, Stark County, Ohio, officials and their acts against the Union and its citizens. October 14, 1863, is the day after the election and indicates that the results, at least locally, were known. Brough's victory as well as victories by other pro-Union governors, allowed Lincoln to make a call for additional troops.

Deaths

Author unknown

[Please note: original punctuation has not been altered.]

Oberlin
went dead
Oct. 14th 1863
Deads his chief
Vallandigham [see 1861.1 and 1863.6]
and not one friend
to care a dam
Sam Lahm [A lawyer; elected to Congress in 1846]
died a hard death
Oct. 14th 1863
Lying and cheating
Was his trade
Now he's dead
The trickey [sic] blade
Fighting Sam Taylor [Probably from Canton, Ohio]
Died unexpectedly Oct 14th 1863
Some living men

A moral draw
But company was
my greatest flaw
Walt Brown [Additional information not found]
Died Oct 14 1863
Drunk was he often
By night and by day
Pour on his grave whiskey
To moisten his grave clay
JJ Hofman [Likely postmaster Massillon, Stark County]
Died Oct 14th 1863
Died in honor
Long ago
John Moline [Additional information not found]
For poor house director
He never was fit
An office in Stark
He never gon git
John Morss [Likely postmaster Limaville, Stark County]
Died Oct 14th 1863
No need to probate
Morsses [sic] Will
He gave it all to Underhill [probably a Stark county judge]
A McGregor [Editor of *Stark County Democrat*]
Died Oct 14th 1863
In life he was not beautiful
No more will he steal
from the peoples hard earnings
No more will he fool us
with twisting and burning
C L Vallandigham
Died October 14th 1863
Oh Vallandigham hang him
On a gallows high W'll hang him
He the traitor vile and hateful
Rest him Devil
On a grate full

1863.18

The Battle above the Clouds

From Levi F. Bauder, *Passing Fancies: Poems*, Cleveland, OH: G.S. Newcomb, 1880.

Levi F. Bauder was born in Cleveland on January 28, 1840, graduated from Central High School in 1858, and attended Oberlin College. At the outbreak of the Civil War he enlisted in the Sprague Cadets, which mustered in as Company B, Seventh Ohio Volunteer Infantry. (His name was misspelled as "Bawder" in the official unit roster.) He reenlisted at Camp Dennison on June 20, 1861, for three years and served until the regiment mustered out, July 6, 1864.

After the war Bauder became a railroad clerk and bookkeeper for the Jackson Iron Company. He was admitted to the Ohio bar in 1891. The following poem from Bauder's only collection recreates the Battle for Lookout Mountain, fought in late November 1863. Union troops scaled the Tennessee mountain in what was called the "battle above the clouds." The confrontation freed up the Confederate stronghold and strengthened the Union plans to forge a path to the sea.

The Right Flank at Lookout

Chattanooga sent Northward a cry of distress,
For the men of the Cumberland, famished and gaunt,
Worn with fighting and vigils and tattered in dress,
Manned their guns in the trenches in peril and want;
For the foe closely pressed them in hostile array,
And their guns shrieked and thundered in demon-like glee,
While Old Lookout's rock front, lined with soldiers in gray,
Threw its shadows of death o'er the blue Tennessee.

But on wings of the lightning that cry for help flew,
To Sherman, to Meade, and from captain to man;
And from Vicksburg marched Sherman's long columns in blue;
And grim Hooker's tried corps, from the swift Rapidan,
Came with bread for the famished, with lead for the foe.
Gleamed Wauhatchie's sweet vale with their bayonets bright;
Torn and bleeding, the ferry guards reeled at their blow,
And dismayed up the mountain side fled in affright.

But the Bar [Confederate] flag still flaunted on Lookout's high peak,
  In defiance above the bright Stripes in the vale;
And the iron shells hurtling with insolent shriek,
  Scarred the great antlered oaks in that beautiful dale.
In the night, lines of watch-fires on Lookout's side,
  Gleamed like comets bespangling the eastern sky,
While the shouts from the heights in derision defied
  The threatened assault for the mastery.

Through the fog shroud, no bugle call echoed that morn
  From the hills in the vale, or the mount's rocky side,
But swift couriers silently mounted to ride
  In the darkness, through thicket and stubble of corn,
To the camps; and battalions, in whispering tones,
  Heard, and fell into ranks with accoutrements bright;
And the strapping of knapsacks, and loading of guns,
  Spoke of marching and battle at dawn of the light.

Through the mist moves the long, silent column, now
  Like a giant snake nearing its dreaming prey,
Fast asleep in their huts on the mountain's brow,
  And no glitter or sound does the peril betray.
Hear ye that? On the left flank the signal guns crash,
  Now the picket shots patter, the batteries boom!
On the right, the troops over the mill-dam dash,
  Unseen and unheard in the mountain-side's gloom.

Forward the Right Flank! but fire not a gun,
  Double-quick, double-quick, now on the run!
Gibraltar is ours if we first reach the top;
  A year more of war if they force us to stop!
On, on, for your comrades famish for bread;
  Forward, for Knoxville still trembles with dread!
Up—over brushwood and rock and ravine,
  Routing the pickets from watch-fire and screen,
Hindered by laurel-bush, cane-brake and log,
  Still firing no shot, but through the dense fog,

Breathless, but desperate, upward we climb,
    For victory hinges on moments of time.
Up, to the precipice guarding the top,
    Not till they reach the great wall do they stop;
Then, forming in battle-line, onward they sweep
    Along the great slope of the mountain's scarred steep,
Still onward, like fox-hounds freed from the leash,
    Though the quick bullets thud in the quivering flesh—
Onward they fight—till a glance of the sun
    Bathes with glory the flags on a battle-field won.

And the Cumberland army, in breathless suspense,
    Heard the battle's fierce roar in the fog-cloud dense;
Now clearer—now fainter—now waver—now stop.
    Repulsed? Or held Hooker, in triumph, the top?
Weak yet with fasting, but with eyes flashing fight,
    They watched long in vain that mist-mantled height,
Till a rift in the cloud showed the mountain top's crag,
    And, like Constantine's cross, in the sky gleamed a flag
But which? Ah, the shout that along the line flew,
    As it showed first the Stripes, then the Star-sprinkled Blue!

'Twas a tale of sweet love that torn banner there told,
    Like the Star in the East in Bethlehem Old;
'Twas an emblem of hope to that suffering host,
    Like the Star of the North to the mariner lost;
'Twas a signal of faith, like the beacon's bright light,
    Safely guiding the ship to the harbor at night;
'Twas a sceptre of power, as upheld on the heights,
    It unfurled its silk folds in the sight of six States;
A forerunner of vengeance to enemies all,
    Like the writing of old on the king's palace wall;
And from that day to this, that dear flag of the Free,
    To the walls of Atlanta, and thence to the sea,
To the fields where surrendered the columns of Lee,
    Ever fluttered in triumph. May God in His might
Ever keep the Old Flag in the pathway of right.

1864

"But even were morals better in America than in Europe, and better in Federal than in the Confederate States, we must frankly tell abolitionists, that that would have nothing to do with right or wrong of slavery . . . The influence of slavery upon the morality of a people can only be a question for the government of that people itself."

James Reddie, Edinburgh University

1864.1

Re-upping for the Cause

From Frank Moore, ed., *The Civil War in Song and Story 1860–1865*, New York: P.F. Collier, 1889.

The Second Regiment of the Ohio Volunteer Cavalry was organized during the summer and fall of 1861 at Camp Wade near Cleveland, Ohio. Of the 1,177 who originally joined the unit, 757 members mustered out on September 11, 1865. During the events described below, the Second was part of the Army of the Cumberland commanded by General Rosecrans.

The following account contrasts the heroic sense of duty, accompanied by the spectacle of initial enlistment, against the stark reality of fighting during the latter stages of the war, when supplies and high morale were in short supply. A sense of camaraderie had to have played a part in an individual's decision to continue on battling for the Union and his survival. Only fifty members of the Second did not reenlist.

A soldier of the Second regiment of Ohio cavalry writes: "On New Year's day, 1864, as our regiment was lying in line of battle beyond Mossy Creek, in East Tennessee, the proposition to reenlist as veteran volunteers was submitted to that grim organization. Peter Longstreet's [James Longstreet, nicknamed "Old Pete," was a Confederate General] ragged but plucky skirmish line was a stone's throw in front, with a forward tendency; snow was on the hills; the Second Ohio cavaliers had drawn no rations from Uncle Sam in fifteen days, and not an average of one eighth ration during the preceding four months; their diaphragms were devoid of burden; they had not 'lived in tents' for an eighth-month; the supply of pone and cerulean hog was failing in that land, and zero was biting at the noses of the cavaliers. Amid all these favorable surroundings the cavaliers said, 'Go to, let us have more of this good thing; give unto us yet thirty and six moons of this goodly service.' Thus the thing was done. Under such circumstances our veteran volunteers enlisted.

"While the cavaliers were signing their names to the enlistment roll, at the rate of a hundred per hour, a ludicrous memory of a former enlistment came to us. Two days after Sumter fell, on a bright April morning, big church full of indignant sovereigns and enthusiastic women; organ thundered, band crashed out 'Hail Columbia;' impromptu banners wagged briskly, and the air was redolent of patriotism. Music ceased. Speeches followed. Roll was opened, and volunteers called for. Five hundred pairs of starry eyes waited to illume the path of the first volunteer. Five hundred pairs of little white hands were nervous to begin clapping at the advent of the first masculine sacrifice. He came, and Emperors have had poorer receptions. He was apotheosized. More followed. The pressure increased. I cowered in my pew, imagining that every woman of sense, and every girl of beauty, was saying to herself, 'Why don't *he* go?' I reasoned with myself, but the clapping and waving of white kerchiefs made me dizzy. With a mighty effort, I made a resolution. I mentally bade adieu to all terrestrial matters. I buried from view all relatives nearer than second cousins, drew the veil of forgetfulness over the dear form of Julia, and most of my outstanding debts, made up my mind to be shot for my country, and began to stride up the aisle. What a path to a graveyard! The male audience yelled—the female audience waved kerchiefs with unexampled energy, and they were perfumed with divine odors. I saw nothing but a dancing sea of snow-white foam, interspersed with smiling stars. I heard nothing but an undefined roar—to me an echo from eternity, to which I regarded myself as rapidly going. I scrawled my name on the elongated foolscap, and thus added my two hundred pounds to the growing hecatomb. I was a volunteer! That night I dreamed of battles. Next day, twenty-seven Testaments, thirteen 'housewifes,' [a sewing kit] eleven pin-cushions, and thirty-eight rolls of bandages, were left at my boarding-house, each with a touching note from the fair donors. Such was three months' soldiering 'in the brave days of old.' Then we were green—how sadly veteran we are now!"

1864.2

A Penny at Your Service

From *The Christian Recorder*, "From the 27th U.S.C.T.," January 7, 1864.

Clara Barton is well known as the "Angel of the Battlefield" for her dedication to nursing soldiers during the war. Other famous nurses of the war include Phoebe Yates Pember, Dorothea Lynde Dix, Sally Louisa Tompkins, and the poet, Walt Whitman. Many of the nurses did not take any pay for their services. Estimates of the number of females who became nurses during the war vary, but as many as 6,000–20,000 women carried out nursing duties for Northern troops. Southern society precluded women from becoming nurses, because the wounded and dying presented sights no women should see. One report lists the number of nurses in Confederate war hospitals around 1,000 in 1865. However, this number seems startlingly low.

The following account of Sister Penny details a rise from slavery to service. She became an integral part of the war effort without any fanfare. She was much like the many nurses whose names weren't remembered, but were present when soldiers were hungry and frightened.

CAMP NEAR RICHMOND, VA.,

December 21st, 1864.

Dear Brother Editor:—Permit me the privilege, through your worthy columns, to give your readers a brief historical introduction to our very worthy and eminent sister and mother in the army, namely, Sister Lydia Penny.

Sister Penny was born a slave, in Blunt County, East Tennessee, in the year of our Lord 1814. At the time of the Indian War, when General Scott and General Wool drove the Indians from their habitations in Tennessee, Sister Penny served two years as a cook. She was, at that time, only a girl; but she informed me, that she subsequently became the mother of a family of children, whose companionship she had long been deprived of through slavery, and that she was left a widow, to suffer the torments of cruel oppression.

She was finally sold to a Dutch butcher, in Memphis, Tennessee. By this time, she had learned to trust in God, who had promised to deliver the oppressed and to open the prison doors to them that are bound. She said, that she had a falling-out with her Dutch mistress, about something, and that she gave her master and mistress both to understand distinctly, that she intended to run away from them, which threat she carried into effect about one week after it was made, by which time they thought that she had become contented to remain with them.

Sister Penny says, that she kept herself concealed among her friends in Memphis, until the Union Army had extended its lines near the city, when she made her way within its lines, and again engaged herself as cook. Here, she said, being a lonely widow, and having no one particularly to befriend or protect her, prudence dictated the propriety of making selection of a companion, which she did, as soon as she found one, who she thought would treat her as a wife, and act the part of a faithful husband by her.

While in the army, she formed an acquaintance with Mr. Penny, a native of Pennsylvania, who had enlisted, as a servant, in the three months' service of 1861. They made a match, and were married while in the service. They finally came to the city of Cincinnati, Ohio, where Thomas Penny [mustered out September 20, 1865], her husband, re-enlisted in the service, and joined the Fifth United States Colored Troops, at Camp Delaware, Ohio. Sister Penny said, that she felt it to be her duty to go along with her husband, not merely on account of the love she had for him, but also for the love which she had for her country—that the cause, which nerved the soldiers to pour out their life-blood, was her cause, and that of her race; and that she felt it to be her Christian duty to do all she could for the liberty of her afflicted and down-trodden race.

This good woman is called, by those who are acquainted with her, "the mother of the army." She well deserves the name; for she has been in the service ever since this rebellion broke out, or very nearly as long.

Sister Penny says, that she is not tired of the service, nor does she think of leaving the field until the last gun is fired, and peace is declared, and every slave is freed from captivity. Many of our officers and men, who were wounded at the Battle of Deep Bottom [Virginia; The Union loss was 160 killed, wounded, and missing. The total Confederate loss was unknown, but 129 of their dead were counted in one field.], will never forget the kind deeds of Sister Lydia Penny, who went among them and administered to their wants as they lay, weltering in their blood, on the banks of the James, near Jones' Landing. There she could be seen, the only woman present, like an angel from above, giving words of cheer, and doing all in her power to relieve the sufferings of the wounded and dying.

Yes, while others stood aloof, thinking themselves too good even to go near enough to give them a drink of water to quench their burning thirst, Sister

Penny was seen, like a ministering angel, or one of those holy women, who, in the primitive days, administered to Christ and His apostles. She gave them water to drink, and bread to eat, and assisted the surgeons in dressing their wounds.

When the wounded were placed on the boats, to be taken to hospitals at Fortress Monroe, she left her tent and all behind, and went on board the boats to minister to their comfort. When they were delivered into the hands of careful nurses, Sister Penny returned to her tent, where she ever waits to administer to the wants of the afflicted soldier. . . .

Very respectfully,

James H. Payne [mustered out September 21, 1865],

Quartermaster-Serg't 27th U.S.C.T.

A Nation at War

On January 8, seventeen-year-old David O. Dodd is hanged as a Confederate spy by Union forces in Little Rock, Arkansas.

1864.3

Freed to Fight

From various sources.

Milton M. Holland, Orderly Sergeant of Company C with the 5th United States Colored Troops (U.S.C.T.), was probably the son of Bird Holland, the owner of a plantation in Texas, and slave Emily Holland. Freed by their owner, Milton and his brother were sent to Ohio to receive an education from the Albany Enterprise Academy, a school run by free African Americans.

While in Ohio, the Civil War broke out and in 1863, Milton enlisted in the 127th Ohio Voluntary Infantry, which later became the 5th U.S.C.T. He rose through the ranks and eventually won the Congressional Medal of Honor for his actions at the Battle of Chaffin's Farm.

The following letters have an air of pride, resulting from the opportunity black soldiers were given to defend the Union. Perhaps, as it has been with many who have faced discrimination, an effort above the norm was necessary to dissuade stereotypes. True equality might not have resulted from fighting in the war, but steps taken on the battlefield eventually led to steps forward in society.

From *The Athens Messenger*, "From the 5th U.S. Col'd Troops," February 4, 1864.

NORFOLK, VA., JAN. 19, 1864.

Dear Messenger:—You will be reminded of the company of colored soldiers raised by myself in the county of Athens, and taken to Camp Delaware, 25 miles north of Columbus, on the Olentangy. It has since been mustered into the service in the 5th Reg't U. S. Colored Troops. The regiment is organized, and has been in active service for three months. Our company is C—the color company—in which you may remember of the flag presentation [see 1863.13.] made by the kind citizens of Athens, through Mr. Moore [E.H. Moore, president of the First National Bank of Athens], at which Mr. Langston [John Mercer Langston initially approached Governor Tod with the idea of creating a black regiment in Ohio.] was present and received it, pledging in behalf of the company, that they would ever be true to that flag, though it might be tattered and torn by hard service, it should never be disgraced. I am happy to say that those colors have been used as the regimental colors for several months, and we had the honor of forming the first line of battle under their floating stars. We now have new regimental colors, and the old ones are laid away in my cabin, and I am sitting now beneath them writing.

The regiment though young, has been in one engagement. The men stood nobly and faced the cowardly foe when they were hid in the swamp firing upon them. They stood like men, and when ordered to charge, went in with a yell, and came out victorious, losing four killed and several wounded. The rebel loss is large, as compared with ours. As for company C she played her part admirably in the charge. Our 4th sergeant, Charles G. Stark, is said to have killed the picket guard while in the act of running away.

I must say of the 5th, that after twenty days hard scouting, without overcoats or blankets, they returned home to camp, which the soldiers term their home, making twenty five and thirty miles per day. Several of the white cavalry told them that no soldiers have ever done as hard marching through swamps and marshes as cheerfully as we did, and that if they had to follow us for any length of time it would kill their horses. During that raid, thousands of slaves belonging to rebel masters were liberated. You are aware that the colored man makes no distinction in regard to persons, so I may say all belonging to slaveholders were liberated. We hung one guerilla dead, by the neck, by order of Brig. Gen. Wilder, a noble and brave man, commanding colored troops—"the right man in the right place." He has but one arm, having lost his left one at the battle of Antietam; but with his revolver hand, he was at the head of our regiment cheering us onto victory.

One of the boys belonging to Co. D was captured and hung. He was found by our cavalry pickets yesterday, and is to be buried to-day. We hold one of their "fair daughters," as they term them, for the good behavior of her husband, who is a guerrilla officer, toward our beloved soldiers. The soldier was found with a note pinned to his flesh. Before this war ends we will pin their sentences to them with Uncle Sam's leaden pills.

The boys are generally well, and satisfied that though they are deprived of all the comforts of sweet home, and laboring under great disadvantage as regards pay, and having families to support upon less wages than that of white soldiers, still trust that when they do return they will be crowned with honors, and a happier home prepared for them, when they will be free from the abuses of northern and southern fire-eaters. Though we should fall struggling in our blood for right and justice, for the freedom of or brothers in bondage, or fall in defence [sic] of our national color, the Stars and Stripes, our home and fireside will ever be protected by our old friend Gov. Tod, by the loyalty of Abraham Lincoln, our Moses, and the all-wise God that created us. Friends at home be cheerful, cast aside all mercenary compensation. Spring forth to the call, and show to the world that you are men. You have thus far shown, and still continue to show yourselves worthy of freedom, and you will win the respect of the whole nation. There is a brighter day coming for the colored man, and he must sacrifice home comforts, and his blood if necessary, to speed the coming of that glorious day. I will close my letter in the language of the immortal Henry—"Give me liberty, or give me death!"

Yours truly,

Milton M. Holland

O.S Co. C, 5th U.S. C.T.

From *The Athens Messenger*, "From the 5th U.S. Col'd Troops," August 4, 1864.

NEAR PETERSBURG, VIRGINIA
JULY 24TH, 1864

Dear Messenger . . . I will commence by stating as I did in my previous communication that Co. C, is principally composed of men from Athens and Ross counties, and have been in active service since entering the Department of Virginia and North Carolina. Last winter we made several successful raids through Virginia and North Carolina, liberating the slaves of both loyal and disloyal masters, and likewise confiscating other property, of those who had neglected to take the oath of allegiance to the Government of the United States. Never have we seen a day, however, disagreeable the weather might be, that we would not go to the assistance of our brothers in bond, and sever the chain that bound them. While I mention that we were engaged in this glorious work, I must not neglect to say that we did not pass the guerillas who lurk in swamps and thickets unmolested. As it is not the style of Black Warriors to allow themselves to be trifled with, you may understand that we disposed of them according to the rules for the disposition of such warriors. . . .

Many things attracted our attention along the bank of the James, too numerous to mention. One I might mention particularly, was the ruins of James town, the spot where the curse of Slavery was first introduced into the United States. A serpent that has inserted his poisonous fangs into the body of this Government, causing it to wither in its bloom. Slowly we worked our way up the winding James, until within sight of City Point, celebrated for being the Department where the exchange of prisoners is made. As we neared the shore at that point Co. C was ordered to take the advance as soon as we landed. Up the hill we marched to where the rebel flag was stationed. Down with it cried the boys, and in a moment more the flag of the glorious free could be seen floating in the breeze. The company banners was the first company flag that waved over the rebel city. Forty prisoners were captured at this place by the provost guard of the division. One plattoon [sic] of our company was deployed as skirmishers and followed a short distance the retreating few that escaped. . . .

Providence seemed to have favored us on this occasion for the casualties of Co. C were very few, only two killed and nine wounded, their names are as follows:

Killed—Daniel Blackburn, of Cincinnati, shot through the head; Benjamin Watson, of Athens county, shot through the Abdomen.

Wounded—William R. Bell, of Chillicothe, right arm; Israel Burles, of Parkersburg, Va., in the right side and lodged in the left; William Gaines of Albany, in the right jaw, passing through the left; Thomas Moore, of Pomeroy, in left shoulder; William Newby, of Belmont county, below the left breast, passing through and breaking his arm; John Wilkins of Cincinnati, in the shoulder; Nathaniel Woods, of Athens county, in the head; James Williams, of Cincinnati in the thigh; Samuel Lett, of Belmont county, severely smashed by a cannon ball. . . .

These were brave boys, and the company lament their misfortune, and also sympathise [sic] with the bereaved wives and friends of the deceased. I will mention also that we mourn the loss of two brave comrades who died at General Hospital, Fort Monroe [Virginia], since this campaign. Geo. Ferris of Athens county of Typhoid fever; Geo. Payne of Athens county, of Pneumonia.

M. M. Holland

O.S Co. C, 5th U.S. C.T.

A Nation at War

On February 20, the largest battle of the war fought in Florida at Olustee Station and Ocean Pond results in a Confederate victory.

1864.4

Sons of Ham for Uncle Sam

From Paul Laurence Dunbar, *The Complete Poems of Paul Laurence Dunbar*, New York: Dodd, Mead, 1922.

Paul Laurence Dunbar was called the "elevator boy poet" because after graduating from Dayton, Ohio's Central High School in 1891, he worked as an elevator operator. The son of two slaves, Dunbar's mother taught him to read and he was the only student of color at his school. Dunbar's father, Joshua, fought in Massachusetts's 55th black regiment during the war. Dunbar's work was published in such mainstream journals as *Century, Lippincott's Monthly,* the *Atlantic Monthly,* and the *Saturday Evening Post*. These publications were read primarily by whites in turn-of-the-century America, but Dunbar also had a large black audience. Dunbar died of tuberculosis on February 9, 1906.

Dunbar's work found a renaissance in the second half of the twentieth century. His writing has been viewed by many scholars as authentic in its depiction of black folk life. However, others claim that his work shows signs of being too derivative of the plantation school. The following piece provides us with Dunbar's look at black soldiers who fought during the war.

THE COLORED SOLDIERS

If the muse were mine to tempt it
  And my feeble voice were strong,
If my tongue were trained to measures,
  I would sing a stirring song.
I would sing a song heroic
  Of those noble sons of Ham,
Of the gallant colored soldiers
  Who fought for Uncle Sam!

In the early days you scorned them,
  And with many a flip and flout
Said "These battles are the white man's,
  And the whites will fight them out."
Up the hills you fought and faltered,
  In the vales you strove and bled,
While your ears still heard the thunder
  Of the foes' advancing tread.

Then distress fell on the nation,
 And the flag was drooping low;
Should the dust pollute your banner?
 No! the nation shouted, No!
So when War, in savage triumph,
 Spread abroad his funeral pall—
Then you called the colored soldiers,
 And they answered to your call.

And like hounds unleashed and eager
 For the life blood of the prey,
Sprung they forth and bore them bravely
 In the thickest of the fray.
And where'er the fight was hottest,
 Where the bullets fastest fell,
There they pressed unblanched and fearless
 At the very mouth of hell.

Ah, they rallied to the standard
 To uphold it by their might;
None were stronger in the labors,
 None were braver in the fight.
From the blazing breach of [Fort] Wagner
 To the plains of Olustee [Florida],
They were foremost in the fight
 Of the battles of the free.

And at Pillow [the Fort Pillow Massacre]! God have mercy
 On the deeds committed there,
And the souls of those poor victims
 Sent to Thee without a prayer.
Let the fulness of Thy pity
 O'er the hot wrought spirits sway
Of the gallant colored soldiers
 Who fell fighting on that day!

Yes, the Blacks enjoy their freedom,
    And they won it dearly, too;
For the life blood of their thousands
    Did the southern fields bedew.
In the darkness of their bondage,
    In the depths of slavery's night,
Their muskets flashed the dawning,
    And they fought their way to light.

They were comrades then and brothers,
    Are they more or less to-day?
They were good to stop a bullet
    And to front the fearful fray.
They were citizens and soldiers,
    When rebellion raised its head;
And the traits that made them worthy,—
    Ah! those virtues are not dead.

They have shared your nightly vigils,
    They have shared your daily toil;
And their blood with yours commingling
    Has enriched the Southern soil.
They have slept and marched and suffered
    'Neath the same dark skies as you,
They have met as fierce a foeman,
    And have been as brave and true.

And their deeds shall find a record
    In the registry of Fame;
For their blood has cleansed completely
    Every blot of Slavery's shame.
So all honor and all glory
    To those noble sons of Ham—
The gallant colored soldiers
    Who fought for Uncle Sam!

1864.5

Funding the War on the Homefront

From *The Elyria Democrat*, "The Sanitary Fair," March 2, 1864.

The United States Sanitary Commission (USSC), 1861–1879, was a civilian organization authorized by the federal government to provide sanitary (health) and medical assistance to the Union volunteer forces during the Civil War. Its predecessor organization, the Woman's Central Association of Relief, was founded in April 1861 and later became a branch of the USSC. After the war, the USSC continued its work of helping servicemen and their families file claims for back pay, pensions, and other benefits.

The Soldiers' Aid Society of Northern Ohio operated between April 1861 and November 1868. Financed by private donations, the organization cared for the sick and wounded, provided ambulance and hospital service, solicited clothing and medical supplies, and sent food to soldiers in the field throughout the war. Later in the war, these aid societies throughout the North began to raise money by holding fairs. The one at Cleveland, described below, netted over $100,000.

We visited the Great Sanitary Fair, at Cleveland, last week and are gratified in being able to announce in all respects our expectations were more than realized. We expected to see a large assortment of fancy articles displayed for sale very much after the exhibition at the State and County Fairs, but we were not prepared to witness the magnificence that met our astonished gaze, as we entered the various halls, decorated as they were in a style surpassing our ideal of oriental splendor.

Our first visit was to the Bazaar, where the greater portion of the fancy articles are exposed for sale, arranged in a large number of Booths, representing nearly all the nations of the earth, and decorated in a style of magnificence and taste that fills the beholder with wonder and admiration. It is utterly impossible to give a description of this hall, as it is impossible to describe a beautiful painting, or a beautiful woman. On entering the hall, after our bewildered senses had been sufficiently collected, we seized our pencil, and commenced taking notes, as we passed around, but soon threw it aside in utter despair, as new beauties and wonders appeared before us. Our readers, therefore must not depend on any description they may read, but visit the Fair themselves, and call on us to pay for all regrets for doing so.

One of the first Booths we came to, on the right, was labelled [sic] "Lorain;" and on approaching, we discovered another near the center labelled [sic] in the same manner. This is evidence that Lorain has contributed her full share, for we did not see the Booths duplicated for any other county. They were both beautifully decorated with devices and curtains of elegant and costly fabric, and filled with the handi-work of our fair and patriotic ladies. We were told that the sales had been fully equal to their expectations.

The ladies in attendance from Lorain, who have charge of the Booths, are Mrs. C.H. Doolittle and Miss M.E. Manter, President and Secretary of the Elyria Aid Society, Mrs. J.C. Hale, of Elyria, Mrs. Haynes, of Oberlin, Mrs. Carpenter, of Wellington, Mrs. Warner, of Huntington, and Mrs. Preston, of Grafton, and Mrs. H.H. Williams, of Avon.

On passing the Floral Hall, the scene was varied, but far more grand and impressive. It is a paradise, with little Edens appearing at every step. The imitations of Mountain Scenery around the Statue of Perry, in the center are real beyond conception. We cannot stop to describe this charming retreat, but simply add, it will pay a person to go a hundred miles to view it.

We went through the Museum and Fine Art Gallery, and—but 'tis no use; we cannot tell half we saw, and only add no citizen of Lorain should let this opportunity pass, without visiting this most magnificent Fair ever held in America. It will pay threefold. The fair is a success, and we rejoice thereat.

A View of the Floral Hall at the 1864 Cleveland Sanitary Fair. From Samuel P. Orth, *A History of Cleveland, Ohio,* Volume 1, Chicago-Cleveland: S.J. Clark, 1910.

1864.5

Death Comes Calling

From John M. Jolly to Mr. Allyn, July 1, 1864; Allyn-Mason Civil War Papers; John M. Jolly, 1864; Hiram College Archives. Courtesy Hiram College Archives, Hiram, Ohio.

During the Civil War, 35,000 Union soldiers died of typhoid. Smallpox was endemic and killed hundreds; malaria, dysentery, measles, and scarlet fever were responsible for thousands of deaths. The description by John Jolly of Edwin Allyn's condition certainly fits with symptoms of dysentery gravitating into typhoid fever. Allyn, a member of the 107th Illinois Infantry, was born in Portage County, Ohio, and had moved to Illinois where he was a school teacher.

In 1853, the "School Law" of Ohio was passed. Among other things, the law established a state property tax to finance free, universal public education throughout Ohio. Many Ohio soldiers could read and write to some degree. The following letter is fraught with spelling and grammatical errors. However, Jolly's letter is genuine, and it portrays a soldier trying to fill, to the best of his ability, the wishes of a comrade.

General Hospital No 1 Knoxville, Tenn
July 1, 1864

Mr. Allyn—having saw a leter [letter] a fiew [few] days ago that you wrote to Hoyt [probably Orrin A. Hoyt of the 107th Illinois Infantry] stating you had allso [also] wrote one to me if you did I never received it but suposing [supposing] that you would expect an answer I take this oportunity [opportunity] after seeing this one that have [has been] received.

I wrote to Mr. Mason [John G. Mason was a resident of Hiram, Ohio, and had married Emily Allyn] informing him of the death of Edwin but had received no answer yet and hardly think I shall. I was more or less with him all the time after he came to the Hospital and was in hopes at first that he would get well but after the first week that he was here he seemed to take some kind of feaver [fever] the doctor did not state what kind it was but I think it was brought on acont [account] of his bowels and stomach beeing [being] so from the efects [effects] of the Diarahea [diarrhea] from whitch [which] he has been suffering for near a year pryor [prior] to his death. He was greatley [greatly] in hopes that he would get to go home before he was taking [taken] so bad, and after he was taking [taken] down to his bead [bed] he had me Telegraph to Mr. Mason to come and [bring] him home. I done so thinking that perhaps he could get here and see him before he died. I think if I recolect [recollect] aright it was

Monday that I sent the Dispatch and on the next Sabeth [Sabbath] the surgeon in charge got one stating that he was at Louisville and would wait there untill [until] he came. I never found out wether [whether] the Surgeon ever returned an answer or not. The day that he died I was with him allmost [almost] all the time and should hav [have] been all the time if the Steward would hav [have] let me staid [stay]. When knight [night] came I was with him all the time. I saw in the morning of the last day that he was but short for this wourld [world] I felt rather dellicate [delicate] about speaking to him about what I thought he ought to no [know] so I got a Delligate [delegate] of the Christian comition [commission] to talk to him. At first he seamed [seemed] to think it allmost [almost] an imposibility [impossibility] that his end was so ner [near] and we left him for an hour or so, and then two of the Delligates [delegates] came back to see and talk with him, he then seamed [seemed] to realise [realize] his situation. They talked to him about the future state he talked very rational he sed [said] he felt that he had done his duty to his country and hoped that if he had don [done] anything rong [wrong] in the eyes of the allmighty [almighty] that he would forgiv [forgive] him. He then requested each of them to pray with him whitch [which] they did and his feeble ways would repeat each word after them and after one or two others he seemed to be entirly [entirely] reconsiled [reconciled] to go, and then cauled [called] to his side to giv [give] me directions within regard to what money and things he had here and his business in Ill. the partickulars [particulars] of whitch [which] I wrote to Mr. Mason, and I shall giv [give] them to you. He had $53.30 fifty three dollars and 30 or 35 cts (I hav [have] just forgoten [forgotten] whitch [which] it was) the money two diaries one pocket knife and some pictures & a Gold pen he wanted sent home to his Brotherinlaws. The pen was to go to his youngest sister these things he wanted me to see to and send them home. I told him I would do the best I could but the morning after his death the Surgeon in charge demanded the money. I first refused to giv [give] it up stating that I could prove that it was his request that I should take care of it, he then wanted to hear my proof. I went and got Hoyt and the nurses but when I brought them in he would not hear them but again demanded the money whitch [which] I again refused. And turned and I left him, but after geting [getting] out and talking it over with Hoyt I saw that they had the power to make me giv [give] it up and more than that send me to the military prison fo [for] not giving it up.

After loocking [looking] at it in that view of the case I went and gave it to him not thinking but what he would let me send the rest as he requested this I was denide [denied]. You may want to know why I did not want to giv [give] them up in the first place it was his request that I should not let them hav [have] them but send them myself to his friends. (whitch [which] to hav [have] done would [have] been a pleasure to me) another was that I thought if they wer [were to] get the mone [money] and things in there [their] hands they would never send them but keep the money and destroy the rest. I may judg [judge] too harshly. (I only hop [hope] I do) I should like to hav [have] received a leter [letter from] Mr. M. to no [know] wether [whether] he got them or not I believ [believe] I hav [have] wrote the particulars if I hav [have] left anything out let me now [know] and I will answer imedatly [immediately].

Let me asure [assur] you that I with all that had bcame [became] acquainted with your brother simpathise [sympathize] with you in your loss we the members of Co B feel that we hav [have] lost a Beloved companion in armes [arms] and a tru [true] and simpathising [sympathizing] friend in times of need. Again let me asure [assure] you that alltho [although] he is with us no more yet we hav [have] not forgoten [forgotten] him neither will we. So long as we live to call up the many tryals [trials] thru [through] whitch [which] we hav [have] passed togeather [together]

I ever remain
Your well wishes
John M Jolly

[Major in the 89th Ohio Voluntary Infantry; mustered out on July 7, 1865.]

Direct John M. Jolly Hospital No. 1 Knoxville, Tenn

1864.6

We Still Need More Troops

From *The Defiance Democrat,* "Proclamation by Governor Brough," August 6, 1864.

In July of 1864, President Lincoln made a call for 500,000 additional Union troops to be enlisted for one, two, or three years' service. Prior to July 4, 1864, many citizens avoided military duty by paying a commutation fee of $300. After that date commutation was amended to include only conscientious objectors, but individuals could still avoid service by hiring substitutes.

Part of the need for more troops stemmed from the losses the Union army endured in the late spring and early summer of 1864. In the battles of Spotsylvania, the Wilderness, and Cold Harbor, the Union killed, wounded, or missing totaled almost 49,000 men. The Confederate army had 41,000 casualties. The following document, an announcement to citizens by Governor Brough, asks Ohioans to come to the aid of the Union with 50,000 troops, including blacks who wanted to enlist.

COLUMBUS, JULY 20, 1864

To the People of Ohio:

The President of the United States has issued a call for 500,000 men for the army of the nation. This call is necessary in order to meet the reduction of our forces by the expiration of the term of service of a large number of men between this time and the middle of October. The quota of Ohio will be a little short of 50,000 men, subject to such credits as may be found on closing up the accounts of former calls.

The quota is to be filled by volunteering up to the 5th day of September, when a draft is ordered to take place for any deficit that may then exist. Recruits may be enlisted for one, two or three years, each recruit receiving a bounty of one hundred dollars for each year of the time of his enlistment. The draft will be for the term of one year.

Under this call I have received authority to organize twenty new regiments of infantry. The field officers, and as many of the line officers of these regiments as practicable will be appointed from men who have heretofore served in the field and honorably retired from such service. The Adjutant-General is preparing, and will issue in a few days, the necessary orders for the organization of the regiments. I have also authority to organize a regiment of representative recruits. I desire the earnest cooperation of our people, who are not liable to draft, in this enterprise. This should be a representative regiment of the State, and if its ranks are promptly filled up it shall be officered with care, in the selection of men to give it character and efficiency. Colored recruits receive the same bounty and pay as white soldiers. The 5th and 27th Regiments of colored troops raised in this State, received several hundred recruits, and if more colored troops enlist than will fill their ranks, an additional Regiment will be organized. It is not necessary to urge the people of Ohio to respond to this call for maintain the forces in the field. The work of closing this war is before us. We have it to do, and of course we cannot avoid recognizing the fact that we must furnish the means to accomplish that purpose. Ohio has fully and nobly responded to all the requisitions that have been made upon her.—Let this call be promptly responded to, that our whole duty may be honorably discharged.

Very respectfully,

John Brough, Governor

A Nation at War

On March 9, Ulysses S. Grant is appointed Lieutenant General and given command of all active United States forces.

On April 20, the Confederate ironclad, *Albermarle* helps the Confederate Navy capture Plymouth, North Carolina.

On May 5–6, General Grant engages Southern troops at the Battle of the Wilderness as part of the Overland Campaign, the bloodiest campaign in American history.

On June 15, Northern forces begin the siege of Petersburg, Virginia, an encounter that would last for ten months.

1864.7

We Can See No Hope

From *The Reports of Committees of the House of Representatives Made during the Third Session of the Fortieth Congress.* Washington, DC: Government Printing Office, 1869.

While there is debate about how responsible the officials at Andersonville Prison (Camp Sumter, Georgia) were for the horrible conditions interred soldiers faced, the prison has taken its place, along with WWII Nazi concentration camps, as examples of man's inhumanity to man. Built in early 1864, and in operation for 14 months, 45,000 Union soldiers passed through its gates. Of those, 13,000 died from disease, poor sanitation, malnutrition, overcrowding, or exposure. Andersonville was constructed to hold 10,000 prisoners, but at one point 32,000 men were held within its stockades.

During the early part of the war, a system of prisoner exchange, the Dix-Hill Cartel, was set up by the combatants. Dix-Hill called for each side to exchange or parole all prisoners of war "in ten days from the time of their capture, if it be practicable to transfer them to their own lines in that time; if not, as soon thereafter as practicable." The rank of a prisoner was taken into account: a lieutenant could be exchanged for four privates and a commanding general was worth sixty privates. Eventually, Northern military leaders decided that the exchanges were detrimental to their cause. The following letter to Governor Brough is a plea from Ohio soldiers at Andersonville to foster their swift release.

Camp Sumter, Georgia, July 30, 1864

To his Excellency Governor John Brough, *of Ohio*:

Dear Sir: We, the undersigned, and other soldiers from Ohio, who were compelled by the misfortunes of war to surrender ourselves to the confederate forces while doing our duty as soldiers, do most respectfully and earnestly entreat and petition that some action be taken soon to alleviate our present suffering condition. We have suffered long, many of us, been patient, hoping for the best results, and yet we can see no hope for us. Therefore we humbly petition you, as our leader and protector, to use your every effort and influence with the national authorities to bring about a speedy exchange. We are almost destitute of clothing, and suffering for shelter from the storm. Disease is raging frightfully, and of almost every character. Very many are dying from long confinement, and disease contracted during that period. Scurvy is the principal disease among those who have been in confinement for ten and twelve months.

Very few of the old prisoners have escaped it. During the next two months, we doubt not but three-fourths of the prisoners will have taken the scurvy. If it is within the power of the federal government, we trust that an exchange or parole may be effected, and our condition bettered. We have stood by the nation in its peril, and now will not our State and government sympathize with its suffering and dying defenders! Will it not lend us a helping hand in our hour of misery and extreme destitution! Governor, may we not expect and effort from you! Just one effort, and you will have the gratitude and sincere thanks of Ohio's soldiers and citizens.

We are, governor, very respectfully, your obedient servants,

H. C. Doddridge, 81st infantry.
Albert Willey, 26th infantry.
W. Lighthizier, 51st infantry.
F. Stone, 26th infantry.
John Krumlaugh, 19th infantry.
Liberty Jinks, 2d infantry.
M. Goss, 90th infantry.
Winfield Neely, 51st infantry.
A. C. Brown, 2d infantry.
N. J. Ramsey, 33d infantry.
A. B. Whitehead, 33d infantry.
John Willey, 33d infantry.
J. Fife, 33d infantry.
George C. Drake, 50th infantry.
Christopher King, 50th infantry.
William Evans, 51st infantry.
J. D. Stonehockerdith, 51st infantry.
M. J. Rogers, 51st infantry.
James Rush, 40th infantry.
N. W. Reed, 94th infantry.
B. Helwig, 51st infantry.
J. H. Hall, 89th infantry.
Gilbert Stork, 32d—
William McMullen,1st—
J. L. Finley, 7th infantry.
P. F. Darnel, 7th infantry.
S. Moss, 7th infantry.
F. H. Marsh, 105th infantry.
Elias Malone, 40th infantry.
P. Freely, 10th infantry.
J. Blackford, 11th infantry.
Wm. H. Hubbell, 23d—
John Hunter, 10th—
A. Sibley, 7th infantry.
W. H. Rinehart, 7th infantry.
J. Randoff, 7th infantry.
J. Smith, 7th infantry.
A. Wickhoff,7th infantry.
Geo. Lewis, 39th infantry.
Wm. Rea, 45th infantry.
A. Vores, 45th infantry.
M. Hockman, 89th infantry.
J. Rickett, 12th infantry.
J. Rose, 2d infantry.
J. O. Young, 7th infantry.
Thomas Jackson, 7th infantry.
J. Imoden, 44th infantry.
E. B. Rutan, 44th infantry.

James Foster, 40th—
J. W. Higgins, 7th infantry.
William Johnson, 7th infantry.
John Foose,7th infantry.
Lysander Ames, 21st infantry.
A. A. Kelly, 40th infantry.
J. A. P. Ferrell, 51st infantry.
L. Baker, 51st infantry.
F. G. Palmer, 2d infantry.
And many others.

A. W. Maynard, 101st infantry.
J. Crawford, 101st infantry.
J. L. Smith, 19th infantry.
W. C. Rose, 113th infantry.
James McCollum, 40th inf'y.
B. Taylor, 18th infantry.
W. J. Kelly, 40th infantry.
J. Robinson, 1st battery.
C. C. McLean, 2d infantry.

A Nation at War

On July 12, Confederate General Jubal Early's troops attack Washington, DC, but are unsuccessful.

On August 18–24, the Battle of the Weldon Railroad (Virginia) results in the Union's permanent capture of Lee's most important supply line.

1864.8

A Chaplain Returns Home

From David Todd to Rev. D. Worcester, September 12, 1864; Oberlin Students, Letters II; David Todd Letters; Oberlin College Archives. Courtesy Oberlin College Archives, Oberlin, Ohio.

The following letter was written by David Todd. Todd, a graduate of Oberlin College, moved to Iowa in 1852 to set up a Christian college, Tabor College, like the one at Oberlin, Ohio. He also established one of the more significant hubs of the Underground Railroad in Iowa. John Brown, the famed abolitionist, paid several visits to Todd and stored guns and ammunition there that would be used in Brown's raid at Harper's Ferry. Todd was not aware of Brown's plans.

Todd enlisted in the Union army as a 100-day recruit when he was 43 years old. He mustered out of the service on September 23, 1864, at Davenport, Iowa. Reverend Todd died in 1894. In this letter, Todd makes a rather universal realization; the terror and stress of fighting tend to bring out the very best or very worst in combatants.

On board Steamer Golden Era
September 12, 1864

Rev. D. Worcester [likely a colleague from Tabor, Iowa]

Dear Br

Yours of the 31st ult. [from the Latin *ultimo*—last or last month] was received on the 7th inst. [instant or this month] It always affords me satisfaction to hear from you & learn of your welfare.

We are now on our way homeward. We left Colliersville [Tennessee] on the 1st. inst. & camped for 9 or 10 days 2 miles S. of Memphis, where we were until Saturday P.M. At 11½ A.M. on the 10 we received order to be ready to move by 3 P.M. & so we were. We were all aboard the boat, bag & baggage, by 6½ P.M. We are on a very slow boat & much crowded—can't tell when we shall reach Cairo [Illinois], but probably not before tomorrow. I fear I shall not be able to attend our Ass. Which has been changed from Sioux City to Lewis [both in Iowa] & will commence on the 22nd inst. I think there is yet some chance for my being there, at least part of the time. We don't yet know whether we shall take the cars at Cairo or proceed on by the river. My health has been good all the time. The Regiment has lost 14 or 15 men, & some are now quite unwell. Three were taken prisoners besides the 14 or 15 who have died. We have on the whole much occasion for gratitude; & altho' I as Chaplain had a good many obstacles to encounter, yet I can but think some good has been accomplished. A few seem seriously endeavoring to live for God, who made no pretension to religion when they enlisted. Others have seemed to withstand evil habits & practices, tho' not pretending to be religious, & others I presume are decidedly more confirmed in vice than when they entered the service. A number of the Regiment will, I presume, reenlist, but not enough to retain the Regimental organization.

I have not learned anything about the draft in Iowa, but presume it has not taken place, & that there will be an effort to induce men to enlist so as to avoid it.

Br. O. Cumings [Origen Cumings, an Ohio acquaintance of Todd]—that good brother—was drowned in the Nishnabotna river on the 20th of August. He, & John [John Morgan Cumings; graduated Oberlin College in 1872] his son, & his hired man were haying on the bottom, & after eating their dinner it was proposed that they wash off, & accordingly they did so, when Br. C. who could not swim got into a hole beyond his depth & could not get out, neither could the others rescue him. It seems very strange, but so it was. The good Lord would have it so, & we are called upon to bow submissively to his righteous will. His death is an irreparable loss to his family—the church & community. No one was better prepared to go than he was, & our loss is doubtless his gain. The spiritual welfare of Burton [son of Origen] lay heavily on his heart for a long time, & yet I cannot chronicle anything very hopeful of him yet. James [Todd's son, member of the 150th Ohio Volunteer Infantry], who we supposed was dead, has so far recovered as to reach his uncle's at Cleveland, Ohio. His recovery to us is as [letter torn, unreadable, probably similar to "rising of"] the dead.

I will see that the necessary certificate of your standing is made out & forwarded to you, & I hope that you may succeed in obtaining some more lucrative post than a private, for I think you deserve it, & ought to have it. Your family needs your presence or your aid to a greater extent than you can afford with the wages of a private. May God open the way before you & conduct you to your appropriate place. Our National prospects seem some brighter. Atlanta is in our possession. Morgan killed—Mobile invested & three forts taken & C. & C. Still the wickedness of our people is the greatest drawback to our complete success. If the Lord delight in us he will bring us into possession of the land. Direct to Tabor.

I remain Yours truly D. Worcester

John Todd

1864.9

Maintaining the Lines

From the diary of Matthew Childs, July 1864–65. Archives of The Summit County Historical Society. Courtesy The Summit County Historical Society of Akron, Ohio.

The formation of the United States Military Telegraph Corps occurred early in the war. The Corps laid down 15,389 miles of line and sent 6,500,000 dispatches. In a report following the rebellion, Secretary of War Edwin Stanton estimated that the cost of constructing, repairing, and operating the military telegraph system amounted to over $3 million. The Northern system operated much better during the war; by the end of the fighting, the Confederate telegraph infrastructure had to be rebuilt, due in part to the lack of funds and materials to repair the system as the war progressed.

The following document consists of excerpts from a diary by Matthew John Childs, a telegraph repairman from Columbiana County, Ohio. Childs kept notes from July 1864 until early 1865. An excerpt is transcribed below, which includes passages from September 3 through September 27, 1864. The diary begins with fairly routine descriptions until reports of the proximity of Confederate forces escalate. Child begins to use code, which is not unusual as ciphers were used by both sides when sending messages. Also included is a passage that illustrates the events taking place around Clarksburg, West Virginia, during the time Childs kept his diary.

Key

Assuming that the telegraph lines ran along the Baltimore and Ohio Railroad tracks in West Virginia in 1864 and since Childs did his work on horseback, the abbreviations in the diary likely indicate the following places:

B Buckhannon, WV
DC Washington, DC
F Fairmont, WV
J Jane Lew, WV
L Lumberport, WV
P Parkersburg, WV

Sept. 3rd

Both lines grounded heavily whent [sic] out towards B water very high had great difficulty in crossing Elk the water run so fast it almost took my horse off his legs, and although [sic] I knelt in the saddle I got my feet and knees whet [sic]—on my way up found the rain had been much heavier than at Clarksburg, I had to go round 3 places it was to deep for me to go through; meadows and corn fields underwater also hay stacks and some buildings, it is the heaviest flood ever seen in this part of the country—found a tree down just beyond the meeting place (on Clarks end) and the line in the brush which I put up, in returning I came back along the road except in one place the water falling very rapidly on my return found the line to F still grounded—got a paper from Jane [likely Childs' wife].

Sept. 4th

Sunday—Whent [sic] out towards J—1 ½ miles out found Insulator Cap off and line on ground—2 miles out found 1 pole down and 1 insulator off—3 ¾ miles out found 1 insulator nearly off, and 1 tie wire off—8 miles out found 1 pole down, the rest of my section was ok.

September 5

Line towards B grounded—Clark [identification unknown, there were several Clarks in the telegraph service] ordered through to DC as he is to change his horse. The Rail Road wires reported broken and down 1 mile east of here, I and Rowe [probably R.D.E. Rowe, see page 187] whent [sic] out found them broken in two and down off one pole mended it and put it up—no news

Sept. 6th

Lines OK—no news—Clark exchanged his horse and returned to day—sent paper to Jane Mr & Mrs Rowe left for Parkersburg

Sept. 7th

Lines OK—John Morgan killed and his staff killed [at Greenville, Tennessee]—drew my rations and packed box to send Jane—took it over to the Express office—wrote to Jane

Sept. 8th

Lines OK—No news of any importance—posted letter to Jane—Rowe returned from P

Sept. 9th

Lines OK—Rebs been on B&O RR again and driven off—indications of a fight on or in vicinity of the R.R.

Sept. 10th

Lines OK—news unimportant—Thomas [possibly Charles J. Thomas] at Wheeling on his return

Sept. 11th

Sunday—lines OK—no news—Thos returned and Dan [identification unknown] started to pay off at F&B, Jolls [probably J. Jolls] and Reger [probably Philip Reger] to meet him at B—heard from Harold by Thomas, he is well

Sept. 12th

Our lines OK. RR wires crossed and one broken west of the office ½ a mile, whent [sic] to repair it and change a pole for Col Parmelee [further information not available] at his coal bank—got paper from mother with notice of G & F's marriage on the 31st ultimo—also got a letter from Jane all well—wrote to Ada and sent paper from Detroit on to Harold at Hagerstown [Maryland].

Sept 13th

Line towards L grounded and very slight circuit—on going out bound tie wire broken and line on ground 1 ½ miles out—3 miles out found a pole down and line on ground. 6 miles out line broken in two and DC end fast to insulator on tree—repaired these places and returned, Rowe and Graham [likely M.B. Graham] left for Cincinnati

Sept 14th

Lines OK—no news—GK Smith came to day

Sept 15th

Lines OK till between 9 and 10 am when the line to B was grounded. I started out at 11 am found tie wire broken and line down 8 miles out repaired it and returned, line not working when I got back and Rebs said to be in vicinity of B, line came OK between 9 & 10 pm when Tull [T.D. Tull] reported line cut at Maxwell mill also between B & X [possibly Weston, West Virginia] Rebs supposed to be in some force in Upshur Co—wrote to Mother—to Jane—and to Harold enclosing Mother's letter

Sept 16th

Lines OK—news unimportant—posted the above mentioned letters

Sept 17th

Lines OK—Report from Potomac army that Rebs are preparing to evacuate Petersburg [Virginia]—to day I received my first message by sound from F total number of words 17—Capt Lynch [Stafford G. Lynch] reports our pay for July and August on the way here

Sept 18th

Sunday—Line towards B grounded heavily Thomas and I started out found it down just by camp at town put it up when line was OK—no news this evening had a heavy storm of thunder lightening and rain altho [sic] the weather was quite cool

Sept 20th

Line towards B grounded whent [sic] over my section could not find anything but a limb of an apple tree against wire—met Clark had dinner and returned—Clark reports a force gone out from B to attack some rebs about 15 miles from there—Rebs said to be 300 strong our force 80—

[At this point, Childs begins to use cipher entries. What follows is the transliteration of the coded passages. Amy Freels, an editor at The University of Akron Press, used rudimentary character substitutions to undo Childs' cipher.]

Sept 20th

Line towards B grounded on going out found my section ok—four hundred rebels reported within twenty nine miles of Buckhanon a man named WG Pierson a union scout was shot dead at his own door in Jane Lew big fight in the valley [Philip Henry] Sheridan lost two thousand and [Jubal] Early twenty five hundred [Part of Sheridan's Valley Campaign during which Sheridan destroyed the "Granary of the Confederacy."]

Sept 21

Lines ok confirmation of battle in the valley five thousand prisoners taken and Early driven thirty miles got a letter from DA

Sept 22nd

Lines ok got letter from Jane all well Mosby the guerilla hung by General Sheridan [This report of Mosby's demise is erroneous] wrote home to Jane

Sept 23rd

Lines ok our picket post of twenty men stationed at Burnt House [West Virginia] was captured this morning posted letters to Jane and Ada

Sept 24

Line towards F grounded on going out found pole down ten miles out also one eleven and a half miles out got dinner and returned

Sept 25th

Sunday lines ok report that Sheridan has captured Early and Breckenridge [General John C. Breckenridge] with nine thousand men gold fallen to qms female spy captured at Buckhannon who says a rebel force is approaching by way of Sutton

Sept 26th

Lines ok at dusk by questions asked we became convinced a strange operator was at F and as a rebel force had been in that vicinity we became sure Weston was captured so arrangements were made for Thomas and me with 12 mounted mem [men; sic] to go as near there as we could and report back over the line just before starting the line to B got open so we strrte [started; sic] for there we left at 11am we went 16 miles and camped till day break I lay on a rail for my bed woke up by Thomas trying to get into a house the folks thought he was a rebel and would not let him in blew their horn for their neighbours to come to assist them before starting I traded my revolver to Thomas for 2 coats and a vest I got another of his to go on this trip

Sept 27

Started at daylight got no news till we got within 2 miles of B where we heard our pickets had been fired on that morning we rode on rapidly got in found the town quiet and the line working put up our horses and whent [sic] to get breakfast was introduced to Captain Hagans [First West Virginia Cavalry] commanding we had been there but a few moments when his pickets were driven in they rode up and reported a heavy force of rebels advancing on the French Creek road then the skedadling began Hagans got his men together and advanced towards them Thomas and I got our horses and whent [sic] back to get our breakfast this we ate on the porch with our horses close by when we got through I left my tools at the hotel after a good deal of fireing the rebs drove Hagans out of town but did not hurt a man they had about 900 men to our 65 so of course they could flank our party as we left town we tore the planks off the bridge to prevent pursuit 2 miles out we got a good view of the town and we could see their guns glisten quite plainly as they marched through town we retreated on towards Beverly...

From William R. Plum, *The Military Telegraph during the Civil War in the United States,* Chicago, IL: Jansen, McClurg & Company, 1882.

On the 26th of September, 1864, the military telegraph office at Weston, on the Bulltown line, was taken possession of by Confederates under Colonel Witcher. R. D. E. Rowe, the operator there escaped by jumping out of a second story window and running to the woods while the enemy were firing on him. Witcher had with him a telegraph operator who, pretending to be the regular Union telegraphist at that post, transmitted in the name of the captured commandant there, a message to the commander at Clarksburg, stating that three thousand rebels under General Basil Duke were advancing on Weston by the Parkersburg pike and asking how many troops were at Clarksburg, and how many could be sent to Weston. Charles J. Thomas, M. B. Graham, Daniel Colestock and George K. Smith were operating at Clarksburg at the time, and the one of them who chanced to answer the call became satisfied from the peculiarity of the telegraphic manipulations at Weston, that the telegram was written by the enemy and transmitted by a stranger, consequently he informed Colonel Wilkinson, commanding at Clarksburg, of his conviction, but wisely OKed the message when sent, without indicating to the rebel operator his suspicions. Wilkinson promptly replied, stating that two thousand troops had just arrived by rail and that more were expected during the night. It subsequently became known that Colonel Witcher's command nine hundred strong, after plundering Weston, retreated southeasterly, striking the Beverly line at Buckhannon, although his original intention was to capture Clarksburg and destroy the large amount of Government property at that depot, which he could have very easily accomplished, as there were but two companies of troops at Clarksburg at that time. This is a clear case of being beaten at their own game, but it is only one of the many bloodless victories won by the telegraph and heralded by nobody. If the place had been saved after great sacrifices in battle, someone would have been promoted.

A Nation at War

On September 2, Atlanta, Georgia, falls to General William Sherman's troops.

On October 19, Confederate Lieutenant Bennett H. Young and his soldiers raid St. Albans, Vermont, and rob three banks.

On November 8, Abraham Lincoln is reelected as President.

1864.10

And What Remains

From John M. Jolly to John Mason, December 26, 1864; Allyn-Mason Civil War Papers; John M. Jolly, 1864; Hiram College Archives. Courtesy Hiram College Archives, Hiram, Ohio.

This letter is a follow-up to Jolly's previous letter (1864.5). Jolly is responding to a letter he received from John Mason of Hiram, Ohio. Jolly helped to return personal belongings of Edwin Allyn, a relative of Mason.

Article 27 of *The Regulations for the Army of the United States* contained provisions to deal with a deceased soldier's effects. In part, an inventory of the deceased's belongings along with a final statement of pay was to be forwarded to the Adjutant-General and colonel of the regiment by the commander of the company to which the deceased belonged. Undoubtedly, the letter of the law could not be followed in many cases as the course of the war escalated. Families could make claims for belongings, but there was no assurance that they would ever be returned.

Knoxville, Tenn
Dec. 26th 1864

Friend Mason

Your note of Nov 28th was received this morning and I hasten to answer. Our communication has been blocaded [sic] by Hood [Confederate General John Bell Hood invaded Tennessee in November 1864] or I should hav [sic] received your letter sooner. I was hapy [sic] to learn that you had received the money and so mutch [sic] of the effects as you have the smaller items I suppose you never will get. I hav [sic] searched for them but cant [sic] find them. I supose [sic] they have been distroyed [sic]. All I can do within regard to the Discriptave [sic] Role wil [sic] bee [sic] to giv [sic] you the officers adress [sic] comanding [sic] the Company Direct to the commanding Officer of Co. B.

107th Ills V.I.

2d Brig 2d Div 23d A.C.

I dont [sic] know the exact day of his enlistment but think about the 5th of August 1862. We wer [sic] musterd [sic] the 4th of Sept 1862 the Regt is near Nashville as present.

Within regard to geting [sic] the remains sent home, my advise [sic] would bee [sic] never move them unless yourself or some one sent by you come to atend

[sic] to it. There would bee [sic] no trouble in getting it started from here but I fear that unless some one was with it that it would never get thru [sic], and eaven [sic] then it will bee [sic] a very trobelsom [sic] undertaking. the reason why is very plain to bee [sic] seen by taking into consideration that there is but one line of railroad to suply [sic] the wants of the armies of the West. Rest asured [sic] I will do all I can to asist [sic] you but those are my views as to my receiving pay for what I hav [sic] done or what I may yet do it is abserd [sic] to think of. I hav [sic] but tried to discharge my duty to a departed fellow soldier and if I hav [sic] done that I feel that it is all the pay that I want.

If I remain here untell [sic] sutch [sic] time as you want to move the body I will atend [sic] to it for you, or if you come or send whitch [sic] I think the better way, I will do all I can to asist [sic] you

for the present I remain

yours with Respct [sic]

John M. Jolly

A Nation at War

On December 15–16, the Battle of Nashville, one of the final large-scale engagements of the rebellion, is fought, effectively ending the Army of Tennessee's role in the war.

1864.11

An Education in War

From L.T. Guilford, *The Story of a Cleveland School: From 1848 to 1881,* Cambridge, MA: John Wilson and Son, 1890.

Camp Cleveland in Tremont was Cleveland's largest and best-developed Civil War camp. Approximately 15,230 troops were trained there. The camp also housed federal units in transit from one assignment to another. In the summer of 1862, a 320-bed Civil War Army hospital was built directly across the street from Camp Cleveland. A total of 3,028 soldiers received care for gunshot wounds, illnesses, and diseases before it closed in July 1865.

The following passage recollects an 1864 visit by members of the Cleveland Academy to soldiers in the Camp Cleveland hospital. The Academy, a school for young women, opened in 1848 on the corner of Ontario and Prospect Streets. The gruesome nature of a hospital ward must have provided an education in reality for the young women.

. . . For two months in the beginning of 1864 little was talked of but the great Sanitary Fair [see 1864.4] in its building in the Park, and teachers and pupils passed hours of enchantment in the bewildering beauties of its bazaar,—hours to be dwelt on long after; while stories of all that the brave soldiers were suffering at the front sank indelibly into memory.

Camp Cleveland hospital, circa 1864. Courtesy the Western Reserve Historical Society.

Several expeditions were made by the school in the summer of that year to visit Camp Cleveland, on the heights, where a number of sick and wounded from Western battle-fields were convalescing. Permission having been gained from the proper officers, an omnibus or two would be chartered, oranges, strawberries, and other delicacies loaded in, and a group of children, with their teacher, would ride over and distribute their gifts under the direction of the surgeons. In no other way could the terrible losses, maimings, and diseases of a military hospital be made to the visitors so real. If they learned little else, the remembrance of particular cases of severely wounded, of individual martyrdom, would be imperishable vouchers of the nation's great deeds when the children in after life should more fully understand the cause for which these things were endured. Many of the school could but share in the general spirit of rash expenditure and luxurious display which pervaded the community, and these hospital visits were a sober corrective. To the soldiers, that short Saturday afternoon diversion and insubstantial treat was too slight for mention.

Lambert's elastic field tourniquet, which was used during the war. From Sir T. Longmore, *Gunshot Injuries*, London: Longmas, Green & Co., 1895.

1864.12

Death and Politics

From L.C. Walton, *Reminiscences of 1864*, Tallmadge, OH: Tallmadge Historical Society, 1865. Courtesy Lawrence Collection, Akron-Summit County Public Library.

On November 6, 1864, Abraham Lincoln and Andrew Johnson defeated George B. McClellan and George H. Pendleton. Lincoln received 212 electoral votes to McClellan's 21. The reelection reflected the realities on the battlefield. Finally, the North was seeing signs that the fighting might end soon. A Confederate attack on Washington, DC, was repulsed in July. William T. Sherman occupied Atlanta in September 1864. General U.S. Grant laid siege to Petersburg, Virginia.

The following document should be compared to 1861.18. After three years of war, the number of soldiers dying had obviously climbed. Typhoid fever deaths highlighted the lack of sanitation within communities. The war would also leave a further mark when soldiers returned home, many infected with venereal disease. In politics, Tallmadge reflected the nation by supporting Lincoln.

Reminiscences of 1864

There have been 23 who have died or been buried in Tallmadge the past year.

George Huber, aged 29, a member of Konkle's Battery of O.V.I. died at Cleveland, Feb. 9th of Typhoid Pneumonia. He was buried with military honors in Tallmadge by several members of the Battery, who were at home on furlough, and by the Tallmadge Co. of O.N.G.

Lorenzo M. Clark, aged 28, died in Springfield Feb. 20th and was buried in Tallmadge.

March 4th David Morris (Welch) died at Brewster's Coal Bank in Coventry, was buried in Tallmadge, his age 20 and his disease Spotted Fever.

March 12th Arthur, son of Mr. and Mrs. John Howe, died of croup and diphtheria—his age 5.

March 26th Mary, daughter of Mr. Richard Cleaton, age 18.

April 11th Mrs. Laura, widow of Mr. Justus Bradley, died at Middlebury and was buried in Tallmadge—her age 78.

April 12th Mrs. Jane C., wife of Mr. Calvin Treat, died of consumption, age 61.

May 25th Henry L. Hart, a member of Co. D., O.N.G. died at Fort Corcoran—was buried in Tallmadge—age 17.

June 6, Christopher Callahan, a member of Co. D., O.N.G.—was buried in Akron.

June 17th infant of Mr. and Mrs. Charles Richardson—age 3 months .

Aug 4th Joseph Guingrich, a member of Co. D, O.N.G. died at Fort Strong, Va. in hospital.

June 27th Samuel C. Means died of Erysipelas age 53.
July 1st Sarah Ann Ire (Welch) died—age 12.
Aug 13th Mrs. Hile was found dead in her bed in the morning.
Oct. 1 Lucinda (Schaff) wife of Charles Hamlin died of Typhoid fever in Portage—was buried in Tallmadge—age 21.
Oct. 21st Emma E. Sparks died of Typhoid fever at Mr. Sylvester Barnes'—age 16.
Oct. 22d Gen. Charles Woodruff died very suddenly of heart disease—age 75.
Oct. 23d in the hospital at Alexandria D.C. Geroge [sic] C. Monks died of congestion of the lungs—age 16. He was a soldier of the 60th Reg't O.V.I. and was buried in Tallmadge with military honors by the Tallmadge Co. of O.N.G. of which the deceased was a member before enlisted.
Nov. 4th Mrs. Miriam M. wife of Mr. Zerah Hinman died—age 66.
Nov. 21 Mr. Adna Sperry died of Spotted fever—age 58.
Nov. 25th Mrs. Betsy C., wife of Mr. Elisha Taylor died—congestion of the lungs—age 68.
Dec. 6th Mrs. Sarah (Hagenbaugh) wife of Samuel Taylor died—age 21.
Dec. 17th Mr. Reuben B. Beach died of typhoid fever—age 66.

The following persons who were former residents of Tallmadge have died.
In Dec 1863 Albert E. Root, a soldier from Wisconsin, died in the army—age 41.
June 25th—Lieut. Henry M. Baldwin of the 6th O.C. was killed in a skirmish with the rebels near Charles City, Va.—age 29. He had received a captains commission but had not taken command.
In July Mr. Wm. Chapman died in Illinois, and Mr. Sydney H Wright in Memphis, Tenn.

Dr. Willis Sperry, a native of Tallmadge, after several years residence in California returned in 1863 and is now practicing his profession with Dr. Wright.

It is well to mention our election. Tallmadge has been noted for many years to be in politics all on one side, like a jug handle. There were 228 votes cast at the Presidential election, of which 216 were for Lincoln and 12 for McClelland.

1865

"The people have reasoned by the logic of the sword, and the ballot, and they have declared the States are inseparable parts of a national government. . . . State right remain; but Sovereignty is a right higher than all others; and that has been made into a common stock for the benefit of all."

Henry Ward Beecher

1865.1

Slavery No More

From "Amendment of the Constitution Regarding Slavery," J. Res., Ohio Leg., Jan. 20, 1865.

Ohio, like other states, instituted "black laws" in the early 1800s to regulate the admission of blacks and mulattos into the state. It wasn't until 1887 that vestiges of the laws, including the prohibition of interracial marriages, were repealed. Also, in 1865, Ohio's "Visible Admixture Law," which required election judges to disqualify any voter who seemed to have African blood, was overturned.

Congress was also codifying the concept of equality. Declaring that "Neither slavery nor involuntary servitude, except as a punishment for crime . . . shall exist within the United States," the 13th Amendment was passed by the Congress on January 31, 1865, and eventually ratified by the states on December 6, 1865. By then the rebellion was over.

AMENDMENT TO THE CONSTITUTION

—

RESOLUTIONS OF
THE LEGISLATURE OF OHIO.
RELATIVE TO

AMENDMENT OF THE CONSTITUTION
REGARDING SLAVERY.

—

JANUARY 20, 1865.
LAID ON THE TABLE AND ORDERED TO BE PRINTED

—

THE STATE OF OHIO.
EXECUTIVE DEPARTMENT

COLUMBUS, JANUARY 12, 1865 . . .

—

JOINT RESOLUTION
INSTRUCTING THE MEMBERS OF CONGRESS FROM THIS STATE IN RELATION TO AMENDING THE CONSTITUTION THE UNITED STATES, RELATIVE TO SLAVERY.

Whereas, the declaration "that all men are created equal, and are endowed by their Creator with certain inalienable rights, among which are life, liberty, and the pursuit of happiness, and to secure these rights all just governments are instituted among men, deriving their just power from the consent of the governed," is as true and self evident now as when first enunciated by the fathers and founders of the republic; and,

Whereas the Constitution of the United States was ordained and established "to form a more perfect union, establish justice, insure domestic tranquility, provide for the common defence, promote, the general welfare, and secure the blessings of liberty to the people of the United States;" and,

Whereas, slavery, or involuntary servitude, except as a punishment for crime, is a violation of the inherent and inalienable rights of men, a crime against justice and humanity, a disturber of the Union and of domestic tranquility, a hindrance to the common defence, a spoiler of the public liberties, has inaugurated civil war, and is the cause of our national calamities; therefore,

Be it resolved by the general assembly of the State of Ohio, That our senators and representatives in Congress be requested to use their influence and vote for the proposition now pending in Congress to amend the Constitution of the United States, so that neither slavery or involuntary servitude, except as a punishment for crime, whereof the party shall have been duly convicted, shall exist within the United States, or any place subject to their jurisdiction, and giving to Congress power to enforce such prohibition by appropriate legislation.

Resolved, That the governor be requested to forward to each of our senators and representatives in Congress a copy of these resolutions.

John Johnston, *Speaker of the House of Representatives.*
Charles Anderson, *President of the Senate.*

A Nation at War

On January 31, Congress passes the 13th Amendment, formally abolishing slavery in the United States.

1865.2

The Beall in the Booth

From Military Commission, *Trial of John Y. Beall as a Spy and Guerrillero*, New York: D. Appleton and Company, 1865.

On September 28, 1864, John Y. Beall and three accomplices boarded the steamboat *Philo Parsons* on Lake Erie. When the boat had nearly reached Kelly's Island that afternoon, about six miles from the Ohio shore, the men drew revolvers and took possession of the vessel. They threw freight overboard, examined the ship's papers, took the money from the clerk's offices, and ran the boat to Middle Bass Island, where the passengers were put ashore. Soon after, a freight and passenger steamboat, the *Island Queen,* came alongside and was promptly seized and sunk. Beall was arrested on December 16, 1864, in Suspension Bridge, New York. He was charged with violating laws by "undertaking to carry on irregular and unlawful warfare as a guerrilla, without lawful authority and for unlawful purposes," and for acting as a spy.

Beall was tried in early 1865, found guilty, and subsequently hanged on February 24, 1865. Before he was executed, many members of Congress and other prominent individuals asked President Lincoln to commute Beall's sentence. Even Jefferson Davis tried to intervene. A less-than-reliable theory existed after Lincoln's assassination that contended Beall was a friend or a distant cousin of John Wilkes Booth and the failure of Lincoln to grant clemency, in part, motivated Booth to kill Lincoln.

The following passage is from Beall's trial. Weston, who is providing the testimony, was eventually awarded a settlement of $621.70 for the belongings he lost in the affair.

The Judge Advocate then called William Weston, a witness for the prosecution, who being duly sworn, in presence of the accused, testified as follows:

EXAMINED BY JUDGE ADVOCATE.

Q State your name, place of residence, and occupation.
A William Weston, Sandusky City, Ohio. I have been fireman for the last five years.

Q Have you ever seen the accused, Capt. Beall, before?
A Yes, sir.

Q When for the first time, and where?
A The first time I saw him was on board the *Philo Parsons* on the 19th of last September.

Q State what you saw him do, and what you heard him say.
A After the capture of the boat, and we got a little excited, he came forward, and told us what they were going to do with us, and the boat; I was a passenger on board; he said they were not going to hurt or harm any of us, and that they would land us as soon as they thought fit; he also stated that he was an escaped rebel prisoner from Johnson's Island, and that they had taken the boat for the purpose of capturing the United States vessel *Michigan*; he said they were going to liberate the prisoners on Johnson's Island [see 1861.16], and were going to destroy the commerce on the Lakes; that is all I recollect he said.

Q Did you see what was done with any of the freight on board the *Philo Parsons* after the boat was seized?
A I did not see them do anything with the freight, only they threw out one of my boxes, that I got afterwards on the beach, that was pitched out; that was after they landed us on the Island; they pitched one of my boxes into the water.

Q Will you state whether Beall, the accused, had any arms about him or not, while on board the *Philo Parsons*?
A I could not state; I did not see.

Q How was he dressed?
A He was dressed in citizens' clothes.

Q Do you remember whether he wore a cap or a hat?
A He wore a kind of a low-sized hat; a low-crowned hat.

Q Where did you next see him after you were landed?
A I did not see him after I was landed on the Island until I saw him here, at Fort Lafayette, when I was brought down to the fort to identify him.

Q Did you hear on board the *Philo Parsons* from himself or others, what was the name of the accused ; what they called him?
A Captain Beall.

Q You heard him called Captain Beall?
A I could not say whether he was the person or not; I heard somebody called Captain Beall.

Q Can you state who appeared to be in command, or charge of the party who seized the *Philo Parsons*?
A I could not state.

The Judge Advocate said he had no further questions to ask the witness.

Cross-examined by the Accused.

Q When you were brought down to Fort Lafayette to point out Captain Beall, did you point out this man?
A Yes, sir, when I saw him.

Q Who was with him?
A I could not state who was with him; I am a stranger, I don't know any of the men around.

Q Didn't you point out another and a different man, who proved to be a man named Smedley?
A No, sir.

Q What was the first you saw of this person; who told you he was a rebel prisoner; where was he?
A He came forward stating what they were going to do with us; that was the first time I saw him.

Q Did you know then that the boat had been captured?
A Not until he spoke.

Q Who was he speaking to?
A He was speaking to the passengers.

Q Were you a passenger on board?
A Yes, sir.

Q Did you notice what kind of a cord or string he had round his hat?
A I could not state.

Q Was there any tassel on it?
A I could not say.

Q Was there any gold in it?
A I don't know.

Q Did you notice what kind of buttons he had on his coat or vest?
A No, sir, I don't recollect.

Q Did the man who said he was a rebel prisoner, say that he was an officer in the Confederate army?
A I don't recollect.

Q Where were you put ashore?
A On Middle Bass Island.

Q Did these persons in possession show any flag at any time while they were aboard?
A I did not see any.

Q Have you ever seen a secession flag?
A No, sir.

Q What kind of a box was this of yours that they threw overboard?
A A large box containing bedding.

Q Who threw it overboard?
A I could not state who threw it overboard, but I saw the man pitch it out.

Q Did either of them say anything at the time as to why they threw it out ?
A No sir, they were out six or seven rods from the shore.

The accused said he had no further questions to ask the witness.
No questions were asked by the Commission.
The testimony being read to him he affirmed the same.

A Nation at War

On February 18, the mayor of Charleston, South Carolina, surrenders control of the city to Union forces.

On March 3, President Abraham Lincoln signs a bill creating the Freedmen's Bureau, a federal agency created to aid African Americans' transition from slavery to freedom.

1865.3

They Laid Aside Their Garments

From Andrew B. Cross, *The War and the Christian Commission,* Baltimore, MD: Publisher unknown, 1865.

The Christian Commission was organized on November 14, 1861, in New York and was designed to supplement the work of the Sanitary Commission [see 1864.4]. The latter organization's aim was to administer to the health of the troops, namely aiding with the wounded and sick. The Christian Commission helped with the spiritual needs of the troops.

The following passage, published in 1865, was written by Bishop McIlvaine of the Cleveland (Ohio) Episcopal Diocese. He was also the president of Kenyon College from 1832–1840. McIlvaine is describing his work as a member of the Christian Commission. As one captain in the Northern army stated, "Take your life, Bishop, out of the life of the Union, and there will be very little left in it."

At Fredericksburg (December 1862) we were set down in the midst of the work. There were from 8,000 to 10,000 wounded men in the various churches, halls and other houses of the town. As some were sent away towards Washington others came in from the field. The application of the work of the commission to those poor sufferers lying in ambulances, just from the battle, and waiting to be placed under shelter, as well as to the thousands in the socalled hospitals, was just the aspect in which it would best exhibit its true character. I joined in it, messed with the delegates, saw the whole interior of how they lived and denied themselves and wrought. The morning was begun and the day was ended with devotional exercises in the open air, for the commission rooms afforded no space for about 270.

They went out to help the surgeons, some of them surgeons themselves, to wash, to feed, to soothe, take part in the most painful operations, to minister in every wise and loving way to the sick, the maimed, the dying, to talk with them about their souls, to point them to the Lamb of God, to pray with them, under all varieties of trying and painful circumstances, to receive their last messages to dear ones at home, to comfort in all ways those dear men to whom the country is so deeply indebted, to bury them when dead.

But I cannot expect to give an adequate idea of their work, or of their spirit in it, for all accounts to me, before I saw it, had greatly failed to make me comprehend it so as to do it any justice, greatly as I had valued it. What particularly struck me in the work was the *individuality* and *personality* of the connection between the commission agent and the wounded sufferers. There was nothing between them to make the application of aid circuitous or doubtful. It did not take the place of, or in the least interfere with, the work of the official men, the army surgeons, &c. It supplemented them. It helped them. It supplied deficiencies in special emergencies, which no government could be ready for, in all the details of such a condition of things as existed at Fredericksburg. It met the wounded on the field; it met them on their arrival at the town long before the appliances of a very overworked corps of excellent army surgeons and nurses could get to them.

I was much struck with the high character of the men, coming from the highest social positions, reinforcements daily arriving as the time of others expired, but not reaching the necessities of the case; [on our way from Fredericksburg we met twenty or thirty on their way down, walking in the hot sun,] and then with how they *laid aside their garments and girded themselves,* and became servants to all for Christ's sake, how laboriously they wrought, and how all along, with ministrations to the body, they carried the gospel, and most of all, sought the salvation of the soldier. And how the poor sufferers welcomed them—how they appreciated their work—how they thanked them! In how many cases did I hear them say: "We should have been dead by this time but for the christian commission men."

Having seen the work, under circumstances which tested it to the uttermost, as to the sort of men it gets, the wisdom of its appliances, and the efficiency and economy of its operations, I can say, and I want to say out of my whole heart, that a work more worthy of the confidence, and affection, and cooperation of a christian public, especially of every loyal heart and hand, cannot be devised. It is wonderful to see what, from a very small beginning, it has arrived at. The sight of it is one of the most refreshing alleviations of the grief of the land, under the tribulations of this awful war, and the wicked conspiracy that originated it.

1865.4

Dreams Don't Always Come True

From Charles Waddell Chesnutt, *The Wife of His Youth, and Other Stories of the Color Line*, Boston: Mifflin and Company, 1899.

Charles Waddell Chesnutt, an African American man of letters, was born in Cleveland, Ohio, on June 20, 1858, the son of free blacks who had emigrated from Fayetteville, N.C. When he was eight years old, Chesnutt's parents returned to Fayetteville. In 1872, he began a teaching career in Charlotte, N.C. In 1883, he moved his family back to Cleveland. There he passed the state bar examination and established his own court-reporting firm. Financially prosperous and prominent in civic affairs, he resided in Cleveland for the remainder of his life.

The following except is from the short story, "Cicely's Dream." Cicely discovers a wounded and unconscious man and her grandmother helps her bring the man back to their home. The incident reminds Cicely of a dream she had, where she found something and the discovery provided her with genuine happiness. The family believes that the wounded man, John, is likely a Southern mulatto forced into service for the Confederate cause. However, Cicely's dream of finding true love is dashed after the war, when Miss Chandler, a Northern schoolteacher, arrives and John recognizes her as his wife.

An Excerpt from "Cicely's Dream"

The two women reached the fence that separated the cornfield from the pine woods.

"How is I gwine ter git ovuh dat fence, chile?" asked the old woman.

"Wait a minute, granny," said Cicely; "I'll take it down."

It was only an eight-rail fence, and it was a matter of but a few minutes for the girl to lift down and lay to either side the ends of the rails that formed one of the angles. This done, the old woman easily stepped across the remaining two or three rails. It was only a moment before they stood by the wounded man. He was lying still, breathing regularly, and seemingly asleep.

"What is he, granny," asked the girl anxiously, "a w'ite man, or not?"

Old Dinah pushed back the matted hair from the wounded man's brow, and looked at the skin beneath. It was fairer there, but yet of a decided brown. She raised his hand, pushed back the tattered sleeve from his wrist, and then she laid his hand down gently.

"Mos' lackly he's a mulatter man f'om up de country somewhar. He don' look lack dese yer niggers roun' yere, ner yet lack a w'ite man. But de po' boy's in a bad fix, w'ateber he is, an' I 'spec's we bettah do w'at we kin fer 'im, an' w'en he comes to he'll tell us w'at he is—er w'at he calls hisse'f. Hol' 'is head up, chile, an' I'll po' a drop er dis yer liquor down his th'oat; dat'll bring 'im to quicker 'n anything e'se I knows."

Cicely lifted the sick man's head, and Dinah poured a few drops of the whiskey between his teeth. He swallowed it readily enough. In a few minutes he opened his eyes and stared blankly at the two women. Cicely saw that his eyes were large and black, and glistening with fever.

"How you feelin', suh?" asked the old woman.

There was no answer.

"Is you feelin' bettah now?"

The wounded man kept on staring blankly. Suddenly he essayed to put his hand to his head, gave a deep groan, and fell back again unconscious.

"He's gone ag'in," said Dinah. "I reckon we'll hafter tote 'im up ter de house and take keer er 'im dere. W'ite folks wouldn't want ter fool wid a nigger man, an' we doan know who his folks is. He's outer his head an' will be fer some time yet, an' we can't tell nuthin' 'bout 'im tel he comes ter his senses."

Cicely lifted the wounded man by the arms and shoulders. She was strong, with the strength of youth and a sturdy race. The man was pitifully emaciated; how much, the two women had not suspected until they raised him. They had no difficulty whatever, except for the awkwardness of such a burden, in lifting him over the fence and carrying him through the cornfield to the cabin.

They laid him on Cicely's bed in the little lean-to shed that formed a room separate from the main apartment of the cabin. The old woman sent Cicely to cook the dinner, while she gave her own attention exclusively to the still unconscious man. She brought water and washed him as though he were a child.

"Po' boy," she said, "he doan feel lack he's be'n eatin' nuff to feed a sparrer. He 'pears ter be mos' starved ter def."

She washed his wound more carefully, made some lint,—the art was well known in the sixties,—and dressed his wound with a fair degree of skill.

"Somebody must 'a' be'n tryin' ter put yo' light out, chile," she muttered to herself as she adjusted the bandage around his head. "A little higher er a little lower, an' you would n' 'a' be'n yere ter tell de tale. Dem clo's," she argued, lifting the tattered garments she had removed from her patient, "don' b'long 'roun' yere. Dat kinder weavin' come f'om down to'ds Souf Ca'lina. I wish Needham 'u'd come erlong. He kin tell who dis man is, an' all erbout 'im."

She made a bowl of gruel, and fed it, drop by drop, to the sick man. This roused him somewhat from his stupor, but when Dinah thought he had enough of the gruel, and stopped feeding him, he closed his eyes again and relapsed into a heavy sleep that was so closely akin to unconsciousness as to be scarcely distinguishable from it.

When old Needham came home at noon, his wife, who had been anxiously awaiting his return, told him in a few words the story of Cicely's discovery and of the subsequent events.

Needham inspected the stranger with a professional eye. He had been something of a plantation doctor in his day, and was known far and wide for his knowledge of simple remedies. The negroes all around, as well as many of the poorer white people, came to him for the treatment of common ailments.

"He's got a fevuh," he said, after feeling the patient's pulse and laying his hand on his brow, "an' we'll hafter gib 'im some yarb tea an' nuss 'im tel de fevuh w'ars off. I 'spec'," he added, "dat I knows whar dis boy come f'om. He's mos' lackly one er dem bright mulatters, f'om Robeson County—some of 'em call deyse'ves Croatan Injins—w'at's been conscripted an' sent ter wu'k on de fo'tifications down at Wimbleton er some'er's er nuther, an' done 'scaped, and got mos' killed gittin' erway, an' wuz n' none too well fed befo', an' nigh 'bout starved ter def sence. We'll hafter hide dis man, er e'se we is lackly ter git inter trouble ou'se'ves by harb'rin' 'im. Ef dey ketch 'im yere, dey's liable ter take 'im out an' shoot 'im—an' des ez lackly us too."

Cicely was listening with bated breath.

"Oh, gran'daddy," she cried with trembling voice, "don' let 'em ketch 'im! Hide 'im somewhar."

"I reckon we'll leave 'im yere fer a day er so. Ef he had come f'om roun' yere I'd be skeered ter keep 'im, fer de w'ite folks 'u'd prob'ly be lookin' fer 'im. But I knows ev'ybody w'at's be'n conscripted fer ten miles 'roun', an' dis yere boy don' b'long in dis neighborhood. W'en 'e gits so 'e kin he'p 'isse'f we'll put 'im up in de lof an' hide 'im till de Yankees come. Fer dey're comin', sho'. I dremp' las' night dey wuz close ter han', and I hears de w'ite folks talkin' ter deyse'ves 'bout it. An' de time is comin' w'en de good Lawd gwine ter set his people free, an' it ain' gwine ter be long, nuther."

Needham's prophecy proved true. In less than a week the Confederate garrison evacuated the arsenal in the neighboring town of Patesville, blew up the buildings, destroyed the ordnance and stores, and retreated across the Cape

Fear River, burning the river bridge behind them,—two acts of war afterwards unjustly attributed to General Sherman's army, which followed close upon the heels of the retreating Confederates.

When there was no longer any fear for the stranger's safety, no more pains were taken to conceal him. His wound had healed rapidly, and in a week he had been able with some help to climb up the ladder into the loft. In all this time, however, though apparently conscious, he had said no word to any one, nor had he seemed to comprehend a word that was spoken to him.

Cicely had been his constant attendant. After the first day, during which her granny had nursed him, she had sat by his bedside, had fanned his fevered brow, had held food and water and medicine to his lips. When it was safe for him to come down from the loft and sit in a chair under a spreading oak, Cicely supported him until he was strong enough to walk about the yard. When his strength had increased sufficiently to permit of greater exertion, she accompanied him on long rambles in the fields and woods.

In spite of his gain in physical strength, the newcomer changed very little in other respects. For a long time he neither spoke nor smiled. To questions put to him he simply gave no reply, but looked at his questioner with the blank unconsciousness of an infant. By and by he began to recognize Cicely, and to smile at her approach. The next step in returning consciousness was but another manifestation of the same sentiment. When Cicely would leave him he would look his regret, and be restless and uneasy until she returned.

The family were at a loss what to call him. To any inquiry as to his name he answered no more than to other questions.

"He come jes' befo' Sherman," said Needham, after a few weeks, "lack John de Baptis' befo' de Lawd. I reckon we bettah call 'im John."

So they called him John. He soon learned the name. As time went on Cicely found that he was quick at learning things. She taught him to speak her own negro English, which he pronounced with absolute fidelity to her intonations; so that barring the quality of his voice, his speech was an echo of Cicely's own.

The summer wore away and the autumn came. John and Cicely wandered in the woods together and gathered walnuts, and chinquapins [nuts] and wild grapes. When harvest time came, they worked in the fields side by side,—plucked the corn, pulled the fodder, and gathered the dried peas from the yellow pea-vines. Cicely was a phenomenal cotton-picker, and John accompanied her to the fields and stayed by her hours at a time, though occasionally he would complain of his head, and sit under a tree and rest part of the day while Cicely worked, the two keeping one another always in sight.

They did not have a great deal of intercourse with other people. Young men came to the cabin sometimes to see Cicely, but when they found her entirely absorbed in the stranger they ceased their visits. For a time Cicely kept him away, as much as possible, from others, because she did not wish them to see that there was anything wrong about him. This was her motive at first, but after a while she kept him to herself simply because she was happier so. He was hers—hers alone. She had found him, as Pharaoh's daughter had found Moses in the bulrushes; she had taught him to speak, to think, to love. She had not taught him to remember; she would not have wished him to; she would have been jealous of any past to which he might have proved bound by other ties. Her dream so far had come true. She had found him; he loved her. The rest of it would as surely follow, and that before long. For dreams were serious things, and time had proved hers to have been not a presage of misfortune, but one of the beneficent visions that are sent, that we may enjoy by anticipation the good things that are in store for us.

Cover image of *The Wife of His Youth.*

1865.5

The War Is Over!

From Augustus J. Ricks, "Carrying the News of Lee's Surrender," in *Sketches of War History: 1861–1865, Papers Read Before the Ohio Commandery* . . . Volume II, 234–46, Cincinnati: Clarke, 1888.

Early on April 9, General Robert E. Lee decided to make one last attempt to escape the Union troops and reach his supplies at Lynchburg, Virginia. At dawn the Confederates advanced, initially gaining ground against Sheridan's cavalry, but the arrival of Union infantry halted Lee's troops. Surrounded on three sides, Lee surrendered to Grant.

Augustus J. Ricks was born in Massillon, Ohio, on February 10, 1843. He attended Kenyon College, but did not graduate, instead joining the war effort. He accepted the commission of first lieutenant in the 104th Ohio Volunteer Infantry. At the end of the war, he was serving as the aid-de-camp under Major-General J.D. Cox (who would become Ohio's Governor) in North Carolina. Ricks eventually became a District Court judge. He died December 22, 1906, while on a visit to New York City. The following is Rick's account of the news of Lee's surrender.

On a bright day in April, 1865, Major-General J.D. Cox, commanding the Twenty-third Army Corps, with his staff and escort, was riding leisurely at the head of the marching column on the road to the capital of North Carolina. The latest news we had had from Grant was of the fierce struggles about Richmond, its evacuation, and Lee's flight toward Central Virginia. We were pushing on toward Raleigh to prevent a consolidation of Johnston's and Lee's armies; and though hourly expecting news of important movements, we had no expectation of decisive victory. As I was riding by the general's side, speculating with him as to [General Joseph E.] Johnston's probable movements, an orderly rode slowly toward us, bearing a message. General Cox opened it in the usual business-like manner, and read it over as he would have done an ordinary official communication. There was nothing in the manner of the messenger to indicate that he was the bearer of any unusual or important news, and he sat listlessly on his horse while a receipt was being written for the message. Happening then to cast my eyes toward the general, I noticed his face suddenly brighten, and in great animation he turned and directed the escort and staff to be drawn up in line, that he might read to them a message from General Sherman. It was done in a hurry, and with head uncovered he read a brief dispatch stating that

General Lee, with his entire army, had surrendered to Grant at Appomattox. It was the message long looked for, long fought for, and though it came to us on the roadside so unexpectedly, its full significance was at once appreciated. It meant home, and wife, and children, and happy meetings, throughout the land. The cheers that rang through that North Carolina pine thicket from the headquarters' staff and escort of a battalion of cavalry spirited enough to fill the whole dome of the heavens above us. Before the message was read, General Cox ordered all hats off and throats cleared for three rousing cheers. Our horses' reins were loosened and thrown on their necks, and hats were off as fast as ready hands could catch them. The cheers rang out, prompt and sharp, my horse, being frightened, whirled quick as a flash, and before I could gather my bridle reins to check him, was at full speed, headed toward the approaching column. I had hardly slackened his rapid strides, when the thought flashed upon me that it would be a glorious thing to carry such news to the twenty thousand men of the Twenty-third Army Corps, who were marching the broad road before me, all unconscious of the glad tidings that awaited them. It needed no second thought. If any additional incentive had been needed, I had it in the clamor of horses' hoofs behind me. Accompanying the corps on that day's march were two correspondents one of the *New York Tribune* and one of the *Cincinnati Gazette*. They noticed the rapid dash of my horse toward the marching troops, and with the quick instinct common to men in their calling guessed that it was my purpose to carry the news to the brave men of the Army of the Ohio. Thinking, perhaps, that it was an unwarranted intrusion in their line of business, they both put spurs to their horses to overtake me and make the ride famous as the achievement of the special correspondent of the *Tribune* or the *Gazette*, whichever should first secure the right of way. But my horse was too fleet for them. Spurring and giving free reins to the excited animal, he flew over the ground like a greyhound, seeming to know that a ride of unusual significance was before him, came in sight of the head of the column, Major-General [Darius N.] Couch and staff leading the Second Division. They had heard our cheers, and as they saw me coming down the road at full speed, with hat off, waving for a clear road by which to pass to the rear, they parted ranks to the right and left, and opened a clear passage in the center of the highway. As soon as I was within shouting distance, I cried out: "Lee, with his whole army, has surrendered to Grant. Make way for the bearer of the glorious news!"

Then their wild cheers rang out to swell those of the staff and the headquarters' escort, which could still be heard at my rear. But a few rods back of General Couch and his staff was the head of the infantry column—the One hundred and Eleventh Ohio Regiment [Organized at Camp Toledo September 5 and 6 1862 and mustered out on June 27, 1865]. The men saw how the right of way had been quickly given to the horse and rider by General Couch and his escort in front of them, and as I waved to them to open ranks and give me the roadway, they responded with a will, and, breaking to the right and left, gave me a straight, open road to the rear. Into this living lane, skirted with lines of anxious faces, I dashed with a quick gallop, leaving my pursuers behind, surrounded by the confused ranks of a wild army, to whom their pleas for right of way were of such utter insignificance as not to even secure them notice. The last I saw of my newspaper friends they had taken to the fields and were trying to get in advance of me in that way; but fences and woods impeded them, and at last, in despair, they stopped to see me forging ahead, followed by the plaudits and tears of a grateful soldiery. At the head of each regiment, with horse at full speed, and as often as I could repeat it to the anxious listeners, I cried out, with the waving of my hat, "Lee has surrendered, with his whole army, to Grant." Onward I pressed my way through the surging ranks—before me the open road, lined on each side with excited men leaning forward to catch the first sound of the good news they were all so impatient to hear—behind me, a wild, tumultuous crowd of soldiers suddenly touched with the lunacy of joy, if they were to be judged by their actions, pounding each other with knapsacks, waving blankets on the points of their bayonets, pounding canteens with belt buckles, and making a pandemonium of sounds and a circus of tumbling and vaulting. It was news that needed no explanation. It carried indescribable joy and relief to those brave men, upon whom the long suspense of weary marches and indecisive battles were fast taxing patience and exhausting strength. It meant a speedy end of marching under a hot southern sun with heavy knapsacks, and a happy reunion at home. It meant but few more, if any, bloody battles, with the chances of war leaving them crippled or dead upon the field, and the wild plaudits of a grateful people released from time throes of war. It meant good bye to tent and camp, and the wild exultation of the homeward march through streets filled with joyous friends and under banners flaunting from every house-top and window in the dear old home town, whence messages of love and prayers for safe return had followed them from the first day of enlistment. It meant but few more nights on picket duty, and a happy final reunion around the old hearth-stone, where home and all its blessings awaited them. This was the meaning of those brief words that I cried out with such wild excitement to 20,000 men; and for eight long miles, through ranks of infantry regiments, through batteries of artillery, by the ambulance and hospital trains, rode the one man to whom every ear was turned—the one bearer of tidings whose voice filled every heart with joy and gratitude. And do you wonder, companions, when I say to you to night, that I look back upon that incident as the happiest and most eventful one of my army life? I wish I had the gift to tell you of all its striking points, of how differently strong men gave expression to their joys. Some were too much overcome to speak; some shouted themselves hoarse, while others cried; some were wild with their demonstrations, while others were calm and thoughtful, and secretly breathed a prayer for their safe deliverance from the long series of dangers to which they had exposed. . . .

At the top of a hill, as I neared the end of my long ride, I saw a general, well known to all regiments in the Army of the Ohio, anxiously looking for the bearer of the good news; for, long before I could be seen, the men could hear the wild cheering from the head of the column gradually growing louder and nearer, and therefore knew that news of unusual importance was coming by the hands of some bearer. As I came within hailing distance he recognized me, and cried out: "Ricks, what is it—for God's sake, what is it?" I had grown so hoarse from constant repetition of the message in the midst of such great noise and confusion that I could scarcely speak aloud; but when near enough I again repeated: "Lee has surrendered with his whole army to Grant." Quick as a flash, and with the agility of a boy, he clapped his heels together, and with a wild yell turned a complete somersault in the road and ran back to his command—a part of the Third Division—which had just drawn off from the road for dinner. The assembly was immediately sounded, and beginning with the field officers and the band, the first regiment, and followed by the line officers and color bearers, we marched down the front of the regiment, and so along the front of each succeeding regiment of the division, the bands playing and colors waving, the triumphal procession being greeted by the men of each command in line with cheers and salutes suitable to the occasion. Before we reached the last regiment we had a royal procession of officers and bands, and color-bearers that in itself was an extraordinary spectacle. . . . After a little rest, I started to slowly retrace my steps toward head-quarters, which I did not reach until late in the day. The ride through the corps, though free from the excitement of the one in the morning, was full of interest, and coupled with incidents always to be recalled with the greatest pleasure. The feeling uppermost in the thoughts of all was that the war was over. All restraint and discipline were for the time abandoned. The strain of four long years of anxiety and suspense was suddenly thrown off, and the few hours of tumult and exultation that had intervened since I had brought them the most welcome news of their lives, had already given place to the more serious considerations of the returning responsibilities of their muster-out, so unexpectedly confronting them. To the large majority of the people throughout the North the day was one of unalloyed joy and relief. The dark clouds of uncertainty that had enveloped their country and business had only to lift, and let the sunlight fall upon their homes, without a vacant chair. While they had shared in the general anxiety for the preservation of the government and the risks that made every business venture during, that period attended with unusual care, they could now feel the new impulse, which restored confidence and rapidly returning prosperity sent into every channel of trade. There had been no break in their family circles, no disarrangement in business relations, and now in the glad day of peace there were no uncertainties for them. But all through the ranks about me, in the midst of the most unstrained revelry, I could catch enough of their connversations [sic] to know that already these men were anxiously discussing the chances that awaited them when they returned to the duties of civil life. There were young men among them who had left their schools and colleges, who were now too old to return to them to finish their education. The day was therefore at hand for them, when their life work was to be chosen. There were men of years and families, who had hastily left valuable situations. Others had taken their places, and the chances their returning to such positions were being discussed. There were men who had left important business interests which others had taken during their absence, and the probabilities of new ventures were to be considered. They had gone out from their peaceful pursuits untrained to the duties of the soldier and unaccustomed to the dangers and privations of army life. They had passed through the perils of battles, the hardships of marches, the exposures of the camp, and had in their respective spheres contributed to the great triumphs of the mightiest volunteer armies ever organized. Some of them, rising to the full measure of the opportunities presented, had demonstrated the wonderful capabilities of the American citizen soldier, and were sure to return to their homes to receive the highest honors and rewards a grateful people could bestow. And so, slowly retracing my steps amid these happy and buoyant men, I learned of their anxieties and expectations for the future.

A Nation at War

On April 9, Lee surrenders to Grant at Appomattox Court House, Virginia.

On April 14, President Abraham Lincoln is shot at Ford's Theater in Washington, DC.

1865.6

Give Them Their Horses

From George Rice Carpenter, ed., *American Prose: Selections,* London: Macmillan & Co., 1898.

Hiram Ulysses Grant was born at Point Pleasant, in southern Ohio on April 27, 1822. The family moved soon after and Grant spent the first seventeen years of his life in Georgetown, Ohio. He was appointed to West Point in 1839 and was entered by mistake as Ulysses S. Grant. Lincoln made him General-in-Chief of the Union Army in March 1864. He was elected President in 1868 and served two terms.

The following comes from Grant's recollections during the surrender of the Confederate Army at Appomattox Court House. The war had ended and the two leaders of the combatants were hammering out an agreement. Grant admits that he was unsure of what the terms of surrender should be. Perhaps, because both men understood the journey their troops had endured, going home was a relief.

When I put my pen to the paper I did not know the first word that I should make use of in writing the terms. I only knew what was in my mind, and I wished to express it clearly, so that there could be no mistaking it. As I wrote on, the thought occurred to me that the officers had their own private horses and effects, which were important to them, but of no value to us; also that it would be an unnecessary humiliation to call upon them to deliver their side arms.

No conversation, not one word, passed between General Lee and myself, either about private property, side arms, or kindred subjects. He appeared to have no objections to the terms first proposed; or if he had a point to make against them he wished to wait until they were in writing to make it. When he read over that part of the terms about side arms, horses and private property of the officers, he remarked, with some feeling, I thought, that this would have a happy effect upon his army.

Then, after a little further conversation, General Lee remarked to me again that their army was organized a little differently from the army of the United States (still maintaining by implication that we were two countries); that in their army the cavalrymen and artillerists owned their own horses; and he asked if he was to understand that the men who so owned their horses were to be permitted to retain them. I told him that as the terms were written they would not; that only the officers were permitted to take their private property. He then, after reading over the terms a second time, remarked that that was clear.

I then said to him that I thought this would be about the last battle of the war—I sincerely hoped so; and I said further I took it that most of the men in the ranks were small farmers. The whole country had been so raided by the two armies that it was doubtful whether they would be able to put in a crop to carry themselves and their families through the next winter without the aid of the horses they were then riding. The United States did not want them and I would, therefore, instruct the officers I left behind to receive the paroles of his troops to let every man of the Confederate army who claimed to own a horse or mule take the animal to his home. Lee remarked again that this would have a happy effect.

Union and Confederate troops sharing rations after Lee's surrender. (*Battles and Leaders of the Civil War*, Vol. IV. New York: The Century Co., 1884.)

1865.7

No School

From Edward P. Church to Francis A. Lord, April 14, 1865; Oberlin Students; Frances Lord Church Letters; Oberlin College Archives. Courtesy Oberlin College Archives, Oberlin, Ohio.

Francis Lord graduated from Oberlin College in 1863, and went on to become a teacher at the Wisconsin Institute for the Blind in September of that year. Edward Church wrote the following letter to Lord, his fiancée. Church had graduated from Oberlin in 1863, taught a year at the Ohio Reform School, joined the 150th Ohio Volunteer Infantry in 1865, and then returned to study theology at Oberlin in 1865. Eventually, Lord and Church would marry and live in Honolulu until 1875. Church was the President of Oahu College, a preparatory institute for the children of Congregational missionaries and Lord was a teacher there.

Oberlin's was one of many victory celebrations taking place in the North. The realization the fighting had ceased is evident, but so is the historic importance of the terms of surrender. The war had not deterred the feelings Frankie and Eddie had for each other.

Excerpt from April 14, 1865 letter

This (Friday) is to be a holiday—no exercises in the Institution. Service in the 1st Church this A.M. This evening grand fire-works, processions, etc., etc., intersperced [sic] with speeches. The boys are making immense preparatorial for illuminating Tappan [Tappan Hall, a building that, at the time, represented the ultimate idea of comfort and convenience in a college dormitory. Torn down in 1885.] and putting transparencies on the top, also on the Chapel. The material is now collecting for a bonfire in front of the Hall. I never saw so much effort made to make a display here. Principal F. [Charles Grandison Finney, president, Oberlin College] approves of it and encouraged the boys to go forward with it. This is to be a great day too in Charleston [South Carolina]—wouldn't you like to hear [Reverend Henry Ward] Beecher's speech? Your *wild* letter came on Wed. We had some rejoicing on the receipt of the news but nothing of much importance—fired the cannon some. I felt as you did about the conditions offered to Lee and his army were too good. It will be impossible for them to collect their scattered forces now should they wish to. And then they cannot equip another army either. Perhaps the conditions granted to the rebels were better than they deserved, but still this is better than another battle and the loss of 3000 or 4000 more of our men. The terms of the surrender will take out of the mouths of the enemy—at home and abroad—all charge of *hard* and *humiliating* terms.

I hope you will have no more such high winds there. I shall advise you to choose some other room. That old wing may fall some of these times. Now love, I must close. You will excuse me for not writing sooner, won't you dear? You know I love you. I know you love me too. And how happy I am in the thought of it. I am still, Frankie, as ever your own loving, hopeful, devoted, betrothed

/s/ Eddie

The first church and chapel at Oberlin College. From Eugene A. Tattle, "Oberlin College," *The Continent* 2, July–December 1882.

1865.8

Slings and Arrows Nevermore

From John James Piatt, *Poems in Sunshine and Firelight,* Cincinnati, OH: R.W. Carroll & Co., 1866

At the age of ten, John James Piatt came to Columbus, Ohio. He eventually attended Capital University before continuing his education at Kenyon College. He began writing poetry during his time there. In early 1861, Piatt was appointed to a clerkship in the Treasury Department in Washington, DC. After six years, he and his wife, the poet, Sarah Piatt [see 1861.10], moved back to Ohio.

"The Unbended Bow" was written after the Confederate surrender. Romantic in its imagery, the piece expresses the hope that war would not come again to the Union. The nation had endured a monumental exchange of bloodshed and death.

The Unbended Bow (1865)

In some old realm, we read, when war had come,
The bended bow a warlike sign, was sent
Across the land—a summoner fierce but dumb;
When peace return'd the bow was pass'd unbent.

Oh, sacred Land! not many years ago
(The symbol breathes its meaning evermore),
Thy holy summons, came the bended bow—
Thy fiery bearers moved from door to door.

Then sprang thy brave from threshold and from hearth;
Their angry footsteps sounded, moving far,
As when an earthquake moves across the earth;
Shone on thy hill the flame-lit tents of war.

O tender wife, in all thy weakness stern
With the great purpose which thy husband drew;
O mother dreaming of thy son's return,
Strong with the arm whose strength thy country knew;

O maiden, proud to hold a hero's name
Close in thy prayerful silence, blameless: lo,
Transfigured in the light of love and fame,
They come, the bearers of the unbended bow!

"The strife is hush'd, O Land!"—this voice is plain—
"The bow of Peace is borne from door to door:
May thy dread power be never tried again;
But let thine arrows shine for evermore."

Lee and Grant at Appomattox Court House. From Adam Badeau, *Grant in Peace*, Hartford, CT: S.S. Scranton, 1887.

1865.9

A Day of Gloom and Sorrow

From *Gallipolis Journal*, Vol. 30, No. 22, April 20, 1865.

On the evening of April 14, 1865, only five days after Lee's surrender, President Abraham Lincoln was fatally shot by John Wilkes Booth while attending a special performance of the comedy, "Our American Cousin." Almost simultaneously, one of Booth's accomplices, Lewis Paine, attacked Lincoln's Secretary of State, William Henry Seward. A metal surgical collar (Seward was recovering from a carriage accident) saved Seward from certain death. Booth was shot and captured while hiding in a barn near Bowling Green, Virginia, and died later the same day, April 26, 1865. Four co-conspirators, Paine, George Atzerodt, David Herold, and Mary Surratt, were hanged on July 7, 1865.

The following editorial appeared in the *Gallipolis Journal*, a weekly publication. The tone is one of revenge. Lincoln's status of hero was cemented for all time.

Friday last was generally observed in Gallipolis, as a day of rejoicing. But alas! how soon it was followed by one of gloom and sorrow. On Saturday morning the news of President Lincoln's death reached us by telegraph. As it spread over town, it seemed as though death had taken the "loved one" from every loyal family. The appalling tidings profoundly affected all classes, and shed tears of unfeigned sorrow. No incident of this great and terrible war, has fallen so heavily upon our people. The universal feeling among loyal men is one of fearful wrath and indignation, and revengeful threats are heard on all sides. Many, who on the day previous, felt as though they could forget all past animosities, and look with kindly regard on the authors of our national woe, seeing that their clemency has been requited by the assassination of the leading men of the Republic, now declare for a total change in the public policy, and that henceforth it, shall be an "eye for an eye, and a tooth for a tooth." Nor is this to be wondered at. Placing out of view the diabolical wickedness of removing by death, men whose sole aims have been the welfare and prosperity of the people, the flagrant insult thus given the people by whose voice these great men were placed in power, is one which cannot be atoned for, by taking the life of the wretched miscreants who performed the bloody deeds. The lives of Wilkes Booth and his accomplice are mean atonements for the lives of Abraham Lincoln and W.H. Seward [obviously the paper was mistaken in assuming Seward had died, too]. Let those both North and South, who instigated the terrible crime and by their teachings and actions for the past four years, encouraged them in their hellish designs, be held to a strict accountability at the bar of public opinion. Let the virtuous indignation of all honest men, be showered upon them without stint, until they shall find their punishment greater than they can bear. Let the mark of Cain be set on them and in all time to come, let them be branded as the accessories before the fact to the greatest crime, recorded in history since the crucifixion of our Saviour. Let the blood of Abraham Lincoln and William H. Seward, rest upon them and their children. Public safety demands it. Human justice demands it. All that is moral, upright and honest in the world demands revenge.

Derringer used by John Wilkes Booth to assassinate Abraham Lincoln. From Library of Congress.

1865.10

The Rod of Correction

From *Summit County Beacon*, "From the 29th," May 1865.

The 29th Ohio Volunteer Infantry was organized from August 14, 1861, to March 13, 1862, at Jefferson, Ohio, for three years service. On the expiration of its term of service, the original members (except veterans) mustered out, and the organization, composed of veterans and recruits, was retained in service until July 13, 1865, when it mustered out.

This letter from the 29th comes after the surrender of the Confederate forces; the reality of going home seems to have set in. However, the joy is tempered with the concerns surrounding Lincoln's assassination. The regiment had been part of Sherman's march across North Carolina that culminated with the battle of Averasboro [50 miles west of Goldsboro]. Of the approximately 25,000 Union and 8,000 Confederate troops who participated in the confrontation, about 650 Union and 800 Confederate troops were casualties.

FROM THE 29TH.

—

HD QBS. REG'T OHIO VOLS,
IN THE FIELD. RALEIGH, N.C.

APRIL 21ST, 1865

Friend Lane:—

Some considerable time has elapsed since I last wrote you, but the delay was unavoidable, and consequently I am exensable [sic] for now boring you with a letter. In the first place, be it remembered, that all the "surplus gas" that I possessed has been expended hurrahing for Grant, the Union, and the Old Flag, and last but not least, the order announcing a suspension of hostilities in this Department, as Joseph E. [Johnston] concludes to follow the example of his predecessor Lee. We feel here, that virtually, the war is at an end, and many are planning the campaign for the first three months at home. Doting mammas will need to get down the "rod of correction" in order that the girls must understand not to be too forward when they see these live heroes. Many have asked me the question "What will be the state of society when soldiers are discharged? Will the gentle influence of the female sex, and home comforts, restore society to its original state, or rather as it was before the war?" I cannot tell but I think in some instances it may. I fancy that the unmarried of both sexes will be about on an equal, as I believe that the female portion of community at home have "advanced" just as much as the soldier. I know we shall all be glad to see the loved ones again, and will be content to live in peace at home. We have no feelings of hatred towards our erring Southern brethren. Their leaders should be punished, and we have men whom we can trust to deal with them.

We have heard that President Lincoln was assassinated, and I never saw the feelings of the army so aroused as they were at the reception of the dispatch. It seemed as though every man would consider it a privilege to have the assassin and avenge the President's death. I have heard men say (and I think such is the case with the mass of the soldiers of the army) that they would willingly have endured the hardships of war one or two years longer if it would have averted the blow which the nation has received in consequence of his (Lincoln's) death.

Many of the soldiers wept upon hearing the tidings. Thus you are the confidence that won reposed in him by us, the "mudsilla." [Mudsill—Applied figuratively in the nineteenth century to the laboring classes, and used by Southerners to express their contempt for Northerners who were such "base mechanics" as to work for a living.] It is impossible for people who have never been in the army to form an idea how dear our national flag has become to every American soldier. It is truly grand to see how. It is revered by the soldiery. Every one of its folds seem [sic] to say "I fan the course of freedom." In future tell us all be ready to protect it from insult.

I suppose the most of your readers have been made acquainted with the principal incidents that occurred during the campaign [January to April 1865] from Savannah [Georgia] to Goldsboro [South Carolina], also the loss sustained by this Regt. A number were killed and captured among the latter, I believe, was the following from Akron and vicinity:

1st Lieut; U.S. Hexter Co K, Private J. Treen Co. G, private Charles Upham Co. G, P. Dennis Co. B., Jacob Foster Co. G., who was taken prisoner on the 25th of May last, was paroled and after died. The others have all been paroled and are now at Annapolis, Md.

The men of the Regt. are generally well and in excellent spirits, and all hope to be at home soon.

Yours in haste,
Dick

A Nation at War

On May 10, Union troops capture Confederate President Jefferson Davis near Irwinville, Georgia.

1865.11

Who's Laughing Now?

From Oscar H. Harpel, "Freedom's Immortal Triumph," Lithograph on woven paper, Cincinnati, OH: 1865.

In 1810, there were approximately 350 newspapers, daily or weekly, published in the United States. By 1856, the number had increased to 2,500, and by 1870, 5,800 newspapers were available. In Ohio, publications included Dayton's *Religious Telescope,* Cleveland's *Waechter am Erie,* Mansfield's *Richland Shield and Banner,* Toledo's *Sunday Journal,* and Zanesville's *Farmers' and Mechanics' Advocate.*

The growth of newspapers also saw the growth of the political cartoon, especially after the Civil War. One of the famous cartoonists was Thomas Nast who took on the powerful Tammany Hall politicians. Below is a cartoon by Oscar Henry Harpel (who used the anagram Charles Porah) who was a Cincinnati printer and typographer. Harpel died when he was about fifty, on November 20, 1881.

Explantion of Harpel's Cartoon

Confederate president Jefferson Davis, dressed in a hoopskirt or crinoline [A blow not only to Davis's masculinity but to Southern chivalry. Also, an unfounded rumor was that Davis tried to escape Northern capture by wearing his wife's skirt.], hangs from a "Sour Apple Tree" at left [Reference to a Northern song that included the verse "Hang Jeff Davis to a sour-apple tree. As we go marching on."], a Bowie knife in one hand and a torn flag in the other. Beneath Davis is an open grave from which peers the devil. At right nooses are suspended over the heads of several "Confederate Mourners." From left to right: Gen. Robert E. Lee; Secretary of War, John C. Breckinridge; Secretary of State and War, Judah P. Benjamin; one of the Southern "Fire-eaters" [vociferous proponents of the war and secession] and members of the Confederate Senate, William Lowndes Yancey; Georgian Robert A. Toombs [a strong disunion supporter], and Louis T. Wigfall [anti-Lincoln advocate]. Lincoln's assassin John Wilkes Booth (far right) rushes to join the group. On the ground lie copperheads (symbols of Peace Democrats), skulls, and broken artillery. The infamous Confederate prisons, Libby and Andersonville, can be seen in the distance. In the upper register, the blindfolded figure of Justice, holding a sword and scales, is enthroned on a bank of clouds. At left, Liberty sits beside an urn partially covered by the Union flag. An eagle is beside her. A grieving soldier and sailor attend the urn, while a slave man, his wife, and child look toward the far right, where the recently assassinated Abraham Lincoln is escorted heavenward by angels.

Harpel cartoon. From Library of Congress.

1865.12

A Separate Land of Their Own

From J.D. Cox, "Gen. Cox's Response," *Reconstruction and the Relations of the Races in the United States,* Columbus, OH: Ohio State Journal Steam Press, 1865.

In July of 1865, a committee of Oberlin men sent a letter to the Union candidate for governor, J.D. Cox, asking him two questions: "Are you in favor of modifying our Constitution so as to give the elective franchise to colored men?" and "In the re-organization of the Southern States should the elective franchise be secured to the colored people?" Cox was a brilliant volunteer officer during the war, serving in the Kanawha Valley campaign and at South Mountain, commanding the 9th Army Corps at Antietam, and the 23d Army Corps late in the Atlanta, Franklin, and Nashville campaigns, and was commissioned major general in 1864. He would go on to be elected governor.

The following is an excerpt from Cox's response to the above questions. Cox had a long relationship with Oberlin College, so the questions he received were not startling. E.H. Fairchild, the Principal of the Preparatory Department of Oberlin College, and Samuel Plumb, a prominent citizen, signed the letter on behalf of the committee. Oberlin had gained a reputation prior to and during the war as a bastion of anti-slavery sentiment. One should compare this letter with the Clement Vallandigham document (see 1861.1).

COLUMBUS, 25 JULY, 1865.

. . . The details of any system of separation could only be determined by careful study and a wide comparison of views. Suppose, however, that without breaking up the organization of any State, you take contiguous territory in South Carolina, Georgia, Alabama and Florida, and there, under the sovereignty of the United States, and with all the facilities which the power and wealth of the Government can give, we organize the freedmen in a dependency of the Union analogous to the Western territories. Give them schools, laws facilitating the acquirement of homesteads to be paid for by their own labor, full and exclusive political privileges, aided at the start, should it be necessary, by wise selection from the largest brains and most philanthropic hearts among anti-slavery men, to give them a judiciary or executive which would command their confidence in the first essay of political existence. There need be no coercive collection of the colored race in the designated region, the majority are there now, and the reward of political power would draw thither the remainder quite as rapidly as their place could be supplied by white immigration into other States. The forts and seaport cities could remain under direct control of the Federal Government as the basis for the common trade and intercourse with other parts of the country and world, which would be necessary. Thc fullest opportunity to develop the highest civilization they are capable of, would there be given. Colored men of talent and intelligence would not there make a vain struggle for the empty name of being lawyers without briefs, or merchants without trade, but would have what a leading journal at the East has frequently demanded for them, the opportunity, as well as the right, to take rank according to their real character and ability. . . .

The magnitude of the problem is immense, but the principles which must decide it one way or the other are simple. When we deal with a whole community, however closely connected with ourselves, it is not by the application of the maxim of municipal law as applied to individuals that we must decide the case, but by a modified form of international law, which so far from ignoring our responsibility to God our common ruler, or the obligation to recognize the fundamental rights of man, necessarily implies them all. Religion, honor, humanity, republicanism, all call upon us to see well it that we do not allow the seething and molten elements to crystallize into a new form of oppression, and I recognize as fully as possibly can the burden of responsibility which this great epoch in the world's history rolls upon all who have even the humblest part in determining the shape of public policy.

I have approached the subject as an antislavery man. I have thought as deeply as I was capable of, and have carefully revised my opinions and tested them by all the fundamental principles of right and justice. If others do not agree with me, and it part me from any whose principles and motives are the same as my own, my deep regret that it should be so cannot change my convictions.

It has seemed to me that the solution I have offered rids us of most of the difficulties in our way. It gives the black man political rights and franchises without onerous terms; it reduces the representation of the Southern whites in Congress to a proper basis, their won number; it secures the permanent peace of the Government and the allegiance of the people by the only sure guaranty, viz: that of common interest and identity of institutions. What more would you have?

1865.13

Penniless and Alone

From A. G. Riddle, *Alice Brand: A Romance of the Capital*, New York: D. Appleton, 1875.

Albert Gallatin Riddle was born in Monson, Massachusetts, on May 28, 1816. His family moved to Geauga County, Ohio, shortly thereafter. Riddle eventually became the prosecuting attorney for Geauga and Cuyahoga counties; a member of the Ohio legislature; a representative of the Cleveland district in the House of Representatives; consul at Matanzas, Cuba, during the Civil War; attorney of the District of Columbia from 1879–89, and the author of many works of fiction and history. He died on May 15, 1902.

Alice Brand is a story of Washington life during the postwar, Johnson administration. The heroine of the story is Alice Brand, a Southern girl, whose property was destroyed or stolen when Vicksburg was taken by Union troops, leaving her penniless. She goes to Washington and obtains a clerkship in the Treasury Department and meets Colonel Warhel, a handsome young officer, who undertakes to obtain compensation for her losses, and also to establish her rights under an old will to much valuable property in Washington. The Riddle novel was hailed at the time for its accurate depiction of the "inside" happenings of the U.S. capitol.

An Excerpt from Alice Brand

In the larger of the two rooms, in state, sat Mrs. Thompson in a creaky rocking-chair, with her feet on an ottoman, flashy, frowsy, and forty, attended by two lady admirers who came to "set" with her, as one of them appropriately called it. Mrs. Thompson's voice had drawled and died away, when with an effort she resumed: "Well, it is a comfort to know that these things was permitted for our shortcoming, an' for our good; though the massy knows what I've did;" and, closing her washed-out eyes, she looked as if she would have preferred to realize the "good" in more convertible funds. "Yis, she takes after her father in her workin' ways—a regular Yank never gits the mean, workin' spirit out on 'em; and, as if we hadn't gone down low enough, she must take this place in the Treasury; I tho't I should 'a died. You see, I know'd nothin' 'bout it till 'twas all did."

"Well, now—I think," remarked one of her friends, "that seventy-five dollars a month is not a bad thing."

"Yis; but then—I'm a Biggs, an' the Biggses never did work," was the sufficient answer.

"Then Alice is not a Biggs? I tho't she was your own niece."

"Bless your soul—no! My husband, who's as good as dead, was a cousin to her step-mother. Her mother an' step-mother was both on 'em Craiks, you see, an' cousins; and the Craiks, though a high-toned Southern family, warn't Biggses, by a right smart. Yer see, 'er father, Commodore Brand, married Helen Craik in the ole country somewhere. The Craikses were all in the ole country, both families. Well, the commodore, then a lieutenant, married Helen, an' when she died, leavin' this Alice a baby, he, like a real Northerner, married her cousin. The Craiks was rich, an' some years after, her father resigned his office, an' went to live on his first wife's plantation, called Magnolia, a spul-endid place! near Vicksburg. Her father an' mother was dead, an' she had mor'n a thousan' niggers, an' no end o' horses an' mules, an' raised cotton, an' a heap o' sugar, an' every thing. Fer some reason, Commodore Brand never went North, an' Alice was raised mostly at the South. Her step-mother died first, an' then, jest afore the war, she lost'er father, an' was left with the plantation, an' niggers, 'an things; an' she not mor'n sixteen. I never sawn her father; my husband took me thar just after he died, an' went on down the river, as I told yer, an' never come back. Men is dreadful unsartin'. Wal, the war come, an' General Grant an' his army of Yanks an' murderers, an', for a time, our General Pemberton made his head-quarters to our house, an' one o' his aides, General Gardé, took a great fancy to Alice; but she was jest as full o' her father's Northern blood as she could hole, an' stood up for the North, an' all we could do an' say, she held out, an' quarreled with General Pemberton an' all on 'em. She had 'er father's boat-flag, an' sword, an' plume, in 'er room, an' when the general threatened to confiscate all the property, she tole him to do it.

"Wal, yer see, we had to fall back inter the city, an' insisted on taking Alice with us, an' she refused to go, an' General Gardé staid with some soldiers to take us in; an' Alice still refused; an' jest as we had got 'er out an' started, the Yanks come up. It was jest at dark. Oh, dear! I fainted clar away! The Biggses always did. I only remember the guns, an' a clash, an' shouts; an' when I come to, we're all back in the house, with Yankee soldiers guardin' on't; and Alice was as wild as a mad thing. Wal, the house stood on high ground, an' the mean Yanks tore it down, an' dug a fort thar, an' settin' all the niggers to work, an' took all the corn an' cotton, mules an' horses. They gave 'er some sort o' papers for 'em all; but Lord! when we come yer, the Linkinites only paid for the corn—the mean, thievin', 'ornary creters, an' we never had a red for the niggers, an' cotton, an' things; and never will have. I don't wonder the Lord took off Linkin; I only wonder that Seward lived, and Stanton was spared; an', as if there could be no end to our misfortins, they put poor Alice in the Treasury to earn her livin', an' I thought she would never git that. Oh, dear! it's a comfort to know that these is permitted fer our good"—sinking back in despairing exhaustion a moment, and then, springing to her feet, with her scrawny person alive with energy—"Massy on us—thar's the dinner!" as the Borum dinnerbell sent its cracked clangor up from the reeking depths, "and me a Biggs !"—as, followed by her companions, she escaped from the room.

A bright-faced yellow girl tidied up the room, and placed a low chair by the cheery grate, whose ruddy light dispelled the gloom of an early winter evening.

A light step, a lithe form, and a young girl's face lingered on the threshold, seeming to bring additional brightness; but, as she stepped flaggingly to the chair into which she rather dropped than sat, and placed her chilled feet to the glowing grate, almost a sigh was breathed out, and her eyes for a moment lost the power of seeing castles and knights in the fire.

It was Alice Brand.

1865.14

The Turtle Has All Kinds of Meat in Him

From *The Christian Recorder*, "Letter from Wilmington," August 19, 1865.

Reincorporating the Confederate states into the Union fell to President Andrew Johnson. In order to bring North Carolina back into the fold, Johnson decided in mid-1865 that a convention would be held to aid the process. Delegates to the convention would include those who had taken an oath of allegiance to the Federal government and those who qualified as state voters prior to secession. Basically, this eliminated the newly-freed blacks from having any contributions.

The writer of the letter, James H. Payne, was a Quartermaster Sergeant. He was appointed to the position on February 23, 1864, and mustered out on September 21, 1865. His views on the North Carolina proceedings indicate an understanding of human behavior and the reality of how blacks would be treated in the Reconstruction South.

Mr. Editor:—After the receipt of your brief letter I sit down to pen for your worthy columns a short communication, trusting it will prove both instructive to the readers of your worthy organ, and beneficial to the religious state of the church. . . .

As to the condition of things as they are, and appear to exist here in the city of Wilmington, and I may say throughout North Carolina. So far as I can learn, trouble and destitution, as well as hatred and revenge, await our poor people in these Southern States, and it is to be regretted that the President has left so much to be decided by the choice of the prejudiced loyal white man of the South in the reconstruction of the States. Here the black man, though having fought to bring peace to the distracted country, after the victory is obtained can have no voice in making the laws which are to govern his future destiny in this country. No; but he must sit in a state of perfect dormancy, as though he were under slavery's cruel power still.

I wonder, as the Southern black man has got sense enough to fight for this country, if he ain't got sense enough to vote, whether he is educated or not. It seems to me, if he knew where to strike with his steel and fire-arms, he will also know where to strike with his vote. The opinion of most white men in reference to the colored man is something like the opinion of some people about the turtle; they say the turtle has all kinds of meats in him. So the white men of this nation, or at least a majority of them, think the same of the colored man: they think he has all kinds of material in him, and seem to be under doubts as to which of these principles will prevail in the colored man, whether this or that. But one principle they seem to be determined shall not prevail, and that is the pure principle of his manhood: for they say, "We will not give him the privilege of developing that principle."

But the President has left the matter of reconstruction with the loyal whites of the South, and now the argument attempted to be deduced is this: that no colored man should be allowed to vote, unless he can read and write. Now, if this is to be the motto, let it be applied to all men, for one unlearned man is just as unqualified to vote as another.

But this would cripple the President's decision, for it would cut off a large portion of the votes of the loyal white men of the South, who must, by their votes, assist in the reconstruction of our State laws. Then, in order to justify themselves in this matter, they plead the colored man's inferiority to the white race. But they forget that we have proved ourselves their superiors in every privilege we have been permitted to enjoy....

There is a great deal to be done yet before the full attainment of our liberty in this country and none can accomplish so great a work but God, and He alone. Then let every minister among us teach his congregation the importance of asking God in every petition to turn the strong current of prejudice away from us. May our God work marvelous things for us now and forever. Amen.

J.H. Payne,

Q.M. Sergt. 27th U.S.C.T.

Wilmington, N.C., Aug. 12th, 1865.

1865.15

Graduating in Peace

From August 24, 1865 Commencement Program; Miscellany; College Miscellany; Oberlin College Archives. Courtesy Oberlin College Archives, Oberlin, Ohio.

After the war's conclusion, Oberlin College graduated its class of 1865. The Ladies Hall, a dormitory for women, was completed in time for the ceremonies and the alumni dinner was held there. In 1861, 199 individuals graduated from the college; by 1865 the number had dropped to 99. Among the 1865 graduates were Fanny Jackson, a leading black educator of the nineteenth century, and James Waite Clarke, a captain in the Ohio Militia and future Cleveland bookseller.

In 1865, the Oberlin Conservatory of Music, an offshoot of the College's religious music program, was founded. The tuition at the time was roughly $12/quarter. The seminary itself would continue to graduate ministers who began to go further west. Citizens, after four years of fighting each other, were only a few years away from being able to ride the rails from coast to coast.

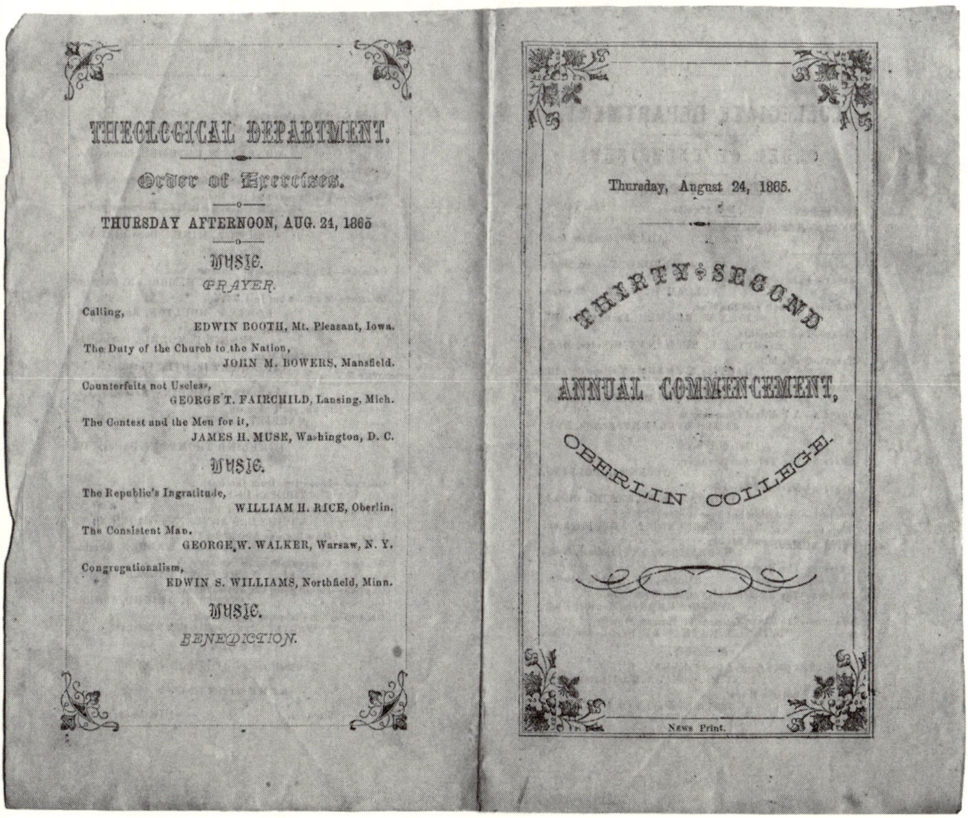

THEOLOGICAL DEPARTMENT.

Order of Exercises.

THURSDAY AFTERNOON, AUG. 24, 1865

MUSIC.

PRAYER.

Calling,
EDWIN BOOTH, Mt. Pleasant, Iowa.

The Duty of the Church to the Nation,
JOHN M. BOWERS, Mansfield.

Counterfeits not Useless,
GEORGE T. FAIRCHILD, Lansing, Mich.

The Contest and the Men for it,
JAMES H. MUSE, Washington, D. C.

MUSIC.

The Republic's Ingratitude,
WILLIAM H. RICE, Oberlin.

The Consistent Man.
GEORGE W. WALKER, Warsaw, N. Y.

Congregationalism,
EDWIN S. WILLIAMS, Northfield, Minn.

MUSIC.

BENEDICTION.

Thursday, August 24, 1865.

THIRTY-SECOND

ANNUAL COMMENCEMENT,

OBERLIN COLLEGE.

News Print.

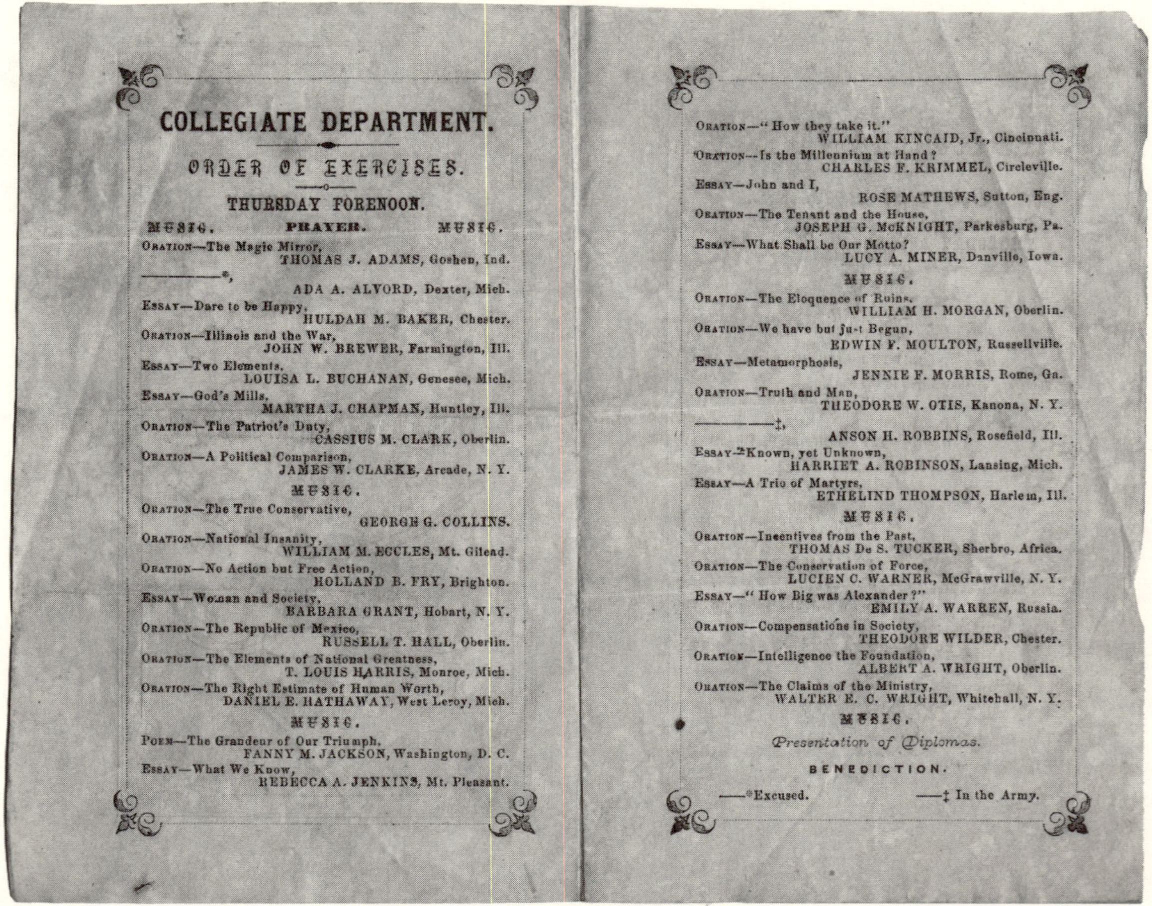

COLLEGIATE DEPARTMENT.

ORDER OF EXERCISES.

THURSDAY FORENOON.

MUSIC. PRAYER. MUSIC.

ORATION—The Magic Mirror,
THOMAS J. ADAMS, Goshen, Ind.

——————*,
ADA A. ALVORD, Dexter, Mich.

ESSAY—Dare to be Happy,
HULDAH M. BAKER, Chester.

ORATION—Illinois and the War,
JOHN W. BREWER, Farmington, Ill.

ESSAY—Two Elements,
LOUISA L. BUCHANAN, Genesee, Mich.

ESSAY—God's Mills,
MARTHA J. CHAPMAN, Huntley, Ill.

ORATION—The Patriot's Duty,
CASSIUS M. CLARK, Oberlin.

ORATION—A Political Comparison,
JAMES W. CLARKE, Arcade, N. Y.

MUSIC.

ORATION—The True Conservative,
GEORGE G. COLLINS.

ORATION—National Insanity,
WILLIAM M. ECCLES, Mt. Gilead.

ORATION—No Action but Free Action,
HOLLAND B. FRY, Brighton.

ESSAY—Woman and Society,
BARBARA GRANT, Hobart, N. Y.

ORATION—The Republic of Mexico,
RUSSELL T. HALL, Oberlin.

ORATION—The Elements of National Greatness,
T. LOUIS HARRIS, Monroe, Mich.

ORATION—The Right Estimate of Human Worth,
DANIEL E. HATHAWAY, West Leroy, Mich.

MUSIC.

POEM—The Grandeur of Our Triumph,
FANNY M. JACKSON, Washington, D. C.

ESSAY—What We Know,
REBECCA A. JENKINS, Mt. Pleasant.

ORATION—"How they take it."
WILLIAM KINCAID, Jr., Cincinnati.

ORATION—Is the Millennium at Hand?
CHARLES F. KRIMMEL, Circleville.

ESSAY—John and I,
ROSE MATHEWS, Sutton, Eng.

ORATION—The Tenant and the House,
JOSEPH G. McKNIGHT, Parkesburg, Pa.

ESSAY—What Shall be Our Motto?
LUCY A. MINER, Danville, Iowa.

MUSIC.

ORATION—The Eloquence of Ruins,
WILLIAM H. MORGAN, Oberlin.

ORATION—We have but just Begun,
EDWIN F. MOULTON, Russellville.

ESSAY—Metamorphosis,
JENNIE F. MORRIS, Rome, Ga.

ORATION—Truth and Man,
THEODORE W. OTIS, Kanona, N. Y.

——————‡,
ANSON H. ROBBINS, Rosefield, Ill.

ESSAY—Known, yet Unknown,
HARRIET A. ROBINSON, Lansing, Mich.

ESSAY—A Trio of Martyrs,
ETHELIND THOMPSON, Harlem, Ill.

MUSIC.

ORATION—Incentives from the Past,
THOMAS De S. TUCKER, Sherbro, Africa.

ORATION—The Conservation of Force,
LUCIEN C. WARNER, McGrawville, N. Y.

ESSAY—"How Big was Alexander?"
EMILY A. WARREN, Russia.

ORATION—Compensations in Society,
THEODORE WILDER, Chester.

ORATION—Intelligence the Foundation,
ALBERT A. WRIGHT, Oberlin.

ORATION—The Claims of the Ministry,
WALTER E. C. WRIGHT, Whitehall, N. Y.

MUSIC.

Presentation of Diplomas.

BENEDICTION.

——*Excused. ——‡ In the Army.

1865.16

1865.16

Time to Go Home

From Hiram Wilson Discharge Papers; William McKinley Presidential Library and Museum Archive Collection. Courtesy William McKinley Presidential Library and Museum, Canton, Ohio.

Starting in June 1865, the Union army was disbanded. Of the 1,000,000 volunteers, 800,000 mustered out by November. A resolution in the U.S. House of Representatives put it best ". . . now 'that grimaged war has smoothed her wrinkled front,' and peace has succeeded din of arms, [Ohio's people] can look back on the events of the past four years and feel just pride for the noble part they have taken in the suppression of gigantic rebellion."

Post-war Ohio was still a heavily agricultural state, but manufacturing was growing rapidly. Prior to the war, Cleveland had been a center for iron manufacturing, and that rise continued. During the Civil War, Procter & Gamble of Cincinnati was awarded several contracts to supply soap and candles to the Union armies, enhancing the company's reputation as soldiers returned home with their P&G products. In 1869, B.F. Goodrich established a small plant to manufacture rubber products, leading to an expansion of the industry in Akron, Ohio.

The following document discharged the 18-year-old Hiram Wilson from the 188th Ohio Volunteer Infantry. His captain, Josephus Cunningham, who signed the document, was only three years older. Hiram, a laborer prior to the war, had been paid in full. Many soldiers and their widows would be forced to make claims for back pay and other benefits for years to come.

A Nation at War

On June 17, staunch secessionist, Edmund Ruffin commits suicide in what is dubbed as the "last shot" of the Civil War.

On July 7, Mary Surratt, a co-conspirator in the Lincoln assassination, is hanged, becoming the first woman executed in the United States.

On August 24, Robert E. Lee accepts the presidency of Washington College in Lexington, Virginia.

On September 12, the Democratic Party of Connecticut recommends that voters reject an amendment to the state constitution that would remove the word "white" as a qualification for voting.

On October 12, President Andrew Johnson indicates to South Carolina delegates that he does not wish to bring former Confederate leader Jefferson Davis to trial for treason.

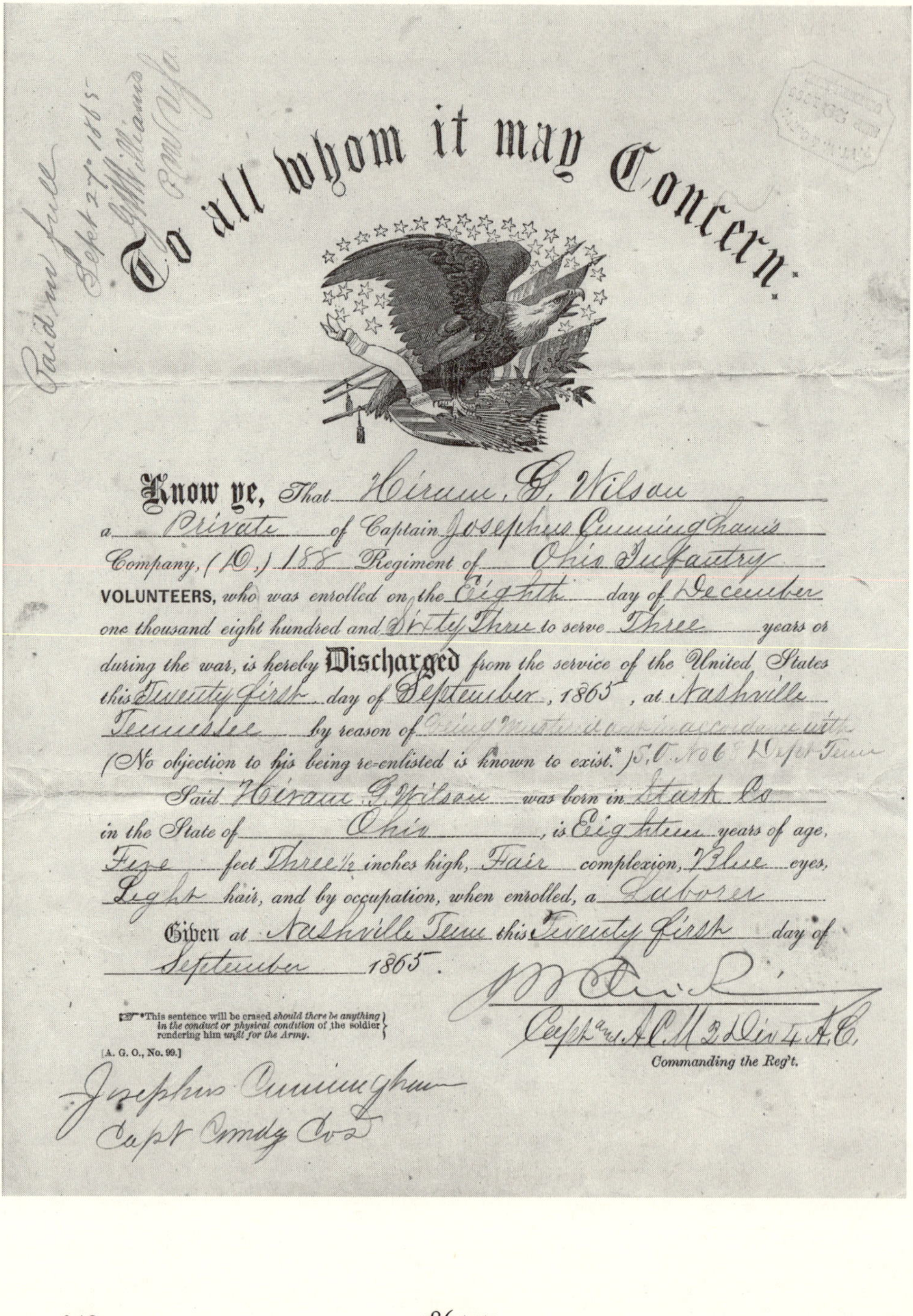

Paid in full
Sept 27th 1865
G.W. Williams
Pm USA

To all whom it may Concern.

Know ye, That Hiram G. Wilson
a Private of Captain Josephus Cunningham's
Company, (D.) 188 Regiment of Ohio Infantry
VOLUNTEERS, who was enrolled on the Eighth day of December
one thousand eight hundred and Sixty Three to serve Three years or
during the war, is hereby **Discharged** from the service of the United States
this Twenty first day of September, 1865, at Nashville
Tennessee by reason of being mustered out in accordance with
(No objection to his being re-enlisted is known to exist.*) S.O. No 68 Dept Tenn
Said Hiram G. Wilson was born in Stark Co
in the State of Ohio, is Eighteen years of age,
Five feet Three ½ inches high, Fair complexion, Blue eyes,
Light hair, and by occupation, when enrolled, a Laborer
Given at Nashville Tenn this Twenty first day of
September 1865.

*This sentence will be erased should there be anything in the conduct or physical condition of the soldier rendering him unfit for the Army.

[A. G. O., No. 99.]

Capt and A.C.M. 2 Div 4 A.C.
Commanding the Reg't.

Josephus Cunningham
Capt Comdg Co D

1865.17

A Free Education

From various sources.

A 1870 Congressional report indicated that Ohio had 20 universities and colleges, 124 professors, 53 tutors, and 5,054 students. The only public institutions were Miami (Ohio) University, Ohio State University, and Ohio University. Tuition at Ohio University in the 1870s was $30/year, plus room and board. Miami University charged $40/year.

The following two documents describe the availability of free tuition to minors (males under 21 years of age) who fought for Ohio in the Civil War. The first document is from an Ohio University administrator clarifying the legislative action, and the second is the act itself. In all likelihood, few soldiers took advantage of the opportunity. Many were not qualified and many stayed home to work on farms.

From *The Coshocton Democrat*, "Interesting to Soldiers," November 21, 1865.

ATHENS, OHIO, NOVEMBER 1865

Editor of the Democrat—

Sir—To meet the constant inquiries of soldiers concerning the free tuition in the Ohio University provided for them by State legislation, will you please to state through your columns:

1. That an honorably discharged Ohio volunteer, who entered the service a minor is entitled to free tuition in the Ohio University for as long a time as he was in the service under age.

2. Soldiers availing themselves of this provision must procure from the Adjutant General at Columbus (it will be furnished on application by letter,) a certificate stating the time spent in the service as a minor. This certificate will be their ticket of admission to the University.

3. Soldiers, as other students, are examined before admission to classes, and classified strictly according to their attainments.

4. All applicants for admission to the Preparatory department of the University are required to be thoroughly acquainted with Arithmetic through vulgar and decimal fractions, and English Grammar through Etymology. The University will gladly welcome to its halls any who have honored their State by fighting under its flag; but it is earnestly recommended to all who may not be advanced as far as indicated above, they spend at least one term at public and

other schools, preparatory to applying for admission to the University.—The next term will commence on the 4th of December.

It may be of interest to your readers to learn that already soldiers from all parts of the State, and representing a large number of regiments, ranking from field officer to private, are attending the University under the above arrangement; and it may interest the soldiers of your county to know that ample provision is made by the officers of the institution to secure to such as may attend the amplest benefit of the gratitude offered them by the State.

Very respectfully

Eli T. Tappan, *Secretary of the Faculty*

From *General and Local Laws and Joint Resolutions, Passed by the Fifty-Sixth General Assembly, of the State of Ohio,* Volume 61, Columbus, OH: Richard Nevins, State Printer, 1864.

An Act

To provide for admission, without charge, into the state universities and common schools of persons, who, when minors, entered the military service of the United States.

Section 1. *Be it enacted by the General Assembly of the State of Ohio, That it shall be* the duty of the clerk in each sub-school district to take, or cause to be taken, annually, between the first and third Monday of September, an enumeration of all male minors who have enlisted or may yet enlist in the military service of the United States during the present war.

Sec. 2. It shall be the duty of the trustees of Miami University, at Oxford, and of Ohio University, at Athens, and of the directors of the several sub-school districts of this State to admit into said universities, and into any of the public schools, without charge, all persons who, when minors, so enlisted in the military service of the United States, and have been honorably discharged therefrom, and to extend to them all the privileges of said institutions and schools for and during a period, equal to the time they have spent in the said service, prior to their arrival at the age of twenty-one years.

Sec. 3. This act to take effect from and after its passage.

JAMES R. HUBBELL, *Speaker of the House of Representatives.*
CHARLES ANDERSON, *President of the Senate.*
February 10, 1864.

1865.18

A Glowing and Delicious Reception Dinner

From *The Holmes County Farmer*, "Soldiers' Reception Dinner," December 21, 1865.

The remaining soldiers of the 19th Ohio Volunteer Infantry mustered out at San Antonio, Texas, on October 21, 1865. The last enlistees of the 51st Ohio Volunteer Infantry mustered out at Victoria, Texas, on October 3, 1865. Both groups made their way home, probably aboard steamers, to Fort Chase in Columbus, Ohio, to get their discharge papers and final payments.

The good people of Berlin Township decided to gather the soldiers together at a reception and dinner, not unlike other towns and cities throughout Ohio. The citizens had sent their boys off to war with fanfare; they were bringing their men home with food and speeches. One of the orators, Noah Yoder, had fought in the war and was a true hero. Yoder had lost one of his legs below the knee and had severely injured his left clavicle. After his return, he carried on as a country physician, as did his brother Samuel, who married Abner Maxwell's daughter, Minerva. Noah's misfortune did not end with his injuries. He accidently drowned in March 1877, on his way to see a patient.

Soldiers' Reception Dinner

The 51st and 19th Reg'ts, the last soldiers from this township, having returned a short time ago, the citizens of Berlin township, according to previous arrangements, held a grand soldiers' reception dinner in Berlin on Friday, Dec. 15th, in which all classes and parties were represented. At 10 o'clock the soldiers marched to the M.E. church headed by the Berlin Brass Band which entertained the meeting with some of the choicest music. Rev. J. Crow was chosen Chairman; Jacob Davidson, Secretary. After prayer by Rev. J. Crow, the Rev. J.C. Gillam delivered an eloquent and befitting reception speech; complimenting the soldiers for the bravery and skill with which they defended their country. Lieut. [Noah] Yoder delivered an accomplished and long to be remembered responding speech in behalf of his comrades and fellow soldiers.—Dr. C.C. Maxwell then delivered a noble, patriotic and pleasing address. Robert Crow of the 120th O.V.I. responded in a highly entertaining speech, in which he thanked the citizens for the honor they conferred upon the soldiers in welcoming them home in such a magnificent style. A speech was delivered in German by Charles Voltz, Esq., full of meaning and patriotism. A splendid and beautiful banner was presented to the returned soldiers by Miss Rosa Fugate, in behalf of the Berlin ladies. Capt. Abner Maxwell, Marshall of the day, then formed the procession and escorted the soldiers with their wives and sweet-hearts to the school house, where they partook of such a glowing and delicious dinner as only the ladies of this township know how to prepare.

John Crow, Chairman.

Jacob Davidson, Secretary.

A Nation at War

On November 11, Mississippi enacts "Black Codes" that supposedly detail the rights of freedmen, but in reality, limit the rights of former slaves.

On December 13, the 39th Congress set up the Joint Committee of fifteen on Reconstruction to monitor post-war activities in the South.

1865.19

The War Will Never Be Forgotten

From "Drawing of Soldiers' and Sailors' Monument," *The Builder* 59, no. 2491, November 1890. From "Drawing of Akron's Soldiers' Memorial Chapel," *The American Architect and Building News*, 2, no. 101, December 1877.

Physical structures dedicated to the Civil War can be found in 85 of Ohio's 88 counties. Among the approximately 269 monuments statewide, the remembrances are varied, from eagles to obelisks, to statues of important soldiers and generals. The war had taken so many and had lasted so long that citizens and surviving soldiers wanted to remember those who had fought to maintain the Union.

In 1894, the Soldiers' and Sailors' Monument opened in Cleveland, Ohio. The structure was designed by prominent Cleveland sculptor-architect, Levi Scofield, who worked on it for over seven years. The monument consists of an elevated base containing a tablet room. The base is surmounted by a column capped with a 15-foot high Statue of Liberty, bringing the total height of the structure to 125 feet. Surrounding the exterior of the base are groupings of bronze sculpture (cast approximately one-third larger than life) depicting various battle scenes. These groupings represent the four main armed services: Infantry, Cavalry, Artillery, and Navy. The tablet room contains lists of Cuyahoga County residents who served in the war, as well as four bronze reliefs representing the "Emancipation of the Slave," "Beginning of the War in Ohio," members of the various soldiers' relief organizations, and "The End of the War—the Peacemakers at City Point."

Akron's Soldiers' Memorial Chapel, in Glendale Cemetery, was dedicated on Decoration Day (now Memorial Day), Tuesday, May 30, 1876. The Victorian-Gothic design was created by Frank O. Weary. Built into its interior walls are fourteen marble slabs, engraved with the names of the fallen brave of Akron and Portage Township. Several beautiful memorial windows highlight the structure and represent three epochs of U.S. History to that point: The George Washington epoch, The Commodore Perry epoch (the opening of Japan), and the Lincoln epoch.

[Drawings on following pages.]

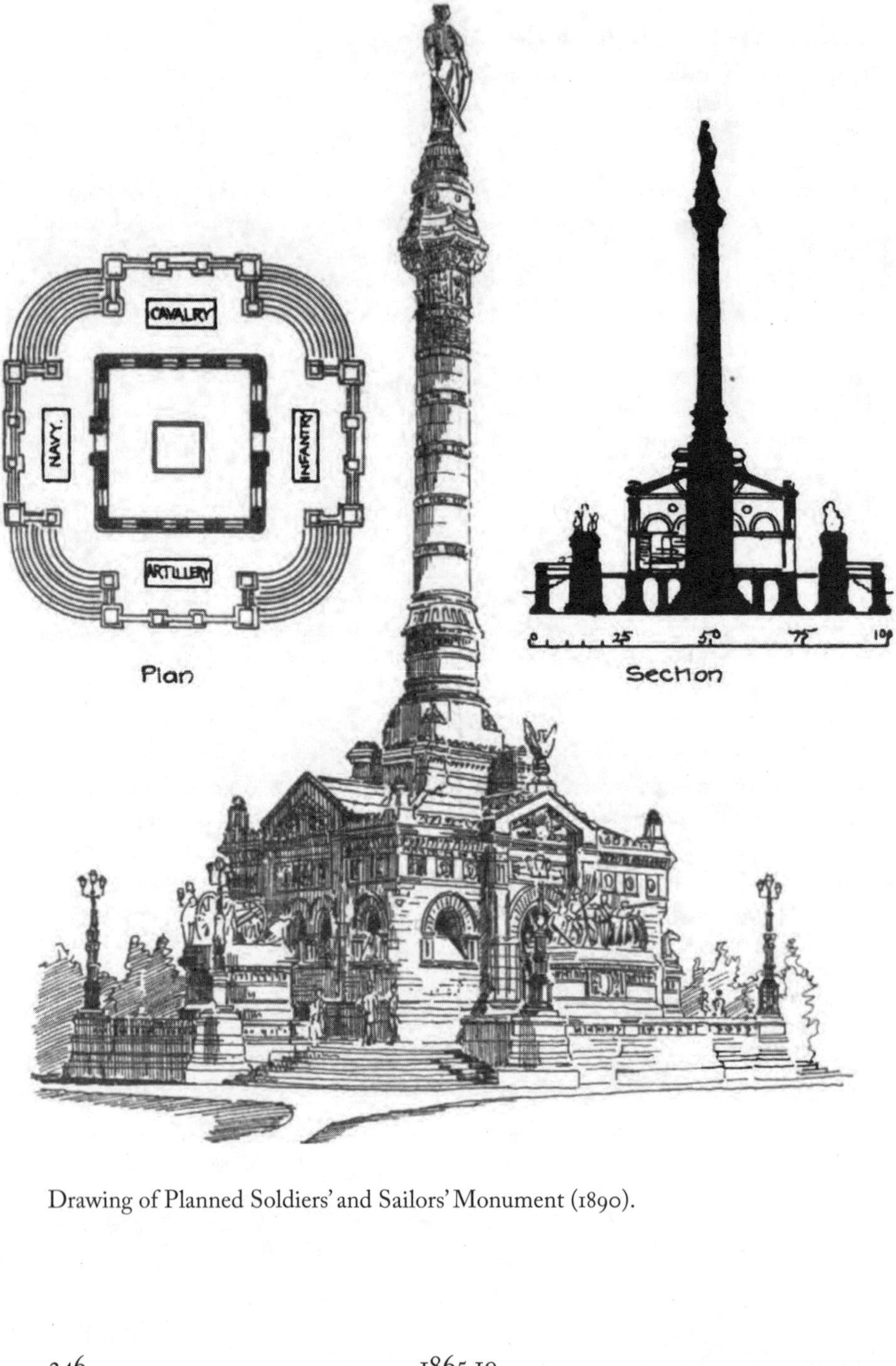

Drawing of Planned Soldiers' and Sailors' Monument (1890).

Drawing of Planned Soldiers' Memorial Chapel (1877).

1865.20

On the Roll of Honor Boys

From Thomas Buchanan Read, *Summer Story: Sheridan's Ride and Other Poems*, Philadelphia, PA: J.B. Lippincott, 1865.

William Rosecrans graduated from West Point in 1842. When war broke out, he was appointed Colonel of the 23rd Ohio Infantry. In September 1863, Rosecrans took Chattanooga, clinching Union control of central Tennessee by blocking Confederate access. He made a tactical error at the battle of Chickamauga, which cost him his reputation. He continued leading troops throughout the war and resigned in 1867. After the war, he moved to California and was a U.S. Representative from 1881 through 1885.

Rosecrans instituted the "Rolls of Honor" to increase the morale of his troops. Regimental rolls of honor consisted of the names of ten sergeants, ten corporals, and fifty privates, most distinguished for bravery, good conduct, and other heroics. In addition, at the brigade level, the rolls included four captains, four lieutenants, and two field officers below the rank of colonel.

Thomas Buchanan Read was born in Chester County, Pa., on March 12, 1822. At the age of seventeen he came to Cincinnati, Ohio. From 1861 to 1867, he lived in the Queen City. In 1862, when Cincinnati was threatened by Confederate troops, Mr. Read was on the military staff of Gen. Lew Wallace, commander of the Union forces in and near the city, and he subsequently contributed to the *Atlantic Monthly* a lucid account of the "Siege" of Cincinnati. Read died in New York City on May 11, 1872. "The Roll of Honor" displays a patriotism and zeal for a just cause attained. The repeated "On the Roll of Honor, boys" echoes a staccato of marching feet.

The Roll of Honor

Dedicated to Major General Rosecrans, who instituted the order of that name in the army of the Cumberland.

Like the lordly Mississippi, we are sweeping to the
South,
A mighty Union river, and the gulf shall be its mouth;
O'er our front wave floats our banner, boys, that leads
to glory's goal,
And at its side, in marital pride, is borne the Honor
Roll.
On the Roll of Honor, boys; on the Roll of Honor,
boys;

Oh, let us see our names shall be on the Roll of Honor,
boys.
Like a great wind we drive Southward, with a storm
of Northern hail,
And our banner rides before us, as a cloud upon the
gale;
We will tear from out the rebel's hold his stolen stars
and bars,
And fame shall see our names enrolled beneath the
stripes and stars.
On the Roll of Honor, boys; on the Roll of Honor,
boys;
And fame shall see our names will be on the Roll of
Honor, boys.

With this great gale sweeping Southward, daily come
the gentle airs
Of our fathers' words of courage, and our mothers'
constant prayers;
With them our wives and sweethearts, with a love
beyond control,
Are reading in their fancy, boys, the names on Honor's
roll.
On the Roll of Honor, boys; on the Roll of Honor,
boys;
Oh, let them see our names will be on the Roll of
Honor, boys.
And when the last armed rebels falls, and bites his
native dust;
When waves o'er every mile of land the banner of our
trust,
We'll return to those whose images are shrined within
the soul,
And proudly listen while they read our names on
Honor's roll.

On the Roll of Honor, boys, on the Roll of Honor,
boys;
Oh, let them see our names will be on the Roll of
Honor, boys.

When the twilight settles round us in life's evening
cool and gray,
Among our children's children we'll describe the
battle day;
They'll cluster to our knees to hear the story never
old,
And watch our trembling veteran hands point out the
names enrolled
On the Roll of Honor, boys; on the Roll of Honor,
boys;
And they shall see our names will be on the Roll of
Honor, boys.
And when at last Death's night comes on and stops
the battle din,
And we have conquered in our hearts the rebel hosts
of sin,
To the fields of Peace above us, may we march there
soul to soul,
And find our names emblazoned on the great Celestial
Roll.
On that Roll of Honor, boys; on that Roll of Honor,
boys;
Oh, let us see our names will be on the Roll of Honor,
boys.